A BRIEF HISTORY
OF LANGUAGES

Jaya S. Nagendra

ATLANTIC
PUBLISHERS & DISTRIBUTORS (P) LTD

ATLANTIC
PUBLISHERS & DISTRIBUTORS (P) LTD
7/22, Ansari Road, Darya Ganj, New Delhi
Tel.: +91-11-4077 5252, 2327 3880
E-mail: orders@atlanticbooks.com
Web: www.atlanticbooks.com

Reprint 2025, 2019

Published by Atlantic Publishers & Distributors (P) Ltd.

Printed & bound in India by Atlantic Print Services

Preface

The origin of languages in human species has been a subject of scholarly debate and discussion for many centuries. There is no consensus among experts regarding the exact origin of human languages because there is no direct evidence and we have to draw inferences from secondary sources like fossil remains and archaeogical findings. It is generally believed that the origin of human languages relates closely to the origin of modern human behaviour.

The book traces the evolution of languages in the history of mankind, and describes a number of hypotheses regarding when, where, why, and how the human languages emerged.

The subject matter is divided into fourteen illuminating chapters for focused study of each pertinent area. The first chapter describes the origin of language in human beings and throws light on various theories regarding spoken language and communication among primitive humans. The primary characteristics of language and root words have been delineated. Animal intelligence and how various animals, like honeybees, dogs, sharks, elephants, dolphins, etc. communicate with other members of their species have been taken up in the next chapter. This chapter also describes how communication permits living beings to use the wisdom of the past and sharpens their perception.

Writing is an integral part of human languages. In the early Neolithic period, people used mnemonics of knot record. Graphic symbols were developed by the people of Mesopotamian civilization around six thousand years ago. Clay tokens used in the Middle East, hieroglyphic writings of the ancient Egyptians and cuneiform signs found in Uruk—an ancient city of Mesopotamia—were all precursors of language. An exclusive chapter has been devoted to such writings, and how they developed into the modern form.

Ancient languages such as Aramaic, Brahmi, Hebrew, Sanskrit, Greek, Chinese, Latin, Arabic, Mayan, and their respective scripts have been discussed in the next chapter.

Language diffusion is the division of one language into two or more languages when the language changes in different methods as new communities develop. Language diffusion in Indo-European languages has been briefly explained in the next chapter.

The dialacts, main characteristics and writing systems of the major living languages, like Vulgar Latin, German, English, French, Spanish, Italian, Hindi, and Japanese have been dealt with in a subsequent chapter.

Grammar is the lifeline of any language. If the rules of grammar are not followed, the communication will not be complete, and confusion will take place. Basic grammar of languages, like German, French, Spanish, Italian, Hindi, Japanese, and their alphabets have also been included in the book. There is an exclusive chapter on the major Indian languages, like Bengali and Marathi, explaining their brief history, writing, dialects, and development through their respective literary works.

Dravidian languages are a family of languages conversed largely in Southern India and parts of Eastern and Central India. They are also spoken in Sri Lanka, Pakistan, Nepal, Bangladesh, Malaysia, and Singapore. Writing, dialects and development of major Dravidian languages, like Kannada, Tamil, Telugu, and Malayalam also find coverage in the book.

Another distinct feature of the book is the inclusion of description of evolutionary timeline of primate language. The importance of Broca and Wernicke portions of the Neocortex in the brain has been explained with illustrations.

Yet another interesting and informative inclusion is about the development of writing materials such as papyrus scrolls, animal skin, stone, bark, and leaves of trees. In India, stone, brick, wood, cloth, copper plates, palm leaves, and birch-bark were used. Manufacture of paper invented in China in 105 AD was kept as a closely guarded secret. Centuries passed before others discovered the Chinese techniques and produced paper. A historical brief-up of the development of printing has also been included in the book.

While describing foreign and Indian languages, only the basic information has been given, including a short list of vocabularies and fundamentals of grammar. The readers should be able to make the best of this fragmentary information as per their need. The grammar section within the chapters provides only the basics of the language covered. For detailed study, the students may refer to other books which contain elaborations. A unique feature of the book has been the inclusion of symbols, dialects, and short expressions used in main languages. The simple phrases and their meaning in English, included in the book, will help travellers and all those who like to know about other languages. The alphabet section includes the alphabets of each language covered, its pronunciation, examples, and general guiding tools for pronunciation. The Appendix provides equivalent words for numbers, days, months, seasons, and colours in each language.

The book aims to provide basic understanding of major world langauges. It will be useful for the students, teachers and scholars in evolutionary linguistics. It will also appeal to those who wish to know about the history of human languages and the basic characteristics of major languages of the world as well as Dravidian languages.

Jaya S. Nagendra

Acknowledgements

I am grateful to University of Maryland's libraries, where I developed my inspiration for languages and started researching for the material to write the book. The staff of the McKeldin library and Hornbake library were extremely helpful in assistance. I am also thankful to all the authors of the books I consulted. I want to thank Wikipedia common sites from where I have taken several photographs. I appreciate Simon Ager for giving permission to use his valuable scripts.

I am grateful to many people who read the manuscript and gave suggestions, but I wish to mention a few who painstakingly read the book and made valuable suggestions. Professor Aswathanarayana of Bangalore University, and Guruswamy Ayya, a Civil Engineer in US, reviewed my manuscript and provided their suggestions encouraging me to proceed. I am very grateful to both of them.

Whenever I had a chance to meet my friends and family, I had the opportunity to discuss about the book. They all liked the subject matter of the book and suggested a few things. I am indebted to them for their opinions.

Special thanks to my spouse B.K. Nagendra for his cooperation and encouragement in all my work.

My personal thanks to Sri Harjeet Singh and Atlantic Publishers and Distributors (P) Ltd. for undertaking this book for publication.

Jaya S. Nagendra

Contents

1

A Brief Study of Evolution of Languages

Evolution of Languages

Every inquisitive mind wants to know the origin of language in the human species and it becomes the topic of scholarly discussion among the intellectual community. There are numerous hypotheses regarding when, where, why and how the language emerged.

Language is a unique characteristic of humans. Humans developed the spoken language in a rudimentary way millions and millions of years ago. In the evolution process when humans and non-human primates were living together, both might have had the capability of communication with sign language first and spoken language later. The special talent of language evolution must have been a long process. Millions of years ago our ancestors were most likely speaking with a slower mode, a smaller vocabulary and simpler grammar than we are using now. Survival of the fittest played a greater part in this struggle. The transfer of more complex information, ideas and concepts from one individual to another was the most valuable evolutionary adaptation for preservation of species.

Language allows broadly spread humans to communicate with one another. It permits us to sample the wisdom of the past. It is an important tool in helping us to sharpen our mental perception to think more clearly. It is an incomparable aid to memory. Language existed long before writing system. Invention of writing played a major role in human success.

Origin of Language

Communication is extremely normal among all species on the planet to interact with each other, whether it is between animals, insects, plants or bacteria. But the human language in general is considered to be relatively very different. Humans also have several communication systems that are not language, but they share many similarities with communication in other species.

Scholars observe an extraordinary feature of human vocal tract that separates from the primate pattern. They explain that human's larynx (voice box) is located slightly low in the throat. Because of this arrangement, humans must synchronize breathing and swallowing cautiously to avoid choking.

This configuration increases the diversity of vowel sounds that we can produce, which in turn increases the information carrying capacity of the vocal channel. In addition to creating a bend in the vocal tract, lowering of the larynx increases the total length of the tract. In humans, male larynx undergoes a second fall around puberty creating a deep voice.

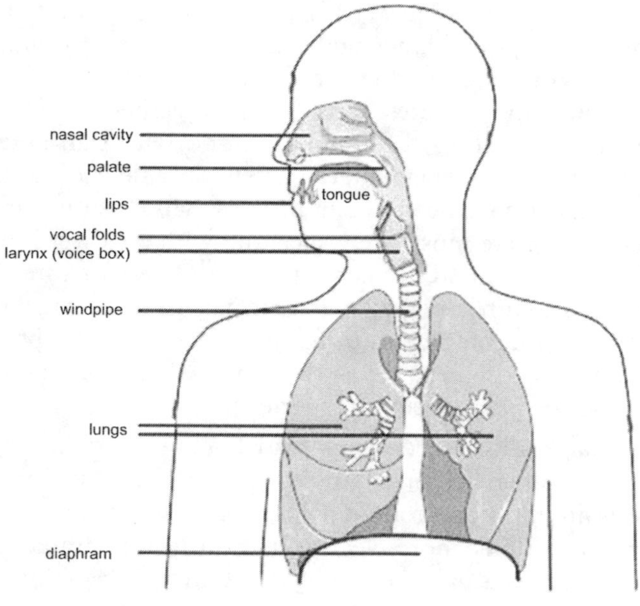

Courtesy: GOSH NHS Foundation Trust

Evolutionary Timeline—Primate Language

By conducting field study in the wild, primatologists have observed and discovered great ape's eccentric communication habits. Their discovery affirms that non-human primates, including the great apes, produce sounds that have delicate levels of emotional conditions in their communication. In detention, apes have been trained basic methods of sign language and have been motivated to use lexigrams on computer keyboards. Some apes were able to learn and use hundreds of lexigrams over a period of time.

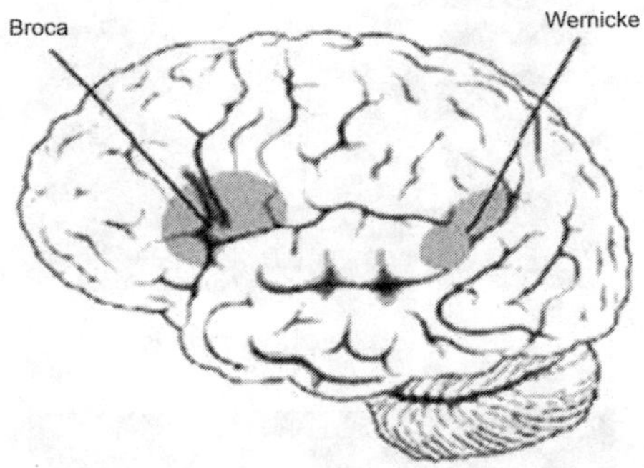

Two Portions of the Neocortex Closely Connected to Speech

As shown in the figure, the Broca's and Wernicke's areas are responsible for controlling the muscles of the face, tongue, mouth, larynx, and recognizing sounds in the primate brain. Scientists have conducted several experiments and have found that primates make vocal sounds, and those sounds are produced by circuits in the brainstem and limbic system.

The Broca's and Wernicke's zones exist both in the primate brain and in the human brain. The Broca's zone executes many cognitive and perceptual responsibilities, while the Wernicke's zone is engaged in language skills. It is understood that human language center is a modification of neural circuit standard to all primates. This modification and its ability for linguistic communication is exclusive to humans, and it indicates that the language organ began after the human stems departed from the primate such as chimps and bonobos' roots.

Early Homo

Fossil records indicate that anatomically modern humans (*Homo sapiens*), first appeared in Ethiopia about 195,000 years ago. The improvement of full modern behavior in *Homo sapiens* occurred about 70,000 to 50,000 years ago.

Australopithecus africanus

Homo neanderthalensis

About articulation, there is huge assumptions about the language proficiency of early Homos around 2.5 to 0.8 million years ago. Anatomically, some researchers consider that around 3.5 million years ago the characteristics of bipedalism, which occurred in australopithecines might have caused changes to the skull allowing an L-shaped vocal tract. The shape of the tract and a larynx located moderately low in the neck are permitting requirements for many of the sounds humans make, chiefly vowels. All vowels a, e, i, o, u, are produced at the lower level in the neck.

Lieberman in his article, "Neandertal and Early Modern Human Mobility Patterns" suggested that the reason for extinction of Neanderthals about 35,000 years ago was due to the larynx situated high in the neck blocking the production of the vowel sounds in complete form like modern day. He infers that this linguistic drawback may be a reason in the Neanderthals' disappearance.

Gestural Theory

The gestural theory states that human language developed from signs that were used for simple communication.

Two kinds of evidence maintain this theory.

1. Gestural language and vocal language depend on same kind of neural systems. The segments on the cortex in the brain interconnect each other that are responsible for hand and mouth movements.
2. Non-human primates also can use signal for archaic communication. Some of their signals are similar to those of humans. Both humans and chimpanzees share each other the traits like begging posture with the hands stretched out.

Grammaticalization Theory

Grammaticalization is a continuous old practice in which unconnected words develop into grammatical associations becoming more specialized. Grammar is a collection of structural rules that controls the composition of clauses, phrases, and words in a given natural language. Also, the same indicates to the study of rules such as phonology, morphology, syntax, semantics, phonetics and pragmatics.

Creativity produces grammatical modification. As Bernd Heine and Tania Kuteva notice, "Grammaticalization requires a linguistic system that is used regularly and frequently within a community of speakers and is passed on from one group of speakers to another." Non-humans do not have that required creativity for this type of communication.

Chomsky argues that, in the mind/brain of speakers, there is a limited set of linguistic rules, which represent gestures. Given a limited supply of random simple signs, these rules can generate an infinite number of complex sentences, whose meaning is compositional. From this view, the aim of linguistic analysis is the finding the mentally represented set of rules that inspire a speaker's linguistic skills. Chomsky uses the term 'grammar' to refer to this mentally represented set of rules.

Max Müller Theory

Max Müller gives a list of hypothetical ideas through his lecture series regarding the origins of spoken language:

- **Bow-wow.** The bow-wow or cuckoo theory, which Müller saw early words as imitations of the cries of beasts and birds. The roots are imitations of sounds. The man, being as yet mute, heard the voices of birds and dogs and cows, the thunder of the clouds, the roaring of the sea, the rustling of the forest, the murmurs of the brook, and the whisper of the breeze. He tried to imitate these sounds, and finding his mimicking cries were useful as signs of the objects from which they proceeded, he followed up the idea and elaborated language.
- **Pooh-pooh.** The pooh-pooh theory saw the first words as emotional interjections and exclamation triggered by pain, pleasure, surprise and so on.
- **Ding-dong.** The ding-dong theory, which states that all things have a vibrating natural resonance, echoed somehow by man in his earliest words.

Once our ancestors had recognized the appropriate imaginative mechanism for linking sounds with meanings, language consequently evolved and changed.

All social animals communicate with each other, from bees and ants to whales and apes, but only humans have developed language skills which are more than a collection of pre-arranged signals.

There are non-human primates very close to the brink of language, eager to learn, fully capable of its use once the language is taught.

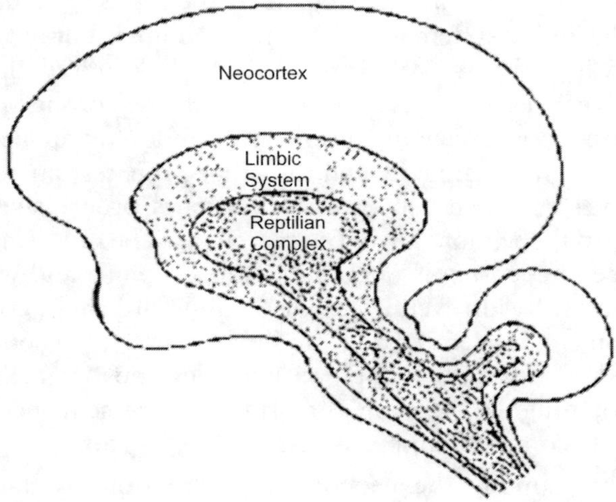

MacLean's Graphic demonstration of the reptilian complex, limbic system, and neocortex in the human brain

MacLean, chief of the Laboratory of Brain Evolution and Behavior, held that the human brain quantifies to three interconnected biological computers, each with its own special intelligence, its own preconception, its own sense of time and space, its own memory, motor, and other functions. Carl Sagan, an astronomer, who has done extensive research on exobiology and other various scientific fields describes:

"Each brain corresponds to a separate major evolutionary step. The three brains are said to be distinguished neuroanatomically and functionally and contain strikingly different distributions of the neurochemicals dopamine and cholinesterase.

"At the most ancient part of the human brain has the spinal cord; the medulla and pons, which comprise the hindbrain; and the midbrain. These combinations of spinal cord, hindbrain and midbrain MacLean calls the neural chassis. The most ancient of them surrounds the midbrain. We share it with the other animals and the reptiles. It probably evolved several hundred million years ago. MacLean calls it the reptilian or R-complex. Surrounding the R-complex is limbic system, so called because it borders on the underlying brain. Our arms and legs are called limbs because they are peripheral to the rest of the body. We share the limbic system with the other mammals but not with the reptiles. It probably evolved more than one hundred and fifteen million years ago. Finally, surmounting the rest of the brain, and clearly the most recent evolutionary accretion, is the neocortex. Like the higher mammals and the other primates, humans have a relatively massive neocortex. It becomes progressively more developed in the more advanced mammals. The most elaborately developed neocortex is ours and of the dolphins and whales. It probably evolved several tens of millions of years ago, but its development accelerated a few millions years ago, when humans emerged. The brain of a human fetus develops from the inside out and, roughly speaking runs through the sequence: neural chassis, R-complex, limbic system and neocortex.

"Chief among the neocortical abstractions is the human symbolic languages, particularly reading, writing and mathematics. These require cooperative activities of the temporal, parietal and frontal lobes, and perhaps the occipital as well. The kind of learning that human youngsters experience during their long childhood seems almost exclusively a neocortical function.

"Human language is controlled in the neocortex. Thus, an essential step in human evolution must have been the transfer of control of vocal language from the limbic system to the temporal lobes of the neocortex, a transition from instinctual to learned communication....

"The development of human language must therefore involve an essentially new brain system and not merely a reworking of the machinery for limbic cries and calls. Some experts in human evolution have suggested that the acquisition of language occurred very late—perhaps only in the last few tens of thousands of years—and was connected with the challenges of the last ice age. But the data do not seem to be consistent with this view; moreover, the speech centers of the human brain are so complex that it is very difficult to imagine their evolution in the thousand or so generations since the peak of the most recent glaciations."

Gradually, humans perfected the language to communicate efficiently. It is an important milestone in human history and human civilization.

Approaches

Scholars use two approaches to understand the origin of languages. These are as follows:

Continuity Theory is established on the idea asserting that because the language is very complex, it cannot appear simply from nothing in its final form. Therefore, it must have developed from previous pre-linguistic systems with our primate ancestors.

Discontinuity Theory is established on a very different idea asserting that because the language is a unique trait, it cannot be associated with anything found with non-humans. Therefore, it must have developed relatively rapidly.

Discontinuity theory advocate Noam Chomsky argues that accidentally a single mutation happened in one individual around 100,000 years ago, triggering the instantaneous occurrence of the language skill in perfect or nearly perfect form. The argument proceeds to explain as follows: (i) in evolution, any biological change in a species arises by a random genetic change in a single individual which spreads throughout its breeding group. (ii) The only change that was needed to develop language was the cognitive ability to construct and process recursive data structures in the mind. This genetic change presented the human mind with the property of distinct perpetuity.

Chomsky explains with an analogy that the development of the language faculty in humans is analogous to the development of a seed crystal in a super-saturated primate brain. On the threshhold of blooming into the human mind, by physical law, a single but crucial key-stone was attached by evolution. This theory supports that language did appear suddenly within the history of human evolution. From this perspective, one can argue that the development of language occurred not innately within the human psyche, but from an earlier trait that was present in the primate brain.

Primary Characteristics of Human Language

Charles Hockett listed sixteen different design features of human language. They are as follows:

1. *Vocal-auditory channel*: Language produced by vocal track and received by ear.
2. *Broadcast-transmission and discretional reception*: Signals transmitted in all directions, but are heard as coming from a particular direction.
3. *Rapid fading*: Spoken sounds cannot be heard long.
4. *Interchangeability*: Members could be speakers and receivers.
5. *Complete feedback*: Receiving back the message.
6. *Specialization*: Triggering effect.
7. *Semanticity*: Signals associated with features.
8. *Arbitrariness*: No connection between sound and meaning.
9. *Discreteness*: Messages broken into separate units.
10. *Displacement*: Messages referred to remote space or time.
11. *Openness*: Messages could freely and easily be understood on the basis of context.
12. *Tradition*: Language learned by teaching and learning.
13. *Duality of patterning*: Ability to make meaningful message from meaningful sounds.
14. *Prevarification*: Forming false or lie based on semanticity.
15. *Reflexiveness*: Copying.
16. *Learnability*: Ability to learn more languages.

Human language and human cognition are dependent on one another. Cognition is a mental process by which one gains knowledge and makes it possible to interpret in a proper language. It is an ability to understand the same thing from different points of view. For English speakers, using pronoun is not a problem, because they address all people 'you'. Other European languages like French, and even in Indian languages, one has to learn the rules when to use the second-person plural (tu or vous for you [French]), (tum or aap for you [Hindi]).

Language has different components. Phonology, study of speech sound was distinguished as word formation and sentence structure, called grammar. Grammar was subdivided into morphology, the study of word structure; and syntax, the study of sentence structure. This theory expands fourth component semantics, the study of meaning.

The sounds of human languages are produced by a set of organs known as speech organs which are primarily for ingestion and breathing. Air expelled by the lungs passes out through the throat, mouth, or nasal passages. When the expelled air is obstructed by the tongue or teeth, it produces various sounds of language. All the sounds produced by speech organs are not used by all languages. Most languages recognize few sounds and combine them to required form.

Phonemes: Speech sounds of a language are called phonemes which cause the accent. They were thought of as the building blocks of languages, unbreakable little atoms. But phonologists discovered that phonemes could be broken into particles, and each phoneme has distinctive features which cause accent.

Morphology is the study of word structure. Words might be defined as a meaning-bearing part in a speech and sentence is a string of words. Some words cannot be broken, some words could be broken. In many languages, the rules of putting words together are different from the rules of English.

Syntax is the study of sentence structure. Sentences are grammatically-ordered strings of words. In English, words could be understood as a part of speech (noun, verb, adverb, adjective, etc.) to which it belongs. Subject-Verb-Object combination is the order of sentence structure in English.

Semantics is the study of meaning, naming a thing, categorizing its origin according to denotation and connotation.

Pragmatics is the study of the way speakers use language to communicate with one another. In linguistic context, the narrow referential context is recognized by traditional semantics, and the sound is created by speech that comes before the word or phrase. Pragmatic makes it possible to understand the meaning outside the sentence. Non-linguistic context consists of objects and activities at the time of speaking.

Prototypes are examples of typical instances, well established in our culture and our language. The term idioms are used to refer these prototypes which all people in a culture can understand without trouble.

Metaphor is a form of thought that asserts a meaningful link between two expressions from different semantic domains. For example, "Arnold is a turkey" states one person and an animal belong to the same semantic domain.

Pidgin is a simplified language when members from different communities meet together without previous contact are forced to create a new form of language which is called pidgin. They are considered to be reduced languages having no native speakers.

Cognition is an open system. Language is not separated from cognitive capacity. Elementary cognitive process is basic human mental ability like abstraction, categorization, and inferential reasoning. In functional cognitive system, these processes are organized. Human cognition involves perceiving, thinking, feeling, and acting.

Certain features in Hockett list, openness, displacement, arbitrariness, duality of parenting, semanticity, and prevarification makes human language distinctive. Among them, openness is creative and it has been considered to be very important.

Openness is absent in ape's communication system. The number of sounds in such system is very few. If food and danger occur at the same time, one of the sounds takes precedence. Displacement is also absent in gorillas and chimpanzees. Human beings can talk about absent or existing objects, and past or future events. Primates cannot do this. Human language has many levels. The pattern that characterizes to one level cannot be changed to any other level. Apes sound system does not have this feature.

Dancing with Root Words

Max Müller in one of his lectures on The Science of Languages argues that language is the creation of humans. It was invented by people as a method for communicating their thoughts when simple looks and gestures were not sufficient. Initially, people must have lived in mute and dumb state. Their methods of communication consisted in gestures of the body only. When their thoughts and ideas increased, they felt it was necessary to discover some kind of symbols which give meaning. Gradually, they decided to find a solution to fix uniform meaning by mutual understanding. Modern day's language perfection is possible through mixing efforts from later generations.

Adam Smith believed that the first artificial words were verbs. He thought that nouns were not necessary in the beginning because things could be pointed at, but actions could not be imitated or expressed. Therefore, inventing verbs was necessary. He gives an example that when people see a wolf coming, they can point at the wolf and simply shout "He comes". Here, the 'He' is Noun and 'comes' is the verb. Noun is standing there. People wanted a verb to express the action.

On the contrary, Dugald Stewart thought that the first artificial words were nouns. His argument was that the verbs could be expressed by gestures. Therefore, when people saw a wolf coming, they shouted "wolf, wolf" and left rest of the action to be imagined.

How can sound convey thought? How can roots become the symbols of popular thoughts? How the conceptual idea of measuring was expressed by *mâ* became the idea of thinking by *man*? How the meanings were attached to *gâ* to going, *sthâ* to standing, *sad* to sitting, *dâ* to giving, *mar* to dying, *char* to walking, *kar* to doing? Max Müller answers these questions as below:

> I shall try to answer as briefly as possible. The 400 or 500 roots which remain as the constituent elements in different families of language are not interjections, nor are they imitations. They are phonetic types produced by a power inherent in human nature. They exist, as Plato would say, by nature. There is a law which runs through nearly the whole of nature, that everything which is struck rings. Each substance has its peculiar ring. We can tell the more

or less perfect structure of metals by their vibrations, by the answer which they give. Gold rings differently from tin, wood rings differently from stone, and different sounds are produced according to the nature of each percussion. It was the same with man, the most highly organized of nature's works. Man, in his primitive state, was not only endowed, like the brute, with the power of expressing his sensations by interjections, and his perceptions by onomatopoeia.[1] He possessed likewise the faculty of giving more articulate expression to the rational conceptions of his mind. That faculty was not of his own making. It was an instinct, an instinct of the mind as irresistible as any other instinct. So far as language is the production of that instinct, it belongs to the realm of nature. Man loses his instincts as he ceases to want them. His senses become dimmer when they become useless, as in the case of scent. Thus, the creative faculty which gave thrilling experience for the phonetic expression first time through the brain, became extinct when its objective was fulfilled. The number of these phonetic types must have been almost infinite in the beginning, and it was only through the same process of natural elimination that clusters of roots were gradually reduced to one definite type.

Numerous number of words we use come from a root word. A root word is a word that does not have a prefix or a suffix. Once you remove any prefix or suffix, the root will be usually at the front or the back of the remaining word. The root of a word is a unit of morpheme, a smallest grammatical unit of a language, and it is an abstraction. Usually, it can be represented as a word in writing. A small digging will reveal the real meaning of root word.

In Sanskrit, to say 'I measure' is *mâ-mi*; to say 'you measure' is *mâ-si*; he measures is *mâ-ti* (or *mimî-te*). In Sanskrit, a measuring instrument is called *mâ-tram*, in Greek metron.

This *mâs* in Sanskrit is obviously derived from a root *mâ*, to measure. The moon was initially called by the farmer as the

1. Onomatopoeia is a word that phonetically imitates or suggests the source of the sound that it describes.

measurer, the administrator of days, and weeks, and seasons and also the controller of the tides.

The name of the Greek God Zeus originally signified the bright heaven or sky as in Sanskrit *Dyaus*.

Max Müller writes, "Indian's achievements in grammatical analysis, which date from the 600 B.C., are still unsurpassed in the grammatical literature of any nation. The idea of reducing a whole language to a small number of roots, which in Europe was not attempted before the 1600 by Henry Estienne was perfectly familiar to the Brahmans, at least 500 B.C." "Hervas was aware of the grammatical similarity between Sanskrit and Greek. He discovered the truth comparing such words as *theos* God in Greek with *Deva*, God in Sanskrit. He identified the Greek auxiliary verb *eimi*, *eis*, *esti*, I am, thou art, he is with the Sanskrit *asmi*, *asi*, *asti*. He even pointed out that the terminations of the three genders in Greek, *os*, *e*, *on* are the same as the Sanskrit, *as*, *â*, *am*. This electric spark was the discovery of Sanskrit. Sanskrit is the ancient language of the Hindus. It had stopped to be a spoken language at least 300 B.C. At that time the people in India spoke Vedic Sanskrit similar to Italian to Latin."

Max Müller gives several beautiful examples regarding the evolution of words. Consider the word *respectable*. In *respectabilis*, we can separate the verb *respectare* and the termination *bilis*. Then separate the prefix *re*, which leaves *spectare*. Word *spectare* can be found as a participial configuration to the Latin verb *spicere* or *specere*, meaning to see, to look. In *specere*, again, separate the changeable termination *ere* and the unchangeable remainder *spec*. Spec is the root word. This root word could be found in Sanskrit and other Aryan languages. In Sanskrit, the word *pas* means to see, without the *s* (*s-pas*). But *spasis* also found in *spasa* in *spashta*, clear, visible. In Old High-German, *spëhôn* meaning to look, to spy, to contemplate; and *spëha*, in English the spy. In Greek, the root *spek* has been changed into *skep*, which occurs in *skeptomai*, I look, I examine; *skeptikos*, an examiner or inquirer. Various ramifications can be found in root spec. Originally, *Respectable* meant a person who deserves *respect*, that is *respect* meaning re-spect *look again*. As *specere*, to see, with the preposition *re* it became respect. With the preposition *de*, down, it forms the Latin *despicere*, meaning to look down, in English it forms *despise*.

As *de* means down from above, so *sus* means up from below, and this added to *specere*, to look, gives us *suspicere, suspicari*, to look up, in the sense of to suspect. From it appears suspicion, suspicious. Some more examples for this root:

(a) As *circum* means round about, *circumspect* means cautious, careful.

(b) With in, *specere* changed to *inspicere*, to inspect. Hence, appeared the words *inspector*, *inspection*.

(c) With *ad*, towards, *specere* became *adspicere*, to look at a thing. Hence, the word *adspectus* becomes the aspect, the look or appearance of things.

(d) With *pro*, *specere* became *prospicere*; and gave rise to words such as *prospectus*, *prospective*.

(e) With *con*, *spicere* forms *conspicere*, to see together, *conspectus*, *conspicuous*.

(f) With *ex*, gives the word in Latin the *expectare*, in English *to expect*, to look out.

(g) *Auspicious* is another word which contains the root word *spec*. The Latin *auspicium* refers for *avispicium* meaning looking for certain birds which bring good or bad omen to the success of any public or private endeavor. Hence the word *auspicious*, which brings luck.

From *specere*, *speculum* was produced to represent looking-glass or looking at oneself. *Speculum* produced *speculari*, and also the English word *to speculate*, and *speculative* appeared.

A root is essentially monosyllabic. Roots comprising more than one syllable can be proved as derivative roots, and even among monosyllabic roots, it is crucial to distinguish between primitive, secondary, and tertiary roots. For example,

A. Primitive roots are those which consist of—

(1) One vowel; for example, *i*, to go;

(2) One vowel and one consonant; for example, *ad*, to eat;

(3) One consonant and one vowel; for example, *da*, to give.

(The primary roots are the most important in the early history of language.)

B. Secondary roots are those which consist of—

Consonant, vowel, and consonant; for example, *tud*, to strike.

In these roots, either the first or the last consonant is alteration.

In the secondary roots, the root retains its usual meaning slightly modified by the changes of the final consonants. So, in addition to *tud* (*tudati*), in Sanskrit there are *topati, tupati,* and *tumpati*, meaning to strike; in Greek, typ-to. Also, according to Sanskrit grammarians there is *tubh* (*tubhnâti, tubhyati, tobhate*). Then there is also a root *tuj* (*tunjati, tojati*), to strike, to excite; another root, *tur* (*tutorti*), to which the same meaning is assigned; another, *tûr* (*tûryate*), to hurt. Then there is the further derivative *turv* (*tûrvati*), to strike, to conquer; there is *tuh* (*tohati*), to hurt, to vex; and there is *tus* (*tosate*), to which Sanskrit grammarians assign the sense of striking.

C. Tertiary roots are those which consist of—

(1) Consonant, consonant, and vowel; for example, *plu*, to flow;

(2) Vowel, consonant, and consonant; for example, *ard*, to hurt;

(3) Consonant, consonant, vowel, and consonant; for example, *spas*, to see;

(4) Consonant, consonant, vowel, consonant, and consonant; for example, *spand*, to shake.

In the third class, one of the two consonants is always a semivowel, nasal, or sibilant. One consonant may be later origin and added to a biconsonantal root in order to make its meaning more special.

Roots may be used as words, each root preserving its full independence. Two roots may be joined together to form words, and in these compounds one root may lose its independence. What applies to two roots, applies to three or four or more.

The principle is the same, though it would lead to a more varied subdivision.

Let us evaluate two words such as *cuckoo* and *raven*. *Cuckoo* in English is clearly a mere imitation of the cry of the bird, it occurs also in Greek, Sanskrit, and Latin. In these languages, the imitative element has received the support of a derivative suffix; we have *kokila* in Sanskrit, and *kokkyx* in Greek, *cuculus* in Latin. The same applies to *cock*, the Sanskrit *kukkuta*. The Sanskrit *kukkuta* is not derived from any root, it simply repeats the cry of the bird such as the French *coquet*, originally strutting about like a cock; *coquetterie*.

In case of raven, the root *ru* or *kru* is not a mere imitation of the cry of the raven; it embraces many cries, from the harshest to the softest, and it may be applied to the nightingale and also to the raven.

In Sanskrit, this root occurs as *ru*, a verb which suggests the sound of rivers including the barking of dogs and the muttering of cows. From *ru* numerous words are derived in Sanskrit.

In Latin, there is *raucus*, hoarse; *rumor*, a whisper; in German *rûnen*, to speak low. This root *ru* has several minor forms such as the Sanskrit *rud*, to cry; the Latin *rug*, to howl; the Greek *kru* or *klu*, in *klaio*, *klausomai*; the Sanskrit *krus*, to shout; the Gothic *hrukjan*, to crow, and *hropjan*, to cry; the German *rufen*.

Even the ordinary Aryan word for hearing is closely related to this root. It is *sru* in Sanskrit (as in *shruthi*), and before it took the recognized meaning of hearing, it meant to sound 'to ring.'

Let us consider the Latin names of cave. A cave in Latin is called *antrum*, *cavea*, *spelunca*. *Antar* in Sanskrit means *between* and *within*. *Antrum*, therefore, meant originally what is within or inside the earth. Thus, we find that the *entrails* were called *antra* in Sanskrit, *enteron* in Greek, meaning things within.

There is a name for man which means simply the thinker. *Mâ* means in Sanskrit is to measure. Man, a derivative root, means to think. From this occurs the Sanskrit manu, originally thinker, the man with manas, the mind (the man with thinking mind). In later Sanskrit other derivatives occur such as *mânava, mânusha, manushya*, all conveying man. In Gothic, there are both man and *mannisks*, in modern German *mann* and *mensch*. Another ancient word for man in the Sanskrit is *marta*, the Greek *brotos*, the Latin *mortalis*, modern name mortal. *Marta* means he who dies.

Another ancient word for cave is *cavea* or *caverna*. In order to call even the first hollow *cavea*, it was necessary that the natural idea of hollow should have been designed in the mind, and should have grasped its vocal expression *cav*. Before a cave was called *cavea*, many hollow things had passed through the eyes of men. At first, hollowed places were intended as a place of safety and protection as a cover, it was called by the root *ku* or *sku*, which gave the idea to cover. Hence, the general idea of covering was in the people's mind before it was used as hiding-places in rocks or trees, the caves were described by the name of *cavea* or hollows.

Another form for cave or cavus was *koilos*, hollow. A hole was called *koilos* because it functioned as a cover. Then *koilos* came to mean a cave, a vault, and therefore the sky was called *coelom* because it was looked upon as a cover for the earth. The word formed in the first instance intended for one object only though it was extended to the whole class to which this object seemed to belong. When a word such as *rivus*, river, was first formed, it was intended for a certain river, and that river was called *rivus* from a root *ru* or *sru*, to run, because of its running water. In many cases, a word meaning river or runner remained the proper name of one river. Thus, *Rhenus*, the *Rhine*, means river or runner, The Ganges is the Sanskrit *Gangâ*, literally the Go-go. The Indus again is the Sanskrit *Sindhu* and means the irrigator, and to sprinkle. If we examine the most ancient word for name, we find it is *namah* in Sanskrit, *nomen* in Latin, *namo* in Gothic. This *namah* stands for *gnaman*, which is preserved in the Latin co-gnomen. The *g* is dropped. *Namah* and name are derived from the root *gnâ*, to know, and signified by which we understand an object.

Other animals have sensation, perception, memory, and, some intellect; but they are familiar with single objects. Man has sensation, perception, memory, intellect, and reason. With this reason man acquires distinct quality to produce general ideas.

The old name given to animals such as cows and sheep, was *pasú*, in Latin *pecus*, which means feeder or nourisher. Animal itself is a later name, and derived from *anima*, soul. Originally, this *anima* again meant blowing or breathing, and it was derived from a root *an*, to blow, which gives us *anila*, wind in Sanskrit, and *anemos*, wind in Greek.

Soul is the Gothic *saivala*, and this is linked to another Gothic word, *saivs*, which means the sea. The sea was called *saivs* from a root *si* or *siv*, the Greek *seio*, to shake; it meant the tossed-about water, in contrary to stagnant or running water.

The Aryan root *da*, to give, exists in Sanskrit as *dâ-nam*, gift. Also, *da* occurs in Sanskrit as *dadâmi*, in Greek *di-do-mi*, I give, as a verb. These roots communicated as the seeds of human speech in the ancient minds.

Max Müller believes that the earlier man, being a mute, heard the voices of birds, dogs, cows, the thunder of the clouds, the roaring of the sea, the rustling of the forest, the murmurs of the brook, and the whisper of the breeze. He struggled to imitate these sounds, and discovering his mimicking sounds and shouts are useful, he pursued the idea of mimicking and elaborated the language gradually.

Max Müller gives a beautiful example with humor to prove his theory.

An Englishman in China saw a dish placed before him at some eating area. Feeling suspicious, he wanted to know whether it was a dish made of duck. He asked the server in a questioning gesture

Quack quack?

The Englishman received the clear and straightforward answer from Chinese server:

Bow-wow!

Indicating it is not a dish prepared from duck. It is a dish prepared from dog!

This conversation applies to any foreign language whether it is a Chinese, French, Mexican, and Indian.

Modern-day Languages

As a result of European colonialism, the Indo-European languages have spread across the globe. Languages continuously creep into each other as words are spread by conquest, trade, religion, technology and global entertainment over the course of history.

A good example of this process is the dividing line in western Europe separating the Romance languages from the Germanic tongues. The Romance family includes French, Italian, Portuguese, Spanish and Romanian. The Germanic group is English, Danish, Dutch, Flemish, German, Icelandic, Norwegian, and Swedish.

This linguistic division precisely reveals the influence of the Roman Empire. Italy, France and the peninsula of Spain were stable territories in the Roman Empire to retain the influence of Latin. The Germanic areas of east and north of the Rhine River were never completely brought under Roman control.

Modern English occupies a middle position within the western European family of languages, with its vocabulary roughly half Germanic and half Romance in origin.

By Wilson Andrews and David Brown, Published: May 6, 2013

While most ancient words are long gone like dinosaurs, a few still live on. A research team led by Mark Pagel at the University of Reading in England has identified 23 "ultraconserved words" that have remained largely unchanged for 15,000 years.

"You, hear me!"

"Give this fire to that old man."

"Pull the black worm off the bark and give it to the mother."

"No spitting in the ashes!"

It's an odd little speech. But if you go back 15,000 years and spoke these words to hunter-gatherers in Asia in any one of hundreds of modern languages, there is a chance they would understand at least some of what you were saying.

That's because all of the nouns, verbs, adjectives and adverbs in the four sentences are words that have descended largely unchanged from a language that died out as the glaciers retreated at the end of the last Ice Age. Those few words mean the same thing, and sound almost the same, as they did then.

A team of researchers has come up with a list of two dozen "ultraconserved words" that have survived 150 centuries. It includes some predictable entries: "mother," "not," "what," "to hear" and "man." It also contains surprises: "to flow," "ashes" and "worm."

As to the origin of the sound of the other ultraconserved words, and who made them up, that's a question best left to the poets.

"The Makers" from "Sentences" by Howard Nemerov

Who can remember back to the first poets,
the greatest ones, greater even than Orpheus?
No one has remembered that far back
Or now considers, among the artifacts,
And bones and cantilevered inference
The past is made of, those first and greatest poets,
So lofty and disdainful of renown
They left us not a name to know them by.

They were the ones that in whatever tongue
Worded the world, that were the first to say
Star, water, stone, that said the visible
And made it bring invisibles to view
In wind and time and change, and in the mind
Itself that minded the hitherto idiot world
And spoke the speechless world and sang the towers
Of the city into the astonished sky.

They were the first great listeners, attuned
To interval, relationship, and scale,
The first to say above, beneath, beyond,
Conjurors with love, death, sleep, with bread and wine,
Who having uttered vanished from the world
Leaving no memory but the marvelous
Magical elements, the breathing shapes
And stops of breath we build our Babels of.

2

Thinking Animals

How Animals Communicate?

Language allows broadly spread humans to communicate with one another. It permits us to sample the wisdom of the past. It is an important tool in helping us to sharpen our mental perception to think more clearly. It is an incomparable aid to memory. Long before the invention of writing, language played a major role in human success.

Animal's vocal signals are usually very consistent. We can rely on their signal by experience that they cannot fake the sound and their signals are not imitateable.

Carl Sagan in his book *Shadows of Forgotten Ancestors* notes that

> The origin of consciousness is imagined to be an unfathomable mystery. Consciousness may not be so mysterious a trait, though, that supernatural intervention is needed to explain it. If consciousness is a lucid awareness of the distinction between the inside of the organism and the outside, between you and everyone else, then, most microorganisms are to this degree conscious and aware. Then the origin of consciousness on our planet dates back more than 3 billion years. There were vast numbers of microscopic creatures then, buffeted by sea swells and ocean currents, reveling in the sunlight, each with a rudimentary consciousness—perhaps only a micoconsciousness, or even a nano- or picoconsciousness.

All life on earth is made from organic molecules, which are composed of carbon and other atoms. In order to arise life, these organic molecules had to be synthesized before the origin of life.

Organic molecules came to earth from both down here and up there. Scientists and primatologists give several examples about animal intelligence. Here are some examples found in some remarkable presentations by them.

- When a honeybee dies it releases a characteristic odor, a death pheromone that warns the survivors to remove it from the hive. The dead body is rapidly pushed out and towed out of the hive by honeybees. The death pheromone is oleic acid, a very complex molecule. If a live bee is applied with oleic acid, it is dragged off for disposal as if it were dead. The oleic acid odor may indicate danger to living insects, triggering them to shun others who have succumbed to disease. How do these bees understand the danger of corpses decomposing in the hive? How do they aware of the connection between death and oleic acid? Do they have any idea what death is?
- When you see an insect closely getting down on your hand or knees, you see the insect raises its head, surveying the location to determine to get a sense of upcoming, immense, three-dimensional gigantic creature in front of it.
- You get down on your hand and knees and look at the insect closely, and you see it raise its head, triangulating you, trying to get a sense of the immense, looming, three-dimensional monster before it. The fly moves unconcernedly. But when you lift an object to strike, it quickly flies off.
- In the night, when you turn on the light, the cockroach stops dead in its path, looking at you eagerly. But, when you move towards it, it runs into the woodwork. Such behavior is due to simple neuronal subroutine. The insect decides whom to eat and whom to run away from.
- The spider builds her web near the porch light. The fine, hard thread reels out from her spinneret. The multi-sided elegant, concentric, polygonal pattern is cautiously

stabilized with a single thread extending to the hood of the lamp, and another to an adjacent railing. She renovates the web even in darkness and bad weather. At night, when the light is on, the spider sits at the very center of her structure, until the unlucky insect whose eyesight is very poor and the web is totally invisible, but it was attracted by the light only. As soon as an insect becomes entangled in the web, the information of this event travels to spider in waves passing through the threads. She hastily goes down, stings it inflicting pain, rapidly wraps it in a white cocoon, saves it for future use, and calmly goes back to her control center. How does the spider know to design, construct, stabilize, renovate and utilize this stylish web? How does she know to construct the web near the lamp, to which the insects are attracted? It is possible its behavior is completely pre-programmed in its ACGT[1] code. But, consider how small that spider's brain is. How much more complex behavior might materialize out of the experience of a much larger brain?

- Bumblebees are most charismatic insects. They detect the polarization of sunlight, invisible to humans.
- Pit vipers, venomous snakes found in Asia and Americas, sense infrared radiation and detect temperature differences of 0.01°C at a distance of half a meter. Many insects can see ultraviolet light.
- Some African freshwater fish generate a static electric field around themselves and sense trespassers by small disturbance produced in the field.
- Dogs, sharks, and cicadas detect sounds completely inaudible to humans.
- Normal scorpions have micro-seismometers on their legs. They can detect the footsteps of a small insect a

1. ACGT stands for the four nucleic acid bases that configure DNA. The A refers to Adenine and pairs with the T, which stands for Thymine. The C refers to Cytosine and pairs with the G, Guanine. These four nucleic acids make up a creature's genetic code, or DNA.

meter away in pitch darkness. Water scorpions sense their depth by measuring the hydrostatic pressure.

- Dolphins, whales, and bats use a kind of sonar for precision echo-location.
- Scent glands are exocrine glands found in most mammals. They produce semi-viscous secretions which contain pheromones and other semiochemical compounds. These odor-messengers indicate information such as status, territorial marking, mood, and sexual power.
- About 80% of the different kinds of mammals are equipped with specialized scent glands. Gazelles have them in front of their eyes, camels on their feet and neck, sheep on their bellies, some pigs on their wrist, chamois behind the horns, pronghorns on the jaw, peccaries on the back, musk deer in front of the genitals, and goats on the tail.
- Water voles[2] dash their hind feet over their flank gland and steadily drum them on the ground. Gerbils and wood rats rub their bellies directly on the ground, secreting their scent mark from a ventral gland. Some animals have five or six different kinds of scent glands in various places on their bodies, each assigned with a different chemical statement. Cats spray carefully measured amounts of urine on the drapes and upholstery, in case some audacious alien cat might enter the living room and curl up before the fire.
- Some animals mark others with these scents. Rats urinate on their partner's bodies—as a sign of ownership over individuals as well as territories. Animals can distinguish male and female, their own group or strain from others, age, individual identity, and the sexual receptivity of females, all by odor alone. This act is related to communication by smell, that is,

2. A vole is a small rodent similar to a mouse but with a sturdy body, a shorter, hairy tail, a little rounder head, smaller ears and eyes, and differently formed molars. It is estimated that there are approximately 155 species of voles.

the perception of molecules borne from one animal to another through air or water which results in a quick alteration of behavior in the receiver animal.

- Animals are busy fulfilling the olfactory communications channels with a richness and excellence of discrimination, which trait is long ago lost to humans.
- Ants can sense earthquakes a day before they happen and the small insects postpone their normal activity until a day after the earthquake. German researchers have discovered that redwood ants like to build their settlements along active faults and breaks where the earth cracks during earthquakes. At the time of their research, during the day ants went on their daily activities and at night the ants rested within the mound. But, before the quake, the ants were awake throughout the night outside their mound. The insects grasp changing gas emissions or local shifts in the Earth's magnetic field. This is possible because the ants have chemo-receptors for carbon dioxide gradients and magneto-receptors for electromagnetic fields.
- Gibbons (a family of apes) are monogamous, a practice of being married to only one person at a time. They marry for life. They create evocative songs heard a kilometer or more away from their place. Adult males sing long solos frequently in the darkness just before sunrise. Bachelors sing longer songs than old married males, and at a different time of the day. Wives like to sing duets with their husbands. Widows endure their grief in silence and they never sing.
- If an infant monkey is riding on its mother, whether it is injured or dead, its mother will continue to carry it. If she stops carrying infant monkey, an adult male goes to bark at her and makes it clear that she should continue carrying the infant. In one case, a mother carried her dead infant for two days and dropped it. Then the dominant adult male of the troop picked the infant up and carried it for two more days before discarding it.

Sagan writes about an incident that happened at the Cape of Good Hope. An officer at animal center had often harassed a certain baboon. The animal seeing the officer approaching for parade on one Sunday, poured water into a hole and quickly made thick mud. Then the baboon skillfully hurled the mud over the officer as he passed by that made many bystanders to burst into laughter. For a long period after that event, the baboon expressed joy about his victory whenever he saw his victim.

In some type of monkeys, males share all parental duties except nursing and usually they are major caretakers of infants. Males in these species are strongly attracted to infants. As soon as the infant's birth, it has been observed that males trying to sniff, touch, or hold the still-bloody newborn, and they sometimes even lick off the covering birth fluids. Within hours of birth, males carry infants on the backs, groom them, and protect them. Most of the time a male's day is devoted to infant care, and the most caring fathers return their infants to the mother only to suckle. Intensely, protective males will secure infants against any real or imagined threat.

Most of the philosophers and thinkers view that humans are fundamentally different from other animals. They apprehend the essential human distinction is our reason, intellect, thought, or understanding. They believe that this distinction arises from something, like matter or energy, within human bodies, which has no evidence. Very few argue that the difference between humans and other animals are only of degree.

According to a Japanese primatologist, an amazing array of events happened in a colony of macaques (a family of old world monkeys widely spread primate group) on a small island called Koshima. In 1953, the normal food supply on Koshima was inadequate. Therefore, primatologists who were observing them provided the monkeys sweet potatoes and wheat dumping on the shore.

As anyone knows, on the shores of beach, sand sticks to food and makes it nastily coarse and impossible to eat. A one-and-a-half-year-old female macaques named Imo realized that she could rinse the sand off her sweet potatoes by dipping them in a nearby stream.

After Imo, her playmates, her mother and other male friends began to wash potatoes in the water. Gradually, sweet potato washing was no longer a new mode of behavior. Practically, almost all folks learned this habit of potato wash through their mothers or playmates when they were infants or juveniles.

But washing sandy wheat was not as easy as sweet potatoes. Imo figured out a technique for this problem also. In 1956, when Imo was four years old, she took a handful of mixed wheat and sand to the stream. When Imo dropped the sandy wheat on the water, the sand sank and the wheat floated. She skimmed off the water's surface and acquired the clean wheat. This placer mining technique was also adopted and learned by more and more animals.

Imo was a primate genius. She was an Archimedes or an Edison among the macaques.

Sometimes features of cultural life such as art, dance, and music are considered to be uniquely human. These features appear in animals also. For example, male bower birds decorate their nests artistically that resembles with ours. They frequently replace decayed flowers, fathers, and fruit with fresh ones in summer. Gibbons play themselves balletically through the high forests, and chimps are seen playing like rock and roll at waterfalls and in rainstorms. Chimps enjoy in resonant drumming, and gibbons enjoy in singing.

Primatologists have observed that chimpanzees often crack open hard-shell seeds and nuts with a stone hammer against a stone or wooden anvil. They will carry the suitable stones over a distance of a kilometer for the purpose. At other times, they use wooden clubs as nutcrackers. It is said that in the Tai forest in the Ivory Coast, chimps select an appropriate club, climb a cola tree, pick the choice of cola nuts, and crack them open using the branch as the anvil and the club as the hammer.

Similar examples occur in other species also. Otters are playful animals, which engage in various behaviors for pure enjoyment, like making waterslides and then sliding on them into the water. The playful and intelligent sea otter consistently dives to the ocean floor, retrieves hard-shelled mussels and a suitable stone, swims to the surface, floats on its back, and then breaks open the mussels using the stone as an anvil. Some birds drop bivalves, a kind of shells, on rocks to break them open. Egyptian vultures drop stone from height on large eggs of emus and ostriches with the intention to dine on the contents.

A chimp breaks off a long stem of a reed so that she can use it later, hundreds of meters away walking more than an hour to attract tasty termites in a log or termite mound. In order to possess this reed, she must remove extra leaves and twigs, shape it, shorten it, insert it into the termite tunnel in a skilfully twisting motion with thorough understanding of the interior contours, shake it to attract termites onto it, and then with great care remove it without scraping off too many termites. Chimps take years to perfect their technique and regularly teach it to their young.

An extraordinary depth of intellect and manual dexterity are needed for chimpanzees to learn termite fishing.

To find out this skill, anthropologist Geza Teleki spent months in Gombe to learn the technique.

He repeatedly observed chimpanzees approach to the mound, their visual scan of the surface, reaching the exact location, and extracting the termites from the mound without losing the termites in this process was unsurpassable. He applied the same techniques. After weeks of experiments, he had to accept the failure to achieve chimpanzees expertise in termite fishing.

We have to consider the chimpanzee's mental retaining power because this intensive probing occurs in short annual season. They have to retain specific information for many years so that they can continue their termite-collecting skills.

The chimpanzee's style of teaching nut cracking and termite fishing to the young is relaxed. They teach by example and not by rote. The learner plays with the tools and tries various approaches, instead of customarily copying every hand movement of the teacher.

Chimps also drop branches of tree on trespasser and offer drinking water with leaves. It has been observed that chimps use leaves as toilet paper and handkerchiefs, and twigs as toothbrushes. They use sticks for digging up roots, for investigating animals in burrows and knotholes. In zoos, chimps attempt to steal the keys from the zoo keeper's pocket. If they are successful, they manage to open the lock. Like human prisoners, they use their intelligence to escape from bondage.

Susan and Robert write an observation they made in North Africa:

> Between 1913 and 1917, Wolfgang Kohler conducted observations and experiments on the intelligence of chimpanzees at a field station in North Africa. In one study a male chimpanzee, Sultan, was led into a room where a banana had been tied to a string and suspended from the ceiling in a corner. A large wooden box had also been placed in the center of the room, open side up. Sultan first tried to reach the fruit by jumping, but this quickly proved futile. He then "paced restlessly up and down, suddenly stood still in front of the box, seized it, tipped it...straight towards the objective...began to climb up it...and springing upwards with all his force, tore down the banana." A few days later Sultan was taken into a room with a much higher ceiling, where again there was a suspended banana, as well as a wooden box and a stick. After failing to get the banana with the stick alone, Sultan sat down with frustration and scratched his head. He then stared at the boxes, suddenly leaped up, seized a box and a stick, pushed the box underneath the banana, reached up with the stick and knocked the fruit down. Kohler was struck with the apparently thoughtful period that preceded Sultan's solution, as well as with his sudden and directed performance.

Animal Intelligence

- Animals have five senses, just like us; they can see, hear, taste, smell, and feel. It has been proved that they also have both sensation and perception. By experiments scientists have found that in the eye of a bird if the roots of the optic nerve are removed from the eye of a bird, the retina in the bird's eye stops to be impulsive or emotional, iris do not move, and it becomes blind because it has lost the organ of *sensation*. On the contrary, if the cerebral lobes are removed within the head, the eye remains perfect, the retina excitable, and the iris movable. However, the bird cannot see, because it has lost the organs of *perception*.

- Animals have sensations of pleasure and pain. A dog that is beaten acts exactly like a child that is punished, whereas a dog that is nursed and loved shows the same signs of satisfaction as a boy under the same situations.
- Animals do not forget. They have good memory. They know their masters, they know their home, and they demonstrate joy on recognizing those who have been kind to them. They bear hatred for years to those who have insulted or ill-treated them.
- Animals are able to compare and to contrast. A parrot will take up a nut, and throw it down again, without attempting to crack it if it found that the nut is light. It discovers this fact by comparing the weight of the good nuts with the bad nuts, and it also knows that the bad nut has no kernel. It has the knowledge to know a light nut, which is hollow.
- Animals show signs of shame and pride. Those who are familiar with dogs know the happiness expressed by dogs wagging their tiles watching their master's arrival or a guily dog of stealing creeping away with his tail between his legs after hearing the sound of the hunter. These signs admit that animals feel shame and pride.
- Animals show signs of love and hatred. There are well-confirmed stories of dogs following their masters to the grave, and refusing food from any one. Some animals will watch their opportunity to take revenge by whom they have been hurt. We hear more such stories about snakes taking revenge, elephants nursing their infants, etc.
- Animals have a will of their own.

There are instincts in man as well as in animals. A child sucks its mother's breast by instinct; the spider interlaces its net by instinct; the bee builds her chamber by instinct. Then, where is the difference between animal and man? Undoubtedly, the answer is that one great obstacle between the animal and man is *Language*. Man speaks, but animal cannot.

Features of Human Language in Animals

Research with apes suggested that apes are capable of using language that meets some of the requirements such as arbitrariness, cultural transmission, discreteness and productivity. However, an experiment was conducted on chimpanzee infant named Gua in order to demonstrate the effects of the environment on language acquisition.

The experiment involved raising a 7.5 month-old chimpanzee child, Gua with a 10 month-old human child, Donald. Chimpanzee infant Gua was introduced to a normal human life at a very early age in order to confirm that the chimpanzee was not exposed to non-human response behaviors. The parents of Donald made sure to treat Gua like a human child, dressing her like a human, refusing to treat her as a pet, feeding her the same way that they fed Donald, and punishing her the same way as Donald. Ultimately, Gua was able to respond to about 95 words and phrases, but she was never able to learn the words or phrases. It was also observed that Gua never babbled or cooed like Donald did. It concludes that both the chimpanzees' vocal cord anatomy and deficiencies in chimpanzees' Broca's areas are responsible for the inability to form a language in animals.

In the forest, chimpanzees have been seen talking to each other warning about approaching dangers. For example, if one chimpanzee sees a snake, he makes a low, rumbling noise, signaling all the other chimpanzees to climb on to nearby trees.

Astronomer Carl Sagan writes that there is a notion that implies animals do not have intelligence. But no examination has been done vigilantly to examine the possibility of animal intelligence. It is said that dolphins and whales sense their surrounding with a fairly complex sonar echo location technique and also converse with each other by a strong and elaborate set of clicks, whose interpretation has failed human attempts to understand it. A dolphin does not say a single word, but instead transmits a set of clicks corresponding to the audio reflection spectrum. We could undoubtedly imagine the extent of such a language from concrete to abstract ideas equivalent to the development of human written languages.

Our speech varies in a physical way from the communication of other animals. It comes from a cortical speech center which does not respond instinctively, but organizes sound and meaning on a logical basis. This section of the brain is unique to humans.

Carl Sagan writes that an extensive attempt to communicate with chimpanzees was conducted in a research center. A newborn chimp was taken into a household with a newborn baby, and both were raised together—twin cribs, twin beds, twin high chairs, twin potties, twin diaper pails, twin baby powder cans. At the end of three years, the young chimp had far surpassed the young human in manual dexterity, running, leaping, climbing and other motor skills. But while the child was happily chatting, the chimp would say with enormous difficulty, Mama, Papa and cup. Then it was concluded that chimpanzees are only minimally capable in language, reasoning and other higher mental functions. They deduced that the pharynx and larynx[3] of the chimp are not suited for human speech. Human beings exhibit a multiple use of the mouth such as eating, breathing and communicating. Insects such as crickets, which call to one another by rubbing their legs, these three functions are performed by completely separate organ systems. Human spoken language seems to be accidental or added organ system. Sagan argues that the development of this organ system with other functions for communication in humans is comparatively recent evolution of our linguistic abilities. Gardeners described that the chimpanzees have substantial language abilities which could not be expressed because of the limitations of their anatomy.

They decided to teach chimpanzees American Sign Language, known by its acronym Ameslan as American deaf and dumb

3. The hollow muscular organ forming an air passage to the lungs and holding the vocal cords in humans and other mammals; the voice box.

language. They trained three chimpanzees Washoe, Lucy and Lana using Ameslan to study. After the study, they came to know that those chimpanzees learned vocabularies of 100 to 200 words, and were also able to distinguish significantly different grammatical patterns and syntaxes. Surprisingly, chimpanzees were astonishingly inventive in the construction of new words and phrases. Some of the examples are given below:

1. Watching a duck land quacking in a pond, Washoe signaled 'water bird' by inventing a new word.
2. Lana had never seen a round fruit other than an apple, but she knew the signs for the major colors. Upon watching a technician eating an orange, she signaled 'orange apple'.
3. Lucy, after tasting watermelon, described it as 'candy drink' or 'drink fruit'.
4. In another occasion when she burnt her mouth on eating radish for the first time, Lucy described that as 'cry hurt food'.
5. When Washoe soiled clothing or furniture, she was taught the sign 'dirty'. Later she used the word as a general term of abuse. Occasionally, Washoe would say "Dirty Jack, give me drink".

To form a word or to signal the meaning of a word requires various mind activities like understanding the concept, eye and mind coordination, and action to produce a symbol that gives meaning of the action.

Apart from Ameslan, chimpanzees and other non-human primates were taught a variety of other gestural languages. At the Yerkes Regional Primate Research Center in Atlanta, Georgia, Lana was learning a specific computer language called "Yerkish." In that center, Lana used to monitor her sentences on a computer display and erase those words with grammatical errors. On one occasion, while Lana was constructing an elaborate sentence, her trainer mischievously and repeatedly interrupted her work and inserted from his computer console, a word that made nonsense to Lana's sentence. She gazed at her computer display, spied her trainer at his console, and composed a new sentence: "Please, Tim, leave room"!!

Carl Sagan assumes that humans may have pushed back the frontiers of intelligence and language ability among the non-human primates. He gives several examples about how we can rectify our mistakes by teaching chimpanzee gestural language and make their brain evolve.

What they are talking?

He wonders if this learning process continued in chimpanzees population, what sort of culture, what kind of oral tradition would they establish after a few hundred or a few thousand years by communal use of a complex gestural language? How would they begin to view the origin of language? Would the gardners and the teachers at the Yerkes Primate Center be remembered as celebrated heroes or gods of another genus? Would there be folklore about divine beings who have given the gift of language to the primates?

60 Minutes' Bob Simon reports a fascinating interview with an extraordinary American scientist named Andrea Turkalo. Here is a brief outlook of the article:

Turkalo said on 60 Minutes: "The Secret Language of Elephants", many of their calls are in some ways similar to human speech.

The Secret Language of Elephants

For two decades, a group of wild African elephants has been watched, studied and protected by an American scientist named Andrea Turkalo.

Elephants communicate in a complicated, sophisticated language that scientists are trying to decipher and compile into the world's first elephant dictionary. When we heard that this is all happening in one of the most magical places on Earth, a remote valley in Central Africa where forest elephants, the rarest, most mysterious, and most threatened member of the species congregate, we simply had to go.

Asked who made the trail, Turkalo said, "This was made by hundreds of years of elephant traffic in this forest. If you look at their feet it is obvious. They do a lot of road work," she explained.

The valley consisted a watering hole, a spa and a sanctuary—a place where elephants take their time, the measured graceful pace of the largest land animal on Earth. They come to the valley for the minerals which they cannot seem to get enough of. It is a place where elephants play, but nobody gets hurt. From an observation deck on the edge of the valley, she collected scientific data for Cornell University and the Wildlife Conservation Society. She watched elephants almost every day, for hours, counting their numbers, monitoring their health, and observing their social behavior.

Turkalo said. "We have to really know a lot more about the behavior of these animals to sort out these different vocalizations and what they mean."

But they can match elephant sounds with behavior they can see, and classify those sounds into distinct categories. Asked what some of them are, Turkalo said, "Well, there are low frequency rumbles. It sounds like a big cat purring. And those are the vocalizations that help keep groups in contact with each other."

"Newborns have a particularly very high cry. And when you hear it, you know it's a very, very young calf," she explained.

Some noises that sound fearsome to human ears are actually elephants greeting one another.

Back in 2000, Turkalo filmed the death of a baby, and the traumatized cries of the other elephants. The elephants kept poking the body, over and over, frantically trying to coax the baby back to life. The elephants formed a procession that marched around the body.

"They would feel it or they would smell it. And then they would vocalize," she explained. "It was like a funeral procession that went on three or four days."

"They seem to recognize death, and it upsets them," she added. But it turns out that these vocalizations are just a small fraction of the sound the elephants make. Until a few years ago, scientists had no idea that what elephants are saying cannot be heard by the human ear.

"The base of their vocalization is infrasonic.[4] In other words, the frequency on which their call is built is below what we can hear," Peter Wrege explained. The elephants use those low sounds to find one another in the dense forests where they spend most of their time. "Elephants are using very low frequencies in their vocalizations which travel far away," Wrege said. Wrege told Simon these low frequency sounds reach about two or three kilometers—more than a mile. Six thousand miles away, in upstate New York at a lab at Cornell University, researchers are listening to everything from the sound of humming birds to the sound of whales.

The Elephant Listening Project grew out of an accidental discovery made by its founder, Katy Payne, one of the world's leading experts on elephant communication. When she went to an elephant cage at a zoo, Payne recollected, "I began to realize that I was feeling a throbbing in my ears and in the air that I couldn't really explain. I said 'You know, do you suppose that elephants are making sounds that are below the pitches that I can hear?' And we recorded for a month and, lo and behold, we found that elephants had a great many sounds that people didn't know about."

4. The term "infrasonic" applied to sound refers to sound waves below the frequencies of audible would, and nominally includes anything under 20 Hz.

"But then how do you discover the meaning of these sounds?" Simon asked.

"You just watch and watch and watch, and record and record and record and keep the two together," Payne explained.

Researchers initially strung nine acoustic recording devices around the valley. As the sound reached each recorder at a different point of time, they could pinpoint the location of the speaking elephant. Picking up sounds too low to hear was another challenge, but recording the sounds normally and playing them back faster was a revelation.

For example, the small valley at night sounds like just like crickets, but play back the recording three times faster, and you can pick up the rumbles of elephants.

But to figure out what the calls mean, the Cornell team spends more time looking than listening. Using computer-generated spectrograms, they can see the low-frequency sounds.

"And what does this visualization tell us?" Simon asked Peter Wrege.

"It tells us that there is an incredible complexity. Many of their sounds are actually similar in some way to human speech," he explained.

3

History of Writing

More than 3000 years ago in Mesopotamia, a proud father told his son's teacher, "My little fellow has opened his hand and you made wisdom enter there. You showed him the fine points of the scribal art." Recognizing that the writing is the pathway to wisdom, it soon spread throughout the ancient Middle East.

Most of us are familiar with only one consonant and vowel alphabetic writing system. But the history of writing has come a long way with many beginnings and alterations.

Before fully-matured perfect writing was developed, ancient people used a number of approaches as marks, graphic symbols and memory tools (mnemonics) in order to store information. Graphic art contained human figures, sun, stars, comets, flora, fauna, and geometric designs.

The fate of writing systems and scripts has been determined by economics, politics, religion and cultural prestige throughout history.

In the beginning, writing was an instrument of power in the hands of small groups of priests, fortune-tellers and scribes-serving monarchs. It was the perfect tool for social ascendency and the expression of a small elite's ideology. With the diffusion of consonantal writing, it could no longer remain the monopoly of the rich and powerful. Eventually, reading and writing spread enormously.

"Writing is the painting of the voice" wrote the French philosopher Voltaire.

There are many ways that writing could be borrowed by different people. For example, only the idea of writing; the idea of writing and its orientation (e.g. linear, right to left, vertical columns); the writing system (logographic, syllabic, alphabet); the writing system and its scripts; parts of writing system; parts of script, etc.

All the writing systems of ancient Afro-Asia seem to relate to one another, either by immediate borrowing and modification or by indirect influence.

Knot Records

One of the early Neolithic, the last period of the Stone Age, people used general mnemonics of knot record. Such records could be simple knots in a single thread or intricate series of colour-coded knots on strings joined to higher-levels of strings. They comprised a complex means of counting: different knots in various positions represented numerical quantities and the knot colours represented separate commodities.

Each knot represented a specific decimal value. If there is no knot in certain place, it meant zero. For example, one knot above two knots above a group of seven knots recorded as the number 127 as shown below. Also, there were specific string places to represent 100, 10 and 1s.

*	1
**	2
*******	7 = 127

Tallies/Marks

Evidently, early humans who were marking memory with knots, realized that a similar process could be done by using marks to record counts. They started to mark on bone to represent different people, a passage of time, and a hunting success. Tally sticks were the oldest form of record keeping. Throughout the European Middle Ages, customs official's marking tools were the tally stick and notching knife. The British Exchequer used tally sticks around 1100 AD to 1826 AD. This system signified the larger the sum of payment, the more wood would be notched from the tally stick.

In ancient India, the first documented coinage was Punch Marked coins issued between 750 BC and 100 AD.

Next came symbols. They were used initially by merchant unions and later by States. The coins represented a trade currency belonging to a period of serious trade activity and urban development in India. They are generally classified into two periods: the first period credited to the Janapadas or small local states and the second period credited to the Imperial Mauryan period. The images on the coins were sun, animals, trees, hills, etc. and some were geometrical symbols.

Graphic Symbols

Around six thousand years ago in the ancient Middle East, southern Mesopotamia Sumer's growing society had to administer and manage its raw materials, manufactured goods, workers, duties, agricultural fields, tributes, royal and temple inventories, incomes and expenditures. Memory tools like notches and tallies were of no use. There was a need to develop something radically.

During 5300-4300 BC, the *Vinča culture* of the Neolithic age in South-eastern Europe produced pottery and other clay objects carving some sort of symbols. A symbol is a graphic mark that stands for something.

Tokens

Clay tokens were also used in the Middle East for thousands of years. Clay is an abundant material in the Middle East. It was easy to work, easy to erase and easy to preserve by drying in the sun or baking it in the oven. Also clay can easily be carved with graphic marks representing stored information. Large numbers of these clay artefacts dating from 8000-1500 BC have been found at archaeological sites from eastern Iran to southern Turkey and Israel. Most come from ancient Sumer, which is modern-day Iraq.

Around 3700 BC Sumerians in Mesopotomia wrote prefixes and suffixes to basic words. In order to read these standalone words, pronouncing the sound was needed to make sense of a spoken statement. When sound adopted priority in the system, imperfect writing became perfect writing. The change expanded writing's capacities, inspired instant adaptations, and diffused to the Nile, the Iranian Plateau and the Indus Valley.

The idea of perfect writing may have emerged only once in the history of humankind, though there are other possible interpretations. Sketching from standardized pictograms and symbols, the refinement from notches to tablets, the Sumerians of Mesopotamia introduced perfect writing system as a useful tool for humans.

New archaeological discoveries show that urban activity occurred as early as 4000 BC in northeastern Syria. There the development of kingdoms might have happened before the appearance of perfect writing. Likewise, Mesopotamian city-states grew into powerful empires once perfect writing appeared in that area.

Hieroglyphic—Egypt Writing

Ancient Egyptians believed that the writing is the gift of God. Their writings were called hierogluphika (sacred carvings).

As writing hieroglyphs were very time-consuming to draw or engrave, cursive hieratic was developed as a practical tool for writing letters, accounts, labels, receipts, invoices, bills, etc., in 2000 BC. It was a common script in Egypt for writing business, administration, and general literary work. Egyptian scribes and writers attained great wealth, prestige and position. Especially, priestly scribes were highly regarded.

Four thousand years ago, an Egyptian bureaucrat Dua-Khety who sailed on the Nile river to take his son to a school of scribe to learn writing technique said, "It is to writings that you must set your mind.... I do not see an office comparable with the scribe's. I shall make you love books more than you love your mother, and I shall place their excellence before you." We can imagine that learning to write is like Information Technology trend in 20th century. All parents wanted their children to learn writing.

All scribes owned their own writing kit: a slate palette with two shallow cups for keeping red and black ink blocks, a connecting string, a thin wooden brush and a small water jug. Red was used for stress and to divide a text. A student scribe had to learn about seven hundred signs seriously over a period of several years. The writing material was papyrus, a kind of paper produced by pounding and beating scraps of the sharp stem of a water plant Cyprus into sheets.

The earliest discovered papyrus sheets are from a first dynasty tomb at Saqqara from 3000 BC. Papyrus was thin, light, flexible and easy to store. Writing on it with ink was quick; it dried easily and required less surface per word.

In Egypt, scribes taught young boys, rarely girls, at special school introducing the world's first formal educational systems. Students began to copy a teacher's sample text—a proverb, a literary fragment, god's names, etc., on the soft clay tablet. Eventually, an entire social class of scribes evolved.

Cuneiform—Mesopotamia Writing

Late 4000 BC cuneiform signs were found in Uruk, an ancient city of Mesopotamia. Most cuneiform writings happened on clay with a reed stylus. A stylus on clay was a fantastic tool. The stylus with triangular tip could be positioned in three dimensions.

Once the tablet was written, it was dried in the sun or baked to preserve. Interestingly, destructive fires have preserved some of the ancient Mesopotamia's greatest libraries because they were made of clay. But all of ancient Egypt's papyrus libraries have burnt leaving only some manuscripts to exist.

Today cuneiform is considered as one of the best scripts of humankind.

The fundamental differences of the two most important cultures are reflected in their respective writing systems: Mesopotamian cuneiforms show abridged usefulness while Egyptian hieroglyphs convey an organized style. In Mesopotamia, the hardware controlled the software: the use of hand-held clay inspired a system of wedge-writing by which picture and symbol yielded the sound; this phonetic expansion later permitted other languages to borrow and adapt this writing, But in Egypt, the software controlled the hardware: rebus[1] writing was produced on surfaces that accepted ink or engraved writing. The cuneiform

1. Representation of words in the form of pictures or symbols.

script was widely borrowed and adapted. But the Egyptian scripts did not have that effect.

Indus Valley Writing

The Indus Valley script, which was used around 3500-1700 BC with no known relationship with other writing system was forgotten entirely for nearly four thousand years until its discovery by European archaeologists in the 1870s. The outstanding Indus Valley Civilization that developed this script was identified only in 1921.

Potters marked their products with special symbols that indicate the contents. Graffiti on these products appear to record ownership or dedicatee.

Indus Valley script has been found in more than fifteen hundred cities and towns. Some 80 per cent of Indus Valley writing appears as seals or seal impressions. The other types are on clay and ceramic ware tablets, bronze tools and utensils, bone and ivory rods and miniature tablets of copper and soapstone. Small writing was done on bone pins, terracotta bangles and gold jewellery. Although most Indus writings are merely one cm in height, an inscription was found at the northern gateway at Dholavira, whose height is over 30 cm. If it had been used as a public sign, it indicates that literacy was widespread in that ancient civilization.

Some 4,200 scripts have been unearthed so far. The longest Indus valley inscription consists of twenty signs in three lines. No papyrus texts have been found. Interestingly, none of the Indus Valley signs resemble either Egyptian hieroglyphs or Mesopotamian cuneiforms. Nevertheless, some resemble Proto-Elamite[2] script.

Probably, the Indus Valley signs were used basically for commercial purposes: stamping packages of commodities with a mark of identification, personal names, titles of office and names of gods. This writing seems it was closely associated with the ruling elite and with the merchants of the Indus Valley's prominent centres.

2. Modern-day Iran.

The archaeological record shows that the Indus Valley script was abandoned at all northern sites when the elite lost authority around 1900 BC. Until recently, it was believed that the people of Indus Valley were driven out of their towns and cities by invaders. If these invaders were Indo-Aryans, then the fundamental language of the Indus Valley script might be of Proto-Dravidian, the mother tongue of the large Dravidian language family now reduced to Baluchistan, Afghanistan and southern India. But archaeological proof for this invasion is not available. Instead, it appears that the fluctuations of the Indus River might have caused floods, which destroyed the civilization's agricultural base along with the Indus script steering into the disruption of trade and economic ruin gradually.

The Indus Valley script developed and perished in its eastern isolation, inspiring no-one and vanishing from human recollection. This is the fate of many earlier writing systems and scripts.

Clay-pressed writing in the Indus Valley flourished for some time and then vanished.

Aramaic Writing

From 1000 BC, North Semitic scripts—Aramaic and Canaanite emerged. Aramaic was as significant as Phoenician, because it was the source not only for Hebrew and Arabic, but also for the hundreds of scripts of Indian subcontinent and outside.

At first, Aramaic speakers used the Phoenician script. During 900 BC, Aramaic speakers were expanding a distinct script of their own called Aramaic. By 800 and 700 BC, Aramaic had become the widely spoken language in the ancient Near East, the interlanguage of the entire region. It eventually became the official language of the Persian Empire (550-330 BC).

The Indic Scripts of India and South-East Asia

Writing did not begin on the Indian subcontinent until 800 BC because Brahmins, India's priestly class, considered writing as inferior to speech. Indus Valley writing had been extinct for thousands of years ago. Even when writing began, oral transmission continued for many centuries. Ultimately, the skill of writing flourished to create great literature in a variety of languages and scripts all over India.

Today India possesses world's richest and most varied literary traditions. Yet, 50% of Indian population is illiterate.

Scholars agree that Semitic writing was the direct source for writing on the Indian subcontinent, possibly the Aramaic script that dominated the Middle East in the 1000 BC. Although some cases of earlier Indian writing are known, the longer inscriptions are the well-known edicts of King Asoka from 253-250 BC, which were carved on stone pillars throughout India. Kharosthi and Brahmi, the two earliest Indian scripts appear in the Asoka inscriptions. This indicate that writing is not native. Even though there are more than two hundred recognized scripts in India, they all derived completely from the single Brahmi script, which is derived from Semitic source.

Initially, northern India inspired by Aramaic used the Kharosthi script, which used right to left for writing and reading. Eventually, Brahmi script replaced Kharosthi script.

Indian scribes deliberately redesigned the Semitic writing according to the well-known phonological principles. Steven Roger recognizes that the Indians were the best linguists. The West did not have Indian level of linguistic sophistication until the early 1800s. Ancient Indian scribes classified their letters according to places of articulation: first vowels and diphthongs, then consonants with default *a,* in the exact back-to-front order as in the human mouth—gutturals (the throat), palatals (tongue), cerebrals (tip of the tongue touches the roof of the mouth), dentals, labials (closing the lips), and semivowels (a vowel like sound that serves as a consonant, e.g. *y*, *w*) and spirants (consonant produced by breath moving against a narrowing of the vocal tract, e.g. *s*, *sh*). Indic writing remained consonantal alphabetic.

Between 700 and 400 BC, the grammarian Panini standardized the language in the book *Aṣṭādhyāyī,* which consists of strict grammar rules.

Gupta script of 400 AD was the Brahmi's first main daughter language. Gupta Empire spread from northern, central and western India, from the early 400 AD to the late 600 AD. The Gupta alphabet became the precursor of most Indic scripts through Devanagari.

Around 600 AD, Gupta script inspired the Nagari, Sarada, Tibetan and Pali scripts. Once Nagari completely developed in the eleventh century, it become Devanagari or heavenly Nagari because of Sanskrit literature. Devanagari alphabet consists of 48 letters: thirteen vowels and 35 consonants. A student must learn many writing conventions: different vowel forms; nasalization; muting of the default *a*; weak aspiration; and other complex details. Word division is known as *sandhi*. A sentence ended with I and a complete passage of text ended with II.

Gradually, Devanagari became India's main script. It is used to convey many other regional languages such as Hindi, Nepali, Marwari, and so on.

Another member derived from Nagari is Proto-Bengali. Proto-Bengali is used to convey a number of important languages: Bengali, Assamese, Manipuri, Maithili, some Tibeto-Burmese languages and Santali.

Sarada script is another Gupta daughter. Another Gupta daughter Pali was parent to many scripts such as Siamese or Old Thai, Burmese, Kavi, Sinhalese that are used for writing Prakrit languages related to Buddhism. As Buddhism expanded, Pali scripts also expanded.

South Indian Dravidian scripts convey the subcontinent's principal native language family. Another consequential Southern Indian script was Grantha.

Chinese Writing

Initially, Chinese writing materials contained brush and ink, bark, bamboo strips, wood in addition to carvings on ivory, ox shoulder bone, turtle shell, and soft wax were used to draw bronze castings. Silk also was used as writing material during 220 AD for writing official documents and correspondence. Afterwards old silk was pulped and the gummy like material was spread thinly on some writing surface to dry, which produced a long-lasting writing substance. Eventually, it presented the world's most useful and commonplace writing material: paper. Another invention from Cai Lun's was cheaper than silk. His paper making was made of old rags, fishing nets and tree bark. In China, paper manufacturing remained a state monopoly until 700s and its technique was a closely protected secret.

To write Chinese character, the writer must follow the fixed number of strokes between 1 and 25 for each character in a given order and with a specified starting point for each stroke. Calligraphy, the art of beautiful writing is very important to the Chinese. Calligraphers should have variety of brushes, paper, a paper weight, an inkstone, a stone mortar for grinding and containing ink, an inkstick and a small bowl of water. Brushes consisted the hairs of marten, goat or hare. They claim it offers the pressure that results in loveliest character lines. Each character exhibits the calligrapher's education, skill and artistry. While Western alphabets are completely functional, Chinese logograms are both functional and artistic at the same time.

Mayan Writing

Previously, it was thought that the remarkable hundreds of Mayan monumental inscriptions found in the ruins of great Mayan civilization were only pictorial decorations. Now it is comprehended that 85 percent of the Mayan hieroglyphic collection identified to be more advanced perfect writing system. This illustrates that the ancient Mayan kingdom was the only historical civilization in the New World with records going back to 300 BC.

All Mayan writing was done on bark-paper and deer-hide using a fresh surface of lime sizing (a specific substance that is applied to other material to act as a protecting filler). First outlines were drawn with red paint and then areas were filled in with various colours. Red colour from iron compounds and other colours were also from other mineral origin. Black paint made of charcoal or soot was used to outline finished figures.

Thousands of bark-paper or deer-hide manuscripts adorned Mayan libraries filled with histories, genealogies, astronomical tables, ritual prescriptions and other types of texts.

Greek Writing

During 500 BC, Herodotus wrote about a legendary Phoenician prince of Tyre and brother of Europa, "The Phoenicians who came with Kadmos...introduced to Greece a number of accomplishments of which the most important was writing, which I believe had not been known to the Greeks until then."

The Greeks borrowed Phoenician writing system and then adapted it to the local needs. All Phoenician words begin with consonants, but many Greek words begin with vowels.

Roman Emperor Constantine I transferred his capital from pagan Rome to Christian Byzantium and renamed it as Constantinople in 330 AD. Consequently, Greek culture and Greek writings experienced a revitalization. The Byzantine Empire preserved and dispersed the teachings of ancient Greece leading the Western world in science and humanities. Also, it influenced Arab scholars and scientists, who carried Greek teachings and translation along with their own compositions to different parts of learning centres. Such transmissions introduced ancient Greek philosophy and science to western Europe. Ancient Greece had inspired Rome, and Byzantine Greece inspired the medieval world through Greek alphabetic script.

It was the Romans who invented the basic forms of our letters. Like Greeks, Romans wrote only in capitals and cursive letter with no upper- or lower-case distinction. Basic Roman letter shapes were originally like Greek letters, with no variation of thick and thin. Nevertheless, the Romans later introduced a light, angled stress to their capitals writing in ink with a broad nib on papyrus.

Written Word Became a Thought

Earlier times people read aloud. Usually, literary texts were chanted or murmured for meditation and for better memorization. Silent reading was practically unknown. In ancient time, the silent reading was always perceived as something extraordinary.

Augustine was wondering when he witnessed his teacher St. Ambrose reading silently to himself. In the early 400 AD, St. Augustine with disbelief and amazement noted:

> When he was reading, he drew his eyes along over the leaves, and his heart searched into the sense, but his voice and tongue were silent. Number of time, when we were present, we still saw him reading to himself, and never otherwise. But with what intent so ever he did it, that man certainly had a good meaning in it.

Silent reading largely replaced loud reading in the middle ages. St Augustine's surprise at watching his teacher reading a text quietly to himself shows a new idea of writing's function in society as a form of information transportation. In the Middle Age, the written word was considered as different from thought. Gradually, the notion changed and written word itself became thought.

Development of Writing Materials

During 500 BC, books consisted of papyrus scrolls, some were more than twenty meter long. In earlier centuries, animal skins had become a cultural curiosity. Several leather documents (any skin tanned with things like acacia shells or oak bark becomes leather) of Egyptian hieroglyphs written around 2500 BC have survived. Then, skin, as a writing material was very popular throughout western Asia, Iraq and Persia. They used goat and sheep skins to write on. For many centuries, Greek, Etruscan and Roman writing was done on stone, leaves, bark, linen, clay and pottery, wall spaces, precious metals, lead, bronze, wood and sometimes animal skins.

With vellum or parchment one could write on both sides of a sheet, which doubled writing capacity. French historian Henri-Jean Martin said, "The appearance of the codex—the work presented on pages written on both sides rather than on one side of continuous scroll—was undoubtedly the most important revolution in the book in the Common Era."

Vellum (skin as a writing material) gradually replaced papyrus altogether. The scripts on Vellum were used to write Homer's work in the Greek world and for Virgil in Rome's classical period. Such writings were highly valued and large numbers of them were also produced.

Who was able to read such works in two thousand years ago? By 100 AD, literacy was common throughout Roman Empire and citizens knew well about reading and writing. Nearly two thousand letters and documents on wooden tablets have been found in England, showing how writing was so common in ancient Roman society, even in this remote place of Roman Empire. Writing retained personal contacts keeping social network and Roman culture even in foreign lands.

In the past, writing material papyrus was expensive. Only few people could afford to buy written texts and not many could read longer works of literature. However, by 200 AD parchment became available in larger quantities. This cheaper writing material inspired increased production of written texts. In fact, parchment was available for many centuries before. In 190 BC, Eumenes II longing to establish a library encouraged his people to perfect a technique of writing material by thinly stretching and drying the skin of sheep and goats. Parchment was named after its place of invention, Pergamum.

In India

In ancient India, various materials were used as writing material. For example:

Stone: Carving inscriptions on stone pillars is a very old tradition.

Brick: A large number of inscribed bricks have been unearthed from archaeological museums.

Wood: Wooden board called phalaka was widely used for writing in ancient India. On it characters were written with ink or chalk. Phalaka was used by the students for learning to write alphabets and for doing elementary calculations.

Cloth: Cotton cloth was also used as writing material in ancient India. Nearchos (c. 326 BC), an admiral of Alexander's navy, has mentioned that the Indians wrote letters on well-beaten cotton cloth. Cloth was prepared for writing by placing a thin layer of wheat or rice pulp and polishing with a smooth stone after the cloth was dried. Black ink was used to write on the pata.

Cloth 2: In Karnataka, processed cloth known as kaditam, was in use. It was covered with a paste of tamarind-seed and afterwards blackened with charcoal-powder. Chalk or a kind of soapstone pencils were used for writing on this black cloth. Alberuni writes, "I have been told that the ancestry of this royal family of Kabul, written on silk, exists in the fortress of Nagarkot."

Copper: Copper was the most commonly used material to write in ancient and medieval India. The copper-plates were known as tamrapata. Fahian (c. 400 AD) records the existence of copper-plates in the Buddhist monasteries dating back to Buddha's time.

Palm-leaf: Palm-leaf was one of the most important materials used for writing purposes. To prepare palm-leaves for writing they were first dried, boiled in water and then dried again. Then they were smoothened and polished with a stone or conch-shell. The leaves were then cut to size. In south India, a pointed stylus was used to incise letters on the palm-leaf, and then black or colour pigment was rubbed into the incised letters. The manuscripts were generally placed between two wooden boards and the cord passing through the holes were wrapped round the boards.

Birch-bark: Another very popular material for writing purposes in ancient India was birch-bark, called *Bhurja-patra* in Sanskrit. The inner bark of this tree was used for writing. The Greek writer of Alexander's time Q. Curtius mentions the tender inner bark of trees was serving the purpose of writing material. Alberuni records the method of preparation of *Bhurja-patra*: "They take a piece one yard long and as broad as the outstretched fingers of the hand and prepare it in various ways. They oil and polish it so as to make it hard and smooth, and then they write on it. The whole book is wrapped up in a piece of cloth and fastened between two tablets of the same size. Such a book is called *Puthi*." A reed pen and specially prepared ink was used for writing.

In India, South-East Asia or East Asia parchment was never used. The idea of writing sacred texts on the skin of butchered animals hurt Hindus and Buddhists. And the Chinese never used it because they already had paper by the 200 AD. But in Europe parchment meant that individual papyrus sheets had no longer needed to roll-up to scrolls; parchment could be collated and bound to create a manuscript or a book. It facilitated written literature's use and conservation like nothing before.

In the 1300s, citizens began to demand education for their children. As a result public schools opened and thousands of boys and girls joined the school and started learning calculations, mathematics, grammar and logic. This new trend transformed all of western Europe in 1300s. With quantity came loss of quality. The writers of the 1300s and 1400s no longer observed the high standards of their ancestors, and their letters being less exact and less elegant.

Something we have not noticed and have taken it granted is that the English handwriting does not resemble to the English printed script. But it should be noted that English writing comprises entirely different scripts even though they all share the Latin alphabet as a writing system. By the 1100s, English scribes were writing an altered Saxon script for English. Shortly, a variety of mixed scripts emerged that integrated features of cursive and book writings.

In English, the use of upper-case and lower-case letters means that every student studying to read and write has to learn not only 26 letters, but 52, in addition to recommended cursive forms and a large number of abbreviations, ideograms and other marks: &, $, +, =, @, % and so on.

Today, the Latin alphabet is world's most preferred writing system.

Punctuation

To conserve precious parchment, complicated abbreviations and restrictions appeared. During twelfth century, the creation of large books and strong, bold, new letters occurred. During thirteenth century, a swift decrease in letter size, compression, a new angularity and slanting strokes refined and developed into hairlines due to great demand for Bibles. In order to conserve space, scribes began to use Arabic numerals 1, 2, 3, 4 instead of Roman numerals i, ii, iii, iv. Arabic numerals are now used worldwide.

Almost all ancient scribes wrote their words together without separation. They seemingly thought that lack of word separation was not a bottleneck in reading their work.

Early Greek, Latin and Sanskrit scribes also left no space between separate words. Only paragraphs were separated as independent components of text. Aristotle (384-322 BC) placed a short horizontal stroke (as in shorthand) under the start of a new line to indicate a break of sentence or the end of a topic. Now, we follow this convention with the rule of capitalizing the first letter of a sentence. The indenting of new paragraphs was introduced from the 1600s.

Because the silent reading increased in mediaeval period, scribes found a necessity to represent the word as an independent unit. So an alphabetic methodology of writing a language was chosen to group letters in units with some space left between the units. Later these units were recognized to be words.

Chinese and Japanese as a rule still do not observe word separation. The earliest word separation in Western writing was not punctuation as we understand the term today. Plato (427-347 BC) used a colon (:) to signify the end of a section of text. Aristophanes of Byzantium (180 BC), director of the Library of Alexandria in northern Egypt, has invented a system of point punctuation: the high point ˙ indicating a full stop (American period); the middle point · an ordinary pause; and the low or line point . a pause between the two, like today's semicolon.

Aristophanes also devised long (¯) and short (˘) syllable marks and the hyphen (-) to signal connection like compound words. Many other reading signs were used in Greek and Latin manuscripts – dieresis (a mark (¨) placed over a vowel to indicate that it is sounded separately, as in *naïve*, *Brontë*, quotation marks, single-letter identifiers, space fillers and so on.

Gradually, Aristophanes' middle point (·) disappeared. The baseline comma was introduced into Greek and Latin texts around 650 AD. The modern full stop or period was introduced by Alcuin of York around 800 AD to indicate the end of long passages of text. By this time, the semicolon (;) already possessed its present value. Afterward, paragraph or chapter endings were marked with : or :-.

The question mark (?) first appeared in Latin manuscripts around the eighth or ninth century but it appeared in English around 1587. Earlier it was abbreviated as Qo—with Q above the o—and then it was written as  and eventually as ?.

In similar fashion, the exclamation mark (!) conveys Latin *io!* Or 'hurrah!' with the i written above the o: .

The apostrophe (`) also credited to Aristophanes was used in ancient, medieaval and later manuscripts to indicate the omission of letters.

Today most of these punctuation marks are used in nearly all alphabetic systems in all languages throughout the world.

Paper

As described earlier, manufacture of paper was invented in China in 105 AD and kept as a closely-guarded secret. Centuries passed before others discovered the Chinese technique and effectively produced paper. The West learned paper-making technique through an indirect and lengthy route.

Samarkand's Muslim governor captured many Chinese during Central Asian Battle in 751 AD. Some captured men were proficient in paper production. Consequently, Samarkand paper composed of linen rags instead of mulberry bark became a valuable export. The knowledge of its manufacture quickly spread throughout the Muslim world: to Baghdad (~793 AD), to Damascus (900 AD), to Cairo (900 AD) and to Sicily (1100 AD). In 1200s, Arab merchants introduced paper manufacture to India.

Paper made a great impact on Western civilization in the beginning and to the whole world later. Parchment and vellum could never have supported mass literacy, worldwide printing, modern offices, newspapers, government records, and general education and so on. These modern facilities are the consequences of paper and the printing press. In the 1800s, as a result of general education, an increased demand for paper caused wood to replace rags as its chief ingredient. By the 1900s, paper had become "the most important, efficient and totally irreplaceable medium of modern information storage. Economically and intellectually our society had become a paper society."

Paper is the world's favoured writing material for the past five hundred years only.

Printing

Steven Roger Fischer writes, "The history of printing is an integral part of the general history of civilization. Printing changed society in a fundamental way. By making almost unlimited copies of identical texts available by mechanical and electronic means, it brought society from limited access to knowledge to almost unlimited access to knowledge. Printing actually enabled modern society. It would be no exaggeration to claim that printing has been as important to humankind as the controlled use of fire and the wheel."

Scribes require more time to copy a book. Even today, to copy Torah, the five books of Moses or Mahabharata, 18 books of Vyasa, can take a scribe/clerk more than a year. Usually, hand copying means books are very expensive and very few readers. Few readers implies low literacy, which is a big disadvantages for a society. Europeans became readers on a large scale only after the printing press appeared in the mid-1400s.

Minoan Greeks are regarded as the original inventors of printing with movable type.

Possibly, they were inspired by existing seals and devised a movable type. Each seal previously used only for names, places or consignments, became a punch of movable type to construct a complete message, syllable by syllable.

China has a long history of block printing. Block printing reproduces whole face of text as the smallest printable unit, while movable type uses smaller exchangeable units such as individual logograms, syllables or letters to produce a face of text. Once they invented paper in 100 AD, they made impression on this new material by means of rubbing and other techniques. In 600 AD, Chinese scribes were producing high quality paper texts with extra care. In order to prevent damaging the original, scribes began to produce an exact copy on wooden blocks, first using negative (backward) characters, then cutting positive ones. Using ink, they produced black script on white paper.

First a text was written down on paper. Then it was turned over and placed on a wooden block to dry. Once it dried, the paper's surface was rubbed away and oil was spread over the block to bring out the characters left behind. Then an engraver cut away the wood around the characters, leaving them in relief, to raise. With a brush, Indian ink was applied to these relief characters. Wet paper was laid over the block of relief characters and rubbed with a special bamboo-fibre tool.

Bi Sheng, alchemist-smith in China, designed another technique for making movable characters in baked clay in 1045 AD for printing purpose. Later came movable type in wood, metal and porcelain. But wood-block printing was preferred in China because of the large number of characters in the Chinese writing system.

In the early 1400s, many book publishers realised that copying and writing books by hand was too slow to satisfy their growing orders because it took too long to copy one book. Therefore, publishers needed a faster and cheaper technique.

The invention of printing by movable metal type and the printing press freed human hand and pen in Europe in 1400s.

Medieval Europe's naturalization of the written word and its superior production transformed Western society and eventually the whole world.

Typewriters

Just like printing, the invention of the typewriter also changed the writing manner, appearance and function in society. The first commercial typewriter was invented by an American Christopher Lathan Scholes in 1867 and put on sale by the Remington Company in 1873. This typewriter with 44 keys was able to type all the capital letters, numbers and some punctuation. Sometime later, the shift key was invented with lower-case letters on the capital letters. Additional copies could also be generated by inserting carbon papers.

Modern electronic typewriters, word processors, and personal computers have overcome many of the hidden drawbacks of the basic typewriter by providing a wide range of typographical options such as fonts, sizes, boldface, italics, underline, justified setting and many special symbols and many more.

Stenography/Shorthand

Stenography or shorthand is a method of fast writing using special symbols or abbreviations for common letters or words. It is designed to manage short-term preservation of speech. It is an ancient practice. It is said that the Greek historian Xenophon 430-354 BC wrote the dialogues of Socrates in a form of shorthand. And also the Roman Marcus Tullius Tiro devised a shorthand to record the speeches of Cicero in 63 BC. For a long time, shorthand was ignored and revived again only in the 1500s. People discovered its benefits during the Industrial Revolution and realized that it will help office work, court works, etc. The two most popular versions of shorthand in English are from Isaac Pitman from England and John Robert Gregg from US.

But shorthand's use has weakened in recent years because of new technology.

Future of Writing

Use of writing in society will change dramatically due to new technology. However, the benefits and joys of reading and writing will still outshine new technology for many centuries because writing is inherent in most educated cultures.

Those people with intelligence and understanding will always appreciate the skills of reading and writing. Once linguist Florian Coulmas wrote, "the skills of reading and writing provide access to knowledge and knowledge is power." Recent studies have shown that the actual act of writing about one's feelings can liberate from depression, boost the immune system and lower blood pressure. Aristotle believed that writing could express 'affections of the soul'.

Four thousand years ago, an Egyptian scribe brushed in ink on some papyrus: "A man has perished and his body has become earth. All his relatives have crumbled to dust. It is writing that makes him remembered."

4

Ancient Languages

Aramaic

Aramaic is the ancient language of the Semitic family group, which includes the Assyrians, Babylonians, Chaldeans, Arameans, Hebrews, and Arabs.

Scholars have found first glimpse of Aramaic language in a small number of ancient royal inscriptions from approximately three thousand years ago (900-700 BC). These inscriptions reveal the history of the early small Aramean kingdoms, in the territories of modern Syria and Southeast Turkey living under the rising Assyrian empire. The inscriptions provide information about dedication to the gods, international treaties, and memorials. After the conquests of Alexander the Great of Macedonia, Aramaic language remained the vernacular of the conquered peoples in Syria, Mesopotamia and the adjacent countries. Eventually, Armaic language yielded to Arabic in the 900 AD.

Aramaic language is believed to have first appeared among the Aramaeans[1] about late 1100 BC By the 800 BC it was accepted by the Assyrians as a second language.

The mass deportations of people by the Assyrians and the use of Aramaic as a *lingua franca* by Babylonian merchants served to spread the language.

Script

The primary Aramaic or Proto-Hebrew alphabet was developed between 1000 BC and 900 BC and replaced Assyrian cuneiform style as a main writing system of the Assyrian kingdom. This Armaic alphabet is considered as the ancestor for

1. Aramaeans were a Northwest Semitic people who originated from modern-day Syria during the late Bronze Age and Iron Age.

a number of Semitic and Kharosthi alphabet families. At the end of the 600 BC the Aramaic alphabet was replaced by the Hebrew square script, which is also identified as the Aramaic alphabet. Actually, a large part of the Hebrew and Arabic languages is borrowed from Aramaic, including the Alphabet.

This is a consonant alphabet with no vowel indication.

Written from right to left in horizontal lines.

Armaic Script

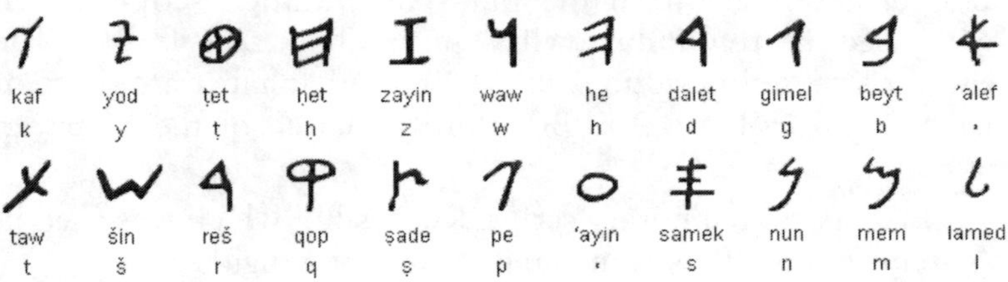

Aramaic Square Scripts

Elephantine Payrus 500 BC

Great Isaiah Scroll 200-100 BC

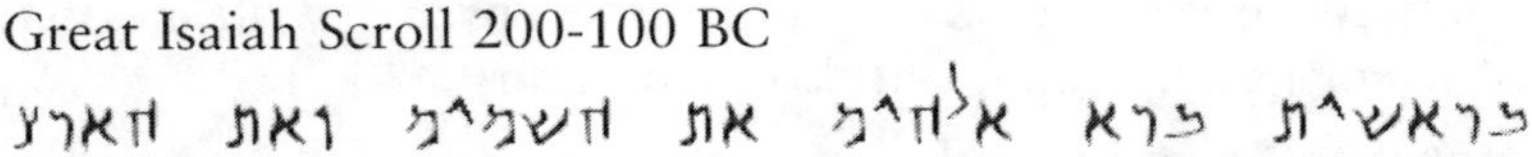

Habakkuk Pesher 150-100 BC

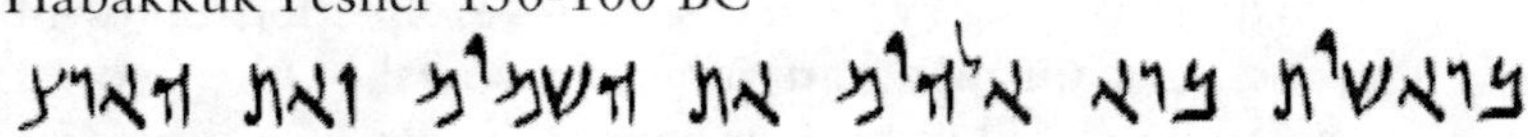

Nabataean Aramaic 100 AD

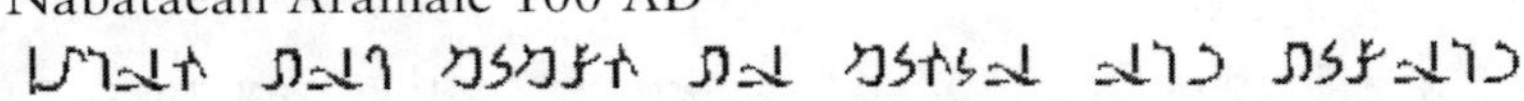

Codex Leningradensis 1010 AD

Modern Hebrew

בראשית ברא אלהים את השמים ואת הארצ

Courtesy: Jack Kilmon

Brahmi Script

The Brahmi script represents the earliest post-Indus form of texts, and some of the earliest historical inscriptions of Brahmi script found in India. It is the ancestor to hundreds of scripts originated in South, Southeast, and East Asia.

One theory suggests that the Brahmi script has been shaped on the Aramaic or Phoenician alphabets, and appeared in India sometime before 500 BC. Another theory is that Brāhmī developed from the Indus or Harappa script, which was used in the Indus valley until about 2,000 BC. The earliest known inscriptions in the Brāhmī alphabet are those of King Ashoka of 270-232 BC, third monarch of the Mauryan dynasty.

Like its contemporary script, Kharoṣṭhī,[2] which was used in Afghanistan and Pakistan, Brāhmī was an abugida.[3]

Indus script inscriptions are found showing coins, pots, etc. with only a small number of alphabets. After the introduction of Brāhmī, Indus script might have developed elaborately keeping the name later Brāhmī.

History: The Brāhmī script was the ancestor for most of South Asian Writing Systems. Brāhmī was used to write a variety of languages, including Sanskrit and Prakrit.

Notable Features

- Type of writing system: abugida—each letter represents a consonant with an inherent vowel. Other vowels were indicated using a variety of diacritics and separate letters.
- Letters are grouped according to the way they are pronounced.

---

2. The Kharoṭṣhī script is an ancient Indic script used by the Gandhara culture of ancient Northwest, primarily modern-day Afghanistan and Pakistan to write the Gandhari language and the Sanskrit language. It was also used in Bactira, the modern-day Tajikstan; Gandhara during Kushan Empire; Sogdina, an ancient civilization of Iranian people, and down the Silk Road.
3. Abugida is a consonant-vowel sequences written as a unit.

- Many letters have more than one form.
- Direction of writing: left to right in horizontal lines.

Brāhmī is usually written from left to right. However, a coin of the 400 BC has been found inscribed with Brāhmī running from right to left, as in Aramaic.

Gupta script on stone Kanheri Caves, one of the earliest descendants of Brāhmī Script.

Over a period of a millennium, Brāhmī developed into many regional scripts, commonly classified as rounded letters in southern India group and an angular letters in Northern India group. Gupta script emerged during the Gupta period with northern Brāhmī style.

Brāhmī is a syllabic alphabet, which means that each sign can be a simple consonant or a syllable with the consonant and the inherent vowel 'a'. Brāhmī and all succeeding Brāhmī-derived scripts indicate the same consonant with a different vowel by drawing extra strokes connecting to the character are called *matra*.

The following chart is the basic Brāhmī script.

And an example of strokes added to indicate different vowels to the consonants *k* and *l*.

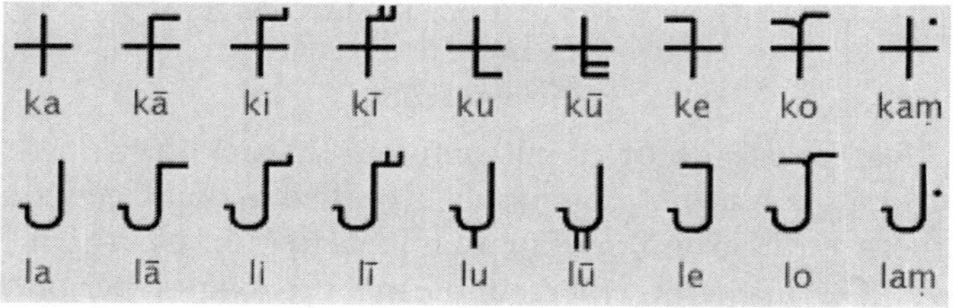

Aramaic Hypothesis on Brāhmī Script

According to the Aramaic hypothesis, the oldest Brāhmī inscriptions demonstrate outstanding equivalents with Aramaic for the sounds that are matching between the two languages, especially if the letters are flipped to imitate the change in writing direction. They suggest more research needs to be done in this field.

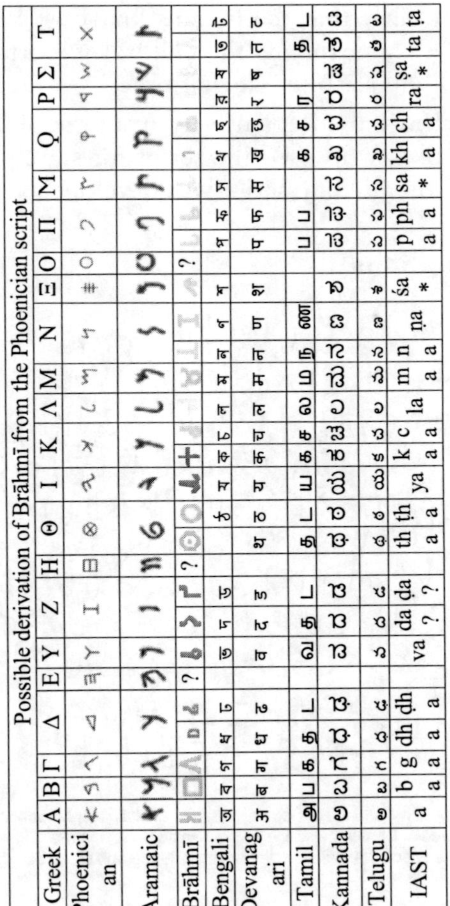

Possible derivation of Brāhmī from the Phoenician script

Courtesy: Wikepedia Common

Pre-Ashokan Epigraphy

Due to the expansion of the Achaemenid Empire[4] under Darius the Great to the Indus valley, the earliest contact of the Hindu Kush area with the Aramaic script happened in the 600 BC. It appears that there was no script to write Indo-Aryan languages before the rule of Emperor Ashoka in the 300 BC in spite of the evidence available about Aramaic. Megasthenes, an ambassador to the Mauryan court a quarter century before

4. First Persian Empire.

Ashoka, noted clearly that the Indians "have no knowledge of written letters". This explains the cultural importance of oral literature for Hindu scripture at that time.

Brāhmī is clearly used extensively from the 300 BC during the rule of Ashoka, who used the script for stately edicts. It is considered that the Brāhmī script was developed at around this time.

Ashoka Inscriptions

9th Major Edict of Ashoka found at Sopara, Vasai, District-Thane, Maharashtra. Original Boulder preserved at Chhatrapati Shivaji Puran-vastu Sangrahalaya (Museum at Mumbai). This image is created by Ashok from the original Photograph of the Boulder.

Semitic Language

The Semitic family is a part of the larger Afro-asiatic[5] family of languages found in north and north-east Africa. Diakonoff opines that the Semitic language originated between the Nile Delta and Canaan as the northernmost branch of Afro-asiatic.

5. Afro-asiatic, also known as Hamito-Semitic is a large language family, including 300 and more living languages. Afro-asiatic languages are spoken predominantly in the Middle East, North Africa and some other parts of Africa. It is estimated that more than 300 million people speak an Afro-asiatic language.

Recent scholars identify the origin of Semitic languages in the Eastern Mediterranean Levant around 3750 BC. It is assumed that Proto-Semitic language reached the Arabian Peninsula by approximately the 4000 BC from which numerous Semitic languages continued to spread externally.

During the 3000 BC, a bulk of ancient Semitic languages practiced cuneiform, a standard logographic script. The authority of written languages was contested by vigorous and innovative oral languages and quickly separated following every minor phonetic shift.

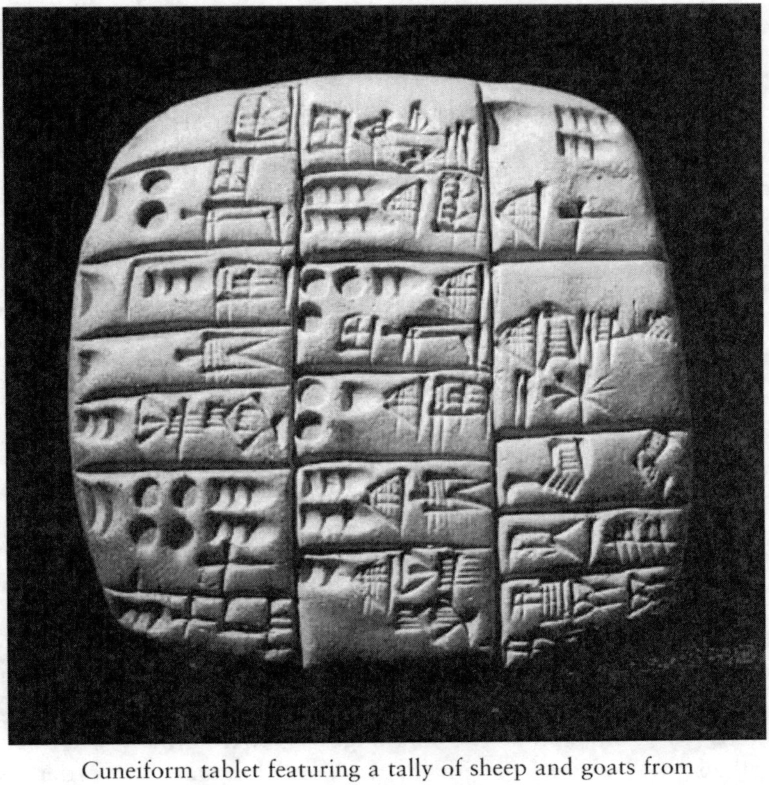

Cuneiform tablet featuring a tally of sheep and goats from Tello, southern Iraq.

Hebrew Language

In the beginning, all humans spoke the same language.

The first type of written language was picture writing. The humans used simple pictures to express the things they wanted to convey in writing.

Cuneiform is the term used to describe the picture writing of early Shemites (i.e. Sumerians and Babylonians).

Hieroglyphics is the term used to describe the picture writing of the early Hamites (i.e. Egyptians, Hittites, and Canaanites).

Another type of written language described as 'sound language' is Phonetic Language. This expression was taken from the Greek word *phone* (English *sound*). The characters of a phonetic language represent 'sounds', instead of 'concepts'.

The table below shows how modern phonetic characters were developed from ancient hieroglyphs.

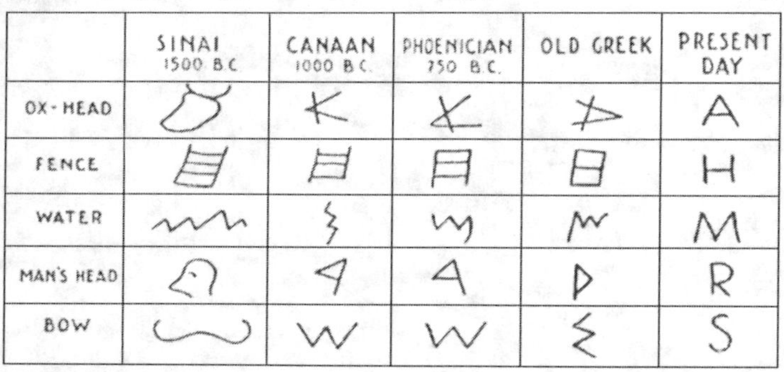

When read as a phonetic expression, the ox-head symbol is pronounced as 'ah', and the fence symbol is pronounced as 'kh'.
Courtesy: Wikipedia

Abraham is the founding father of the Israelites with a prominent role in Judaism, Christianity, and Islam. It is believed that Abraham spoke the language of Eber, which was also called the Hebrew. He invented 'sound language' in order to communicate with the people of other nations with whom he came in contact during his migration from Ur to Egypt. Using his twenty-two letter alphabet, he was able to convert any word into a sound representation.

The table below shows original twenty-two letter alphabet used over 3,000 years ago.

The original Torah[6] and the original books of the Old Testament were written in this same ancient Hebrew script. At present, very little physical evidence exists about this ancient Hebrew script.

The figure below shows the modern Aramean letters currently used to read and write the Hebrew language.

6. The word Torah in Hebrew means 'to guide or to teach'. The meaning of the word is teaching, doctrine, or instruction.

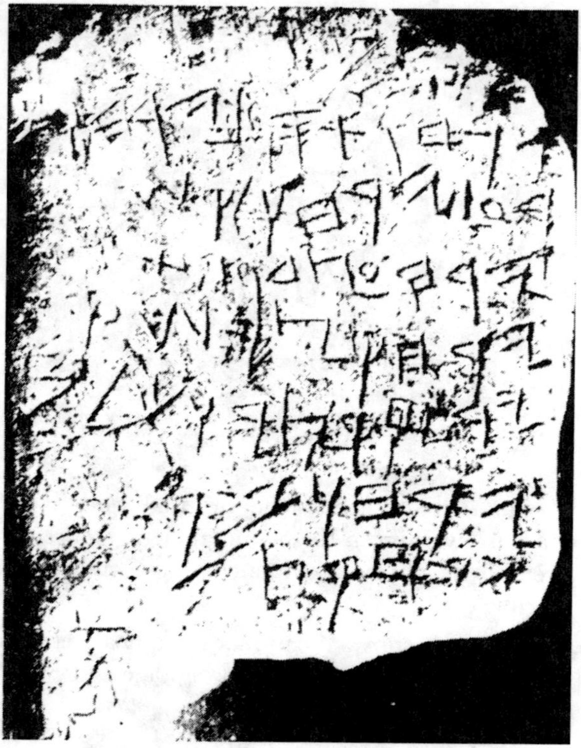

Courtesy: http://www.zaqen.info/hislangu.htm

The artifact shown above is a rare example of ancient Hebrew script. It is a part of what is known as the Gezer Calendar. Named after the city in which it was found, this highly prized ancient clay artifact, written about 925 BC demonstrates two things:

(1) The ancient Israelites wrote in ancient Hebrew script,

(2) The ancient Israelites used a calendar.

Modern Hebrew is written from right to left without vowels using the Hebrew alphabet, which is consonant-only script of 22 letters. Modern scripts are based on the square letter form, known as *Ashurit* (Assyrian), which was developed from the Aramaic script.

A cursive Hebrew script is used in handwriting.

The table below illustrates the Hebrew characters in alphabetical order. The Hebrew is written from right to left. Alef is the first letter of the Hebrew alphabet and Tav is the last. The Hebrew alphabet is called the 'alefbet', because of its first two letters Alef and Bet.

Letters of the Alefbet

ט	ח	ז	ו	ה	ד	ג	ב	א
Teit (T)	Cheit (Ch)	Zayin (Z)	Vav (V/O/U)	Hei (H)	Dalet (D)	Gimel (G)	Beit (B/V)	Alef (Silent)
ס	ן	נ	ם	מ	ל	ך	כ	י
Samekh (S)	Nun (N)	Nun (N)	Mem (M)	Mem (M)	Lamed (L)	Khaf (Kh)	Kaf (K/Kh)	Yod (Y)
ת	ש	ר	ק	ץ	צ	ף	פ	ע
Tav (T/S)	Shin (Sh/S)	Reish (R)	Qof (Q)	Tzadei (Tz)	Tzadei (Tz)	Fe (F)	Pei (P/F)	Ayin (Silent)

The Hebrew Alphabet

Courtesy: Wikipedia

Vowels and Points

Like most early Semitic alphabetic writing systems, the alefbet has no vowels.

After the Romans ousted the Jews from Israel, Hebrew literacy declined and the rabbis recognized the need for aids to pronunciation. Therefore, they developed a system of dots and dashes called *nikkud* (points). These dots and dashes are written above, below or inside the letter. Most *nikkud* are used to indicate vowels.

The Hebrew Alphabet

consists of 22 (2 × 11) letters, so the five finals were added to make up three series of 9, or 27 in all:

Aleph	א	= 1	Yod	י	= 10	Koph	ק	= 100	
Beth	ב	= 2	Kaph	כ	= 20	Resh	ר	= 200	
Gimel	ג	= 3	Lamed	ל	= 30	Shin	ש	= 300	
Daleth	ד	= 4	Mem	מ	= 40	Tau	ת	= 400	
He	ה	= 5	Nun	נ	= 50	Koph	ך	= 500	Finals
Vau	ו	= 6	Samech	ס	= 60	Mem	ם	= 600	Finals
Zayin	ז	= 7	Ayin	ע	= 70	Nun	ן	= 700	Finals
Cheth	ח	= 8	Pe	פ	= 80	Pe	ף	= 800	Finals
Teth	ט	= 9	Tsaddi	צ	= 90	Tsaddi	ץ	= 900	Finals

Sanskrit

Sanskrit is derived from the root *saṃ-skar*—"to put together, compose, arrange, prepare" where *saṃ*=together and *(s) kar*=do, make.

Another meaning for *saṃskṛta* is the cultured language. Sanskrit was used for religious and learned discourse in ancient India, and contrasted with the *prākṛta* a sort of natural, artless, normal, ordinary languages spoken by the people.

Sanskrit is a member of the Indo-Iranian sub-family of the Indo-European family of languages. Its closest ancient relatives are the Iranian languages such as Old Persian and Avestan.

In order to explain the common features shared by Sanskrit and other Indo-European languages, many scholars have proposed migration hypotheses asserting that the original speakers of Sanskrit arrived India from the north-west some time during the early 2000 BC. Evidence for such a theory comprises the close relationship of the Indo-Iranian tongues with the Baltic and Slavic languages, vocabulary exchange with the non-Indo-European Uralic languages, and the nature of the confirmed Indo-European words including plants and animals.

The earliest confirmed Sanskrit texts are Brahmanical texts of the Rigveda, which date to the mid-to-late 2000 BC. No written records from that early period exist today. However, scholars are confident that the oral transmission of the texts is reliable because they were ceremonial literature whose correct pronunciation was considered crucial to its religious efficacy.

Sometime between the 700 and 400 BC, the grammarian Panini standardized the language into a new form, referred to as Classical Sanskrit. In addition to the Vedas, many religious works, influential Indian poetry and drama, and early scientific and mathematic documents were originally written in Sanskrit.

Standardization by Panini

The oldest surviving Sanskrit grammar is Panini's *Aṣṭādhyāyī* consisting of eight chapters on grammar. It basically consists of a strict grammar rules, an authority that defines correct Sanskrit. Classical Sanskrit became fixed with the grammar of Panini, approximately 500 BC and remains in use as a learned language until the present day.

Classical Sanskrit is the standard rules arranged by the grammar of Panini around 4000 BC. It has significantly influenced most modern languages of the Indian subcontinent, particularly in India, Pakistan, Sri Lanka and Nepal.

The pre-Classical form of Sanskrit is known as spoken Vedic Sanskrit, with the language of the Rigveda being the oldest and most archaic stage preserved.

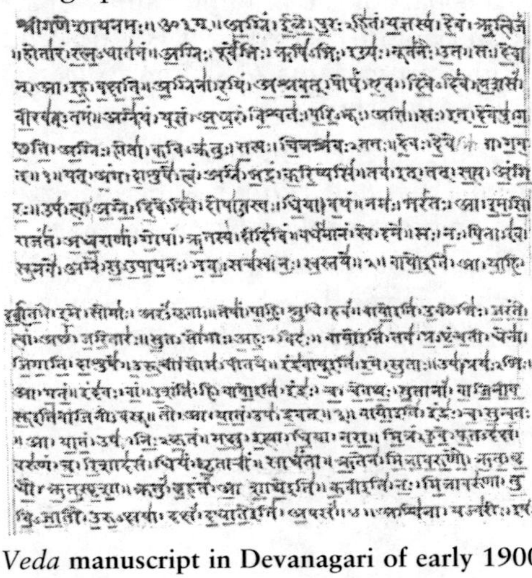

Rig-Veda **manuscript in Devanagari of early 1900 AD.**

Courtesy: Wikipedia

Sanskrit, as defined by Panini, had evolved out of the earlier "Vedic" form. The beginning of Vedic Sanskrit can be traced as early as 1500-1200 BC. Scholars often distinguish Vedic Sanskrit and Classical or "Pāṇinian" Sanskrit as separate 'dialects'. Though they are quite similar, they differ in a number of essential points of phonology, vocabulary, grammar and syntax. Vedic Sanskrit is the language of the Vedas, a large collection of hymns, incantations, Samhitas, theological and philosophical discussions in the Brahmanas and Upanishads.

A significant form of post-Vedic Sanskrit is found in the Sanskrit of the Hindu Epics—the Ramayana and Mahabharata.

According to Tiwari (1955), there were four principal dialects of classical Sanskrit: *paścimottarī* (Northwestern), *madhyadeśī* (middle India), *pūrvi* (Eastern) and *dakṣiṇī* (Southern), arose in the Classical period.

Phonology

Classical Sanskrit distinguishes about 36 phonemes. However, some allophones (as in English p and pH are allophones) and the writing systems used for Sanskrit generally indicates that there are 46 sounds.

Devanagari is part of the Brahmic family of scripts of India, Nepal, Tibet, and South-East Asia. It is a descendant from the Gupta script. Eastern variants of Gupta called *nāgarī* are first attested from the 800 AD.

Sanskrit *nāgarī* is the feminine form of *nāāgara*, means superior. It means that *nāgarī lipi* is superior script. It also may mean that the language spoken by city people because *nāgara* means a city. From time immemorial, all civilized people used to live in a city where royals ruled and gave support to languages and other arts making languages to flourish.

Vowels

अ a आ ā इ i ई ī उ u ऊ ū ऋ ṛ ॠ ṝ
ऌ ḷ ए e ऐ ai ओ o औ au

ṁ (anusvāra) ḥ (visarga)

Consonants

Gutturals:	क ka	ख kha	ग ga	घ gha	ङ ṅa
Palatals:	च ca	छ cha	ज ja	झ jha	ञ ña
Cerebrals:	ट ṭa	ठ ṭha	ड ḍa	ढ ḍha	ण ṇa
Dentals:	त ta	थ tha	द da	ध dha	न na
Labials:	प pa	फ pha	ब ba	भ bha	म ma
Semivowels:	य ya	र ra	ल la	व va	
Sibilants:	श śa	ष ṣa	स sa		
Aspirate:	ह ha	ऽ = ' (avagraha) - the apostrophe			

Courtesy: www.psychedelicjunction.com

The use of the name Devanagari is relatively recent. The rapid spread of the term Devanagari may be related to the exclusive use of this script to publish sacred Sanskrit texts. This has led to such a close connection between Devanagari and Sanskrit that Devanagari is now widely thought to be the Sanskrit script. However, before the colonial period there was no standard script for Sanskrit, which was written in whatever script was familiar to the local population.

The letter order of Devanagari, like all Brāhmī scripts, is based on phonetic principles that consider both the method and place of articulation of the consonants and vowels they represent. This arrangement is usually referred to as the *varṇamālā* (garland of letters).

Writing System

Writing was not introduced to India until after Sanskrit had evolved into the Prakrits. When it was written, the choice of writing system was influenced by the regional scripts of the scribes. Therefore, Sanskrit has no native script of its own. Therefore, virtually all of the major writing systems of South Asia have been used for the writing of Sanskrit manuscripts. Since the late 1900 AD, Devanagari has become the definite standard writing system for Sanskrit publication, perhaps because of the European practice of printing Sanskrit texts in this script. Devanagari is written from left to right and is recognizable by a distinctive horizontal line running along the tops of the letters that links them together.

The earliest known inscriptions in Sanskrit date to the 100 BC. They are in the Brāhmī script, which was originally used for Prakrit, not Sanskrit. When Sanskrit was written down, it was first used for texts of an administrative, literary nature.

Through the development of early classical Sanskrit literature, the oral tradition was maintained. Sanskrit was spoken in an oral society and the writing was not introduced to India until after Sanskrit had evolved into the Prakrits. The regional scripts of the scribe influenced the choice of writing system. Devanagari has been considered as the effective writing system for Sanskrit since the late 1900 AD. The reason for this could be the European practice of printing Sanskrit texts in this script. The Kharosthi script was used in the northwest of the subcontinent. The Gupta script that has been derived from Brāhmī, became prevalent around the 400-800 AD. The Bengali script and the Oriya script were used in Eastern India. In the south, Kannada, Telugu, Tamil, Malayalam and Grantha were the scripts used for Sanskrit.

Transcription	śivō rakṣatu gīrvāṇabhāṣārasāsvādatatparān
Bali	[illegible]
Baybayin	[illegible]
Bengālī	শিবো রক্ষতু গীর্বাণভাষারসাস্বাদতৎপরান্
Devanāgarī	शिवो रक्षतु गीर्वाणभाषारसास्वादतत्परान्
Grantha	[illegible]
Gujarātī	શિવો રક્ષતુ ગીર્વાણભાષારસાસ્વાદતત્પરાન્
Gurmukhī	ਸਿਵੋ ਰਕ੍ਸਤੁ ਗੀਰ੍ਵਾਣਭਾਸਾਰਸਾਸ੍ਵਾਦਤਤ੍ਪਰਾਨ੍
Java	[illegible]
Kannaḍa	ಶಿವೋ ರಕ್ಷತು ಗೀರ್ವಾಣಭಾಷಾರಸಾಸ್ವಾದತತ್ಪರಾನ್
Malayāḷam	ശിവോ രക്ഷതു ഗീർവാണഭാഷാരസാസ്വാദതത്പരാൻ
Oṛiyā	ଶିବୋ ରକ୍ଷତୁ ଗୀର୍ବାଣଭାଷାରସାସ୍ବାଦତତ୍ପରାନ୍
Sinhala	ශිවෝ රක්ෂතු ගීර්වාණභාෂාරසාස්වාදතත්පරාන්
Tamil	ஷிவோ ரக்ஷது கீர்வாணபாஷாரஸாஸ்வாததத்பராந்
Tĕlugu	శివో రక్షతు గీర్వాణభాషారసాస్వాదతత్పరాన్
Tibetan	ཤི་ཝོ་ རཀྵ་ཏུ་ གཱིརྦཱཎ་བྷཱཥཱ་ར་སཱ་སྭཱ་ད་ཏ་ཏྤ་རཱན
Thai	ศิโว รกฺษตุ คีรฺวาณภาษารสาสฺวาทตตฺปรานฺ

Courtesy: Wikipedia Common

Sanskrit in modern Indian and other Brāhmī scripts.

May Śiva bless those who take delight in the language of gods. (Girvana Bhasha = Sanskrit language.)

(Kalidasa)

European Research

European research in Sanskrit instigated by Heinrich Roth during 1620-68 AD and Johann Ernst Hanxleden 1681-1731 AD is regarded as responsible for the discovery of the Indo-European language family by Sir William Jones. This scholarship played an important role in the development of Western philology or literary study of historical linguistics. Sir William Jones, speaking to The Asiatic Society in Calcutta on February 2, 1786, said:

> The Sanskrit language, whatever be its antiquity, is of a wonderful structure; more perfect than the Greek, more

> copious than the Latin, and more exquisitely refined than either, yet bearing to both of them a stronger affinity, both in the roots of verbs and in the forms of grammar, than could possibly have been produced by accident; so strong, indeed, that no philologer could examine them all three, without believing them to have sprung from some common source, which, perhaps, no longer exists.

It was perceived that the languages of the principal European nations—ancient and modern—bore a close resemblance to the languages spoken by the Brahmans of India and the followers of Zoroaster. And from this affinity of the Indo-Germanic languages, it followed inevitably that all these languages must be the off-shoots or dialects of a single primitive tongue, and the assumption of such a primitive language further implied the existence of a primitive Aryan people.

Greek

Mycenaean (1600-1100 BC) is the most ancient known form of the Greek language, spoken on the Greek mainland and on Crete.

Courtesy: http://e-ducation.net/thehistoryoflanguage.htm

The history of the Greek Language begins with the Mycenaean civilization around 1300 BC. The earliest texts are written in a script called Linear B. After the collapse of the Mycenaean civilization around 1200 BC. writing disappeared from Greece. In the late 900 to early 800 BC, a script based on the Phoenician syllabary was introduced. The oldest surviving alphabetic inscriptions are written using this new system and date from the late 800 BC.

In the classical or Hellenic period, Greek existed in several major dialects, each of which has its own significance for the history of the language.

The earliest records of written Greek are inscribed on baked mud tablets found in the ruins of the palace of Knossos on Crete and, later, at sites on the Greek mainland. Written in a syllabic script known as Linear B in which each symbol represents a consonant plus vowel combination. They can be dated to the period about 1450 BC. Most of the tablets are inventories of property or deal with agricultural production and produce. However, they represent the earliest records of any European language.

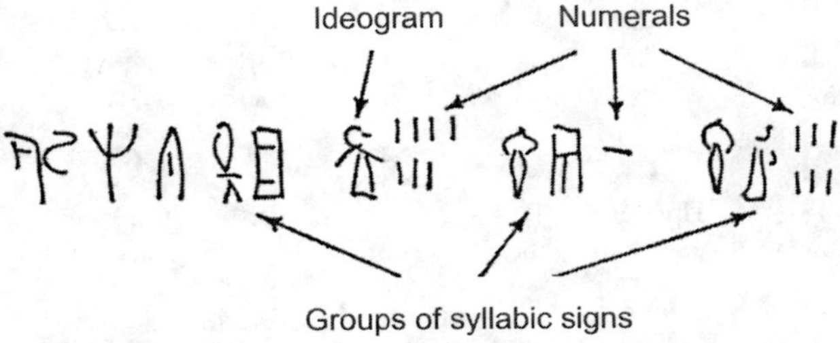

Linear B was essentially a syllabic script with each symbol representing a consonant-vowel combination.

Courtesy: Wikipedia

After the conquests of Alexander the Great (approximately 336-323 BC), the language underwent great changes. Alexander carried the Attic-Ionic form of the language, along with Greek culture as far as into the Near East where it became the standard language of commerce and government, existing side by side with many local languages. Greek was adopted as a second language by the native people of these regions and was ultimately transformed into the Hellenistic Koine or common Greek.

Difference between 'Hellenistic' and 'Hellenic' Greek

1. **Hellenic** Greek refers to the same period as 'Classical Greek.' It is the time of Homer and later the great Greek philosophers, Socrates, Plato, and Aristotle.
2. **Hellenistic** Greek refers to the period after Alexander the Great's conquests that spread the Greek language around the Mediterranean Sea and far into the East in the 300 BC.

For many centuries Greek was the *lingua franca* of the eastern half of the Roman Empire.

Α	Β	Γ	Δ	Ε	Ζ
Alpha (al-fah)	Beta (bay-tah)	Gamma (gam-ah)	Delta (del-ta)	Epsilon (ep-si-lon)	Zeta (zay-tah)
Η	**Θ**	**Ι**	**Κ**	**Λ**	**Μ**
Eta (ay-tah)	Theta (thay-tah)	Iota (eye-o-tah)	Kappa (kap-pah)	Lambda (lamb-dah)	Mu (mew)
Ν	**Ξ**	**Ο**	**Π**	**Ρ**	**Σ**
Nu (new)	Xi (zie)	Omicron (om-e-cron)	Pi (pie)	Rho (roe)	Sigma (sig-mah)
Τ	**Υ**	**Φ**	**Χ**	**Ψ**	**Ω**
Tau (taw)	Upsilon (up-si-lon)	Phi (fie)	Chi (kie)	Psi (sigh)	Omega (oh-may-gah)

Clip Art Credit: Phillip Martin

Homer together with Hesiod the earliest of the famous writers of ancient Greece is the subject of a vast scholarly literature. It is generally held that parts of the Iliad use language that long predates the 800 BC and that some of the descriptions of weapons and fighting techniques are consistent with the archaeological evidence from Mycenaean sites contemporary with the fall of Troy in about 1250 BC.

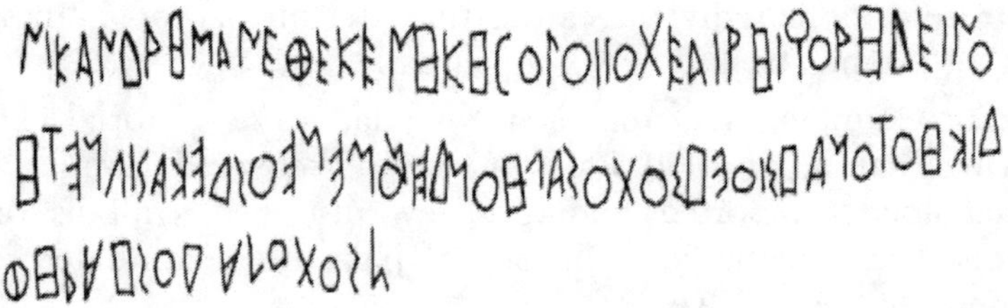

A very early Greek (around 650 BC) inscription with the text running from left to right then doubling back to run from right to left. This form of writing, resembling the path of the ox-drawn plough across a field, is known as *boustrophedon*.

Chinese

Most linguists classify modern spoken Chinese language as a part of the Sino-Tibetan language family. They believe that there was an original language, termed Proto-Sino-Tibetan, from which the Sinitic and Tibeto-Burman languages descended.

Old Chinese language, sometimes known as Archaic Chinese, was the language common during the early and middle Zhou Dynasty (1122 BCE-256 BCE), inscriptions on bronze artifacts, the poetry of the *Shūjīng*, the history of the *Shūjīng*, and portions of the *Yìjīng* (*I Ching*). The phonetic elements found in the majority of Chinese characters provide hints to their Old Chinese pronunciations. The pronunciation of the borrowed Chinese characters in Japanese, Vietnamese and Korean also provide valuable insights. Linguists have found that Old Chinese was not wholly uninflected. It possessed a rich sound system in which aspiration or rough breathing differentiated the consonants, but probably was still without tones. They suggest work on reconstructing Old Chinese started with Qīng dynasty philologists.

Mandarin is the official standard language used by the People's Republic of China, the Republic of China (Taiwan), and Singapore where it is called Huayu.

In recent decades, inscriptions have been found on Neolithic pottery and on bones at a various locations in China, including Banpo and Hualouzi near Xi'an. These simple, often geometric marks are similar to some of the earliest known Chinese characters, potentially indicating that the history of Chinese writing extends back over six millennia.

For example, at Damaidi in Ningxia, 3,172 pictorial cliff carvings dating to 6000-5000 BC were discovered. Similarly, archaeologists reported finding a few inscribed symbols on tortoise shells at the Neolithic site of Jiahu in Henan dated to around 6600-6200 BC.

Gradual evolution and the coexistence of two or more scripts was more often the case. As early as the Shang Dynasty, oracle-bone script coexisted as a simplified form alongside the normal script of bamboo books (preserved in typical bronze inscriptions), as well as the extra-elaborate pictorial forms found on many bronzes.

Left: Bronze fāngzūn (方樽) ritual wine container dated about 1000 BC. The written inscription cast in bronze on the vessel commemorates a gift of cowrie shells used as currency in China, presumably from an elite status in Zhou Dynasty society. Right: Bronze fāngyí (方樽) ritual container dated about 1000 BC. A written inscription of some 180 Chinese characters appears twice on the vessel. The written inscription comments on state rituals that accompanied court ceremony, recorded by an official scribe. *Courtesy*: Wikipedia

Chinese Characters

Chinese characters evolved over time from earlier forms of hieroglyphs. The idea that all Chinese characters are either pictographs or ideographs is not true. Most characters contain phonetic parts, and are mixtures of phonetic components and semantic radicals. Only the simplest characters such as *ren* 人 (human), *ri* 日 (sun), *shan* 山 (mountain; hill), *shui* 水 (water), may be wholly pictorial in origin. In 100 AD, the famed scholar *Xǔ Shèn* in the Hàn Dynasty classified characters into six categories, namely pictographs, simple ideographs, compound ideographs, phonetic compounds and derivative characters. There are about 214 radicals recognized in the Kangxi Dictionary.

There are currently two systems for Chinese characters. The traditional system, and the Simplified Chinese character system, developed by the People's Republic of China in 1954 to promote mass literacy. It simplifies most complex traditional glyphs to fewer strokes, many to common *caoshu* shorthand variants.

A well-educated Chinese reader recognizes approximately 5,000-7,000 characters. Approximately 3,000 characters are required to read a mainland newspaper. The PRC Government defines literacy amongst workers as a knowledge of 2,000 characters, though this would be only functional literacy. A large unabridged dictionary, like the *Kangxi Dictionary*, contains over 40,000 characters, including obscure, variant, rare, and archaic characters. Less than a quarter of these characters are now commonly used.

Written Styles

The earliest known Chinese texts, in the Oracle bone script, display a fully developed writing system, with little difference in functionality from modern characters. It is assumed that the early stages of the development of characters were dominated by pictograms, which were the objects depicted, and ideograms, in which meaning was expressed iconically.

The English word 'mandarin' (Portuguese *mandarim,* Malay [ˈməntəri] *menteri,* Hindi *mantri,* from Sanskrit *mantrin,* means 'minister or counsellor') originally meant an official from the Chinese empire. Because these dialects were often mutually unintelligible, the officials communicated using a koiné based on northern dialects. When Jesuit missionaries learned this standard language in the 1600 AD, they called it Mandarin.

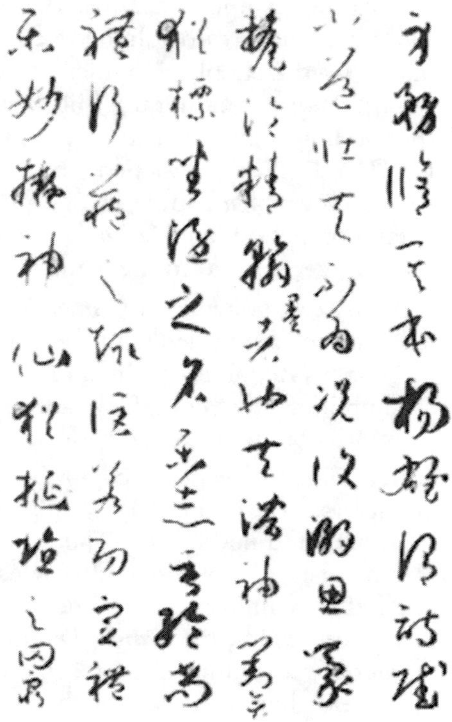

Example of the cursive script by Chinese Tang Dynasty calligrapher Sun Guoting, c. 650 AD.

Courtesy: Wikipedia Common

Writing System

The relationship between the spoken and written Chinese language is very complex. Its spoken varieties evolved at different degrees, while written Chinese remained unchanged. Written records have been discovered as far back as the 1400 to 1100 BC. Shang dynasty used oracle bone scripts.

The Chinese orthography centers on Chinese characters, *hanzi*, which are written in imaginary rectangular blocks. The characters are arranged in vertical columns, and they are read from top to bottom down a column, and right to left across columns.

Latin

Latin was limited to Latium, a small region on the coast of west central Italy.

Latin is a member of the broad family of Italic languages. The Latin alphabet emerged from the Old Italic alphabets, which were derived from the Greek and Phoenician scripts.

Historical Latin came from the prehistoric language of the Latium region, specifically around the River Tiber, where Roman civilization first developed. Various influences on Latin are from Celtic dialects in northern Italy, the non-Indo-European Etruscan language in Central Italy, and the Greek of southern Italy have been detected.

The name Latin derives from the Italic tribal group named Latini that settled at some time in Latium, and the dialect spoken by these people.

Vulgar Latin

Vulgar Latin, as in this political graffiti at Pompeii, was the language of the ordinary people of the Roman Empire, distinct from the Classical Latin of literature.

Vulgar Latin is a comprehensive term covering vernacular dialects of the Latin language spoken from earliest times in Italy until the latest dialects of the Western empire.

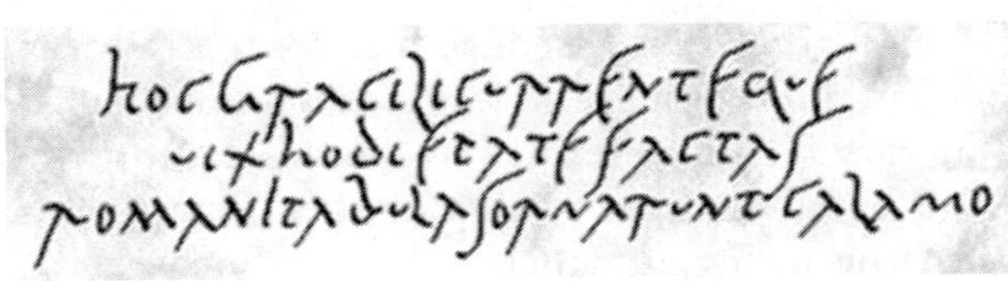

A replica of the Old Roman Cursive inspired by the Vindolanda tablets.

Romance Languages

The Romance languages, a major branch of the Indo-European language family, comprise all languages that descended from Latin, the language of the Roman Empire.

All Romance languages descend from Vulgar Latin, the language of soldiers, settlers, and slaves of the Roman Empire, which was substantially different from the Roman *literati*. Between 200 BC and 100 AD, the expansion of the Empire and the administrative and educational policies of Rome made Vulgar Latin the dominant vernacular language over a wide area which stretched from the Iberian Peninsula to the west coast of the Black Sea. During the Empire's decline in the 500 AD, Vulgar Latin began to evolve independently within each local area, and eventually diverged into dozens of distinct languages.

Ecclesiastical Latin (sometimes called Church Latin) is a broad and analogous term referring to the Latin language as used in documents of the Roman Catholic Church.

Medieval Latin refers to the literary and administrative Latin used in the middle ages. It exhibits much variation between individual authors, mainly due to poor communications in those times between different regions.

Renaissance Latin is a name given to the Latin written during the European Renaissance in the 1400-1600 AD, particularly differentiated by the distinctive Latin style developed by the humanist movement.

Ad fontes[7] was the general cry of the humanists. Therefore, their Latin style sought to purge Latin of the Medieval Latin vocabulary and stylistic additions that it had acquired in the centuries after the fall of the Roman Empire.

Surviving Latin literature consists almost entirely of Classical Latin in its broadest definition. It includes a polished and highly stylized literary language termed as Golden Latin, which spans the 1000 BC and the early years of the 1000 AD. However, throughout the history of ancient Rome the spoken language differed in both grammar and vocabulary from that of literature, and is referred to as Vulgar Latin.

7. to the sources, first principles.

Phonology

Vowels

Proto-Italic inherited all ten of the early post-Proto-Indo-European simple vowels: **a, *e, *i, *o, *u, *ā, *ē, *ī, *ō, *ū.* Long vowels were largely unaffected in general except in final syllables, where they had a tendency to shorten. It indicates short and long vowels.

Ancient Latin alphabet

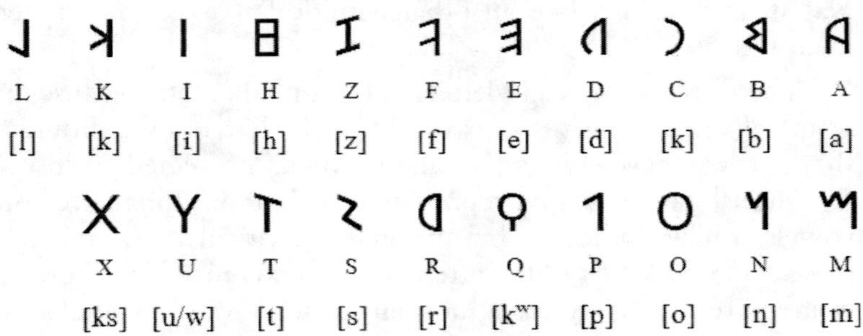

Roman Alphabet for Latin

The Romans used just 23 letters to write Latin:

A	B	C	D	E	F	G	H	I	K	L	M
ā	bē	cē	dē	ē	ef	ģē	hā	ī	kā	el	em
[a:]	[be:]	[ke:]	[de:]	[e:]	[ɛf]	[gə:]	[ha:]	[i:]	[ka:]	[ɛl]	[ɛm]
N	O	P	Q	R	S	T	V	X	Y	Z	
en	ō	pē	qū	er	es	tē	ū	ex	ī Graeca	zēta	
[ɛn]	[o:]	[pe:]	[kʷu:]	[ɛr]	[ɛs]	[te:]	[u:]	[ɛks]	[i: ˈgrajka]	[ˈze:ta]	

Courtesy: http://www.omniglot.com/

Arabic Language

Before the appearance of Islam, Arabic language was a minor member of the southern branch of the Semitic language family, used by a small number of largely nomadic tribes in the Arabian Peninsula, with poorly-documented textual history.

Arabic language belongs to the Semitic language family. Once the Arabian Peninsula was thought to have been the 'cradle' of proto-Semitic, but nowadays many scholars advocate the view that it originated somewhere in East Africa, probably in the area of Somalia/Ethiopia.

Arabic is a name applied to the descendants of the Classical Arabic language of the 600 AD. It is a 'Semitic,' language and is most closely related to Aramaic and Hebrew.

Writing System

The Arabic alphabet derives from the Aramaic through Nabatean.[8] Arabic, like all other Semitic languages, is written from right to left.

There are twenty-eight letters in the alphabet, but because the script of the alphabet is cursive, 22 of the letters take different shapes when they are in initial, middle, final, or isolated positions. The three long vowels are represented within the alphabet. Short vowels can be indicated by optional diacritical markings, but these are most often not written. Those texts in which they are written are usually of a religious nature and they are included to ensure that the proper pronunciation is made for all the words.

Historically, the North Arabic script, the earliest extant copies of which date to the 400 BC, is descended from the Nabatean Aramaic script. However, because the Aramaic script represented less than the required number of consonants for Arabic, the use of some shapes was extended by placing dots on the letters.

Modern dictionaries and other reference books do not use the *'abjadī* order to sort alphabetically. Instead, the newer *hijā'ī* order (with letters partially grouped together by similarity of shape) is used:

ا ب ت ث ج ح خ د ذ ر ز س ش ص ض ط ظ ع غ ف ق ك ل م ن ه و ي

y w h n m l k q f gh ʻ ẓ ṭ ḍ ṣ sh s z r dh d kh ḥ zh th t b ʼ

Courtesy: http://www.shariahprogram.ca/Arabic-alphabet.shtml

8. Border land between Arabia and Syria, and from the Euphrates to the Red Sea.

Arabic Consonants

ر	ذ	د	خ	ح	ج	ث	ت	ب	ا
راء	ذال	دال	خاء	حاء	جيم	ثاء	تاء	باء	ألف
rā'	ḏāl	dāl	ḫā'	ḥā'	ǧīm	ṯā'	tā'	bā'	'alif
r	ḏ	d	ḫ	ḥ	ǧ	ṯ	t	b	'(a)
[r]	[ð]	[d]	[χ]	[ħ]	[ʤ]	[θ]	[t]	[b]	[ʔ]

ف	غ	ع	ظ	ط	ض	ص	ش	س	ز
فاء	غين	عين	ظاء	طاء	ضاد	صاد	شين	سين	زاي
fā'	ġayn	'ayn	ẓā'	ṭā'	ḍād	ṣād	šīn	sīn	zāy
f	ġ	'	ẓ	ṭ	ḍ	ṣ	š	s	z
[f]	[ʁ]	[ʕ]	[ðˤ]	[tˤ]	[dˤ]	[sˤ]	[ʃ]	[s]	[z]

ء	ي	و	ه	ن	م	ل	ك	ق
همزة	ياء	واو	هاء	نون	ميم	لام	كاف	قاف
hamza	yā'	wāw	hā'	nūn	mīm	lām	kāf	qāf
	y	w	h	n	m	l	k	q
	[j]	[w]	[h]	[n]	[m]	[l]	[k]	[q]

Mayan Language

The Maya is a Mesoamerican[9] civilization, which flourished during the pre-Classic period 2000 BC to 250 AD. According to the Mesoamerican chronicle, many Mayan cities reached their highest state of development during the Classic period 250-900 AD, and continued throughout the post-Classic period until the arrival of the Spanish. The Maya civilization shares many features

9. **Mesoamerica** (Spanish: *Mesoamérica*) is a region and cultural area in the Americas, extending approximately from central Mexico to Belize, Guatemala, El Salvador, Honduras, Nicaragua, and northern Costa Rica, within which a number of pre-Columbian societies flourished before the Spanish colonization of the Americas in the 15th and 16th centuries.

with other Mesoamerican civilizations due to the high degree of interaction and cultural diffusion that characterized the region.

Mayan Script—Origin

Writing in the Mayan script dates from about 250 BC, but the script is thought to have developed at an earlier date. Recent archeological finds indicate that the Mayan civilization started around 3,000 BC.

The Mayan script is logo syllabic combining about 550 logograms, which represented whole words and 150 syllabograms, which represented syllables. The script was commonly written in paired vertical columns reading from left to right and top to bottom in a zigzag model.

In about 1566 AD, the first bishop of Yucatan, Diego de Landa, compiled a key to the Mayan syllabary consisting of 27 Spanish letters and the Mayan glyphs with similar sounds.

For a long time many scholars believed that the script did not represent a language at all, or that it wasn't a complete writing system. The first major breakthrough in decipherment came during the 1950s when a Russian ethnologist, Yuri Valentinovich Knorosov, proposed that the Mayan script was at least partly phonetic and represented the Yucatec Mayan language.

A fascinating interpretation of the decipherment of the Mayan script can be found in breaking the Maya Code, by Michael D. Coe.

The Yucatec Maya continued to use the Mayan script until 1600 AC. Recently, Mayan have started to learn the script once again from the scholars who have deciphered it.

Notable Features

- The Mayan script is logosyllabic combining about 550 logograms (which represent whole words) and 150 syllabograms (which represent syllables). There were also about 100 glyphs representing place names and the names of gods. About 300 glyphs were commonly used.
- Examples of the script have been found carved on stone and written on bark, wood, jade, ceramics, and a few manuscripts in Mexico, Guatemala and northern Belize.

- Many syllables can be represented by more than one glyph.
- The script was usually written in paired vertical columns reading from left to right and top to bottom in a zigzag pattern.

The Mayan Syllabary

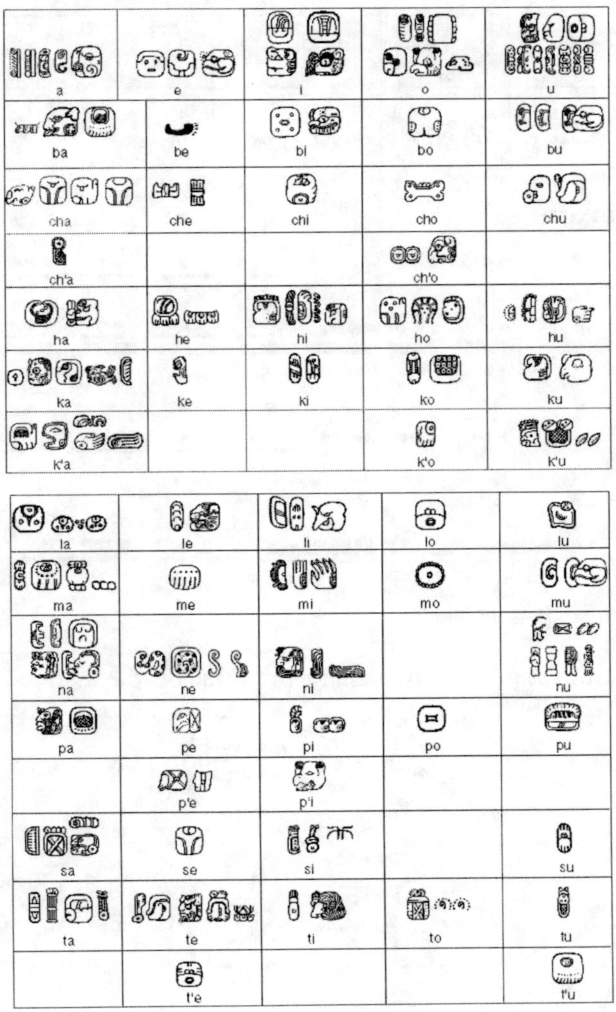

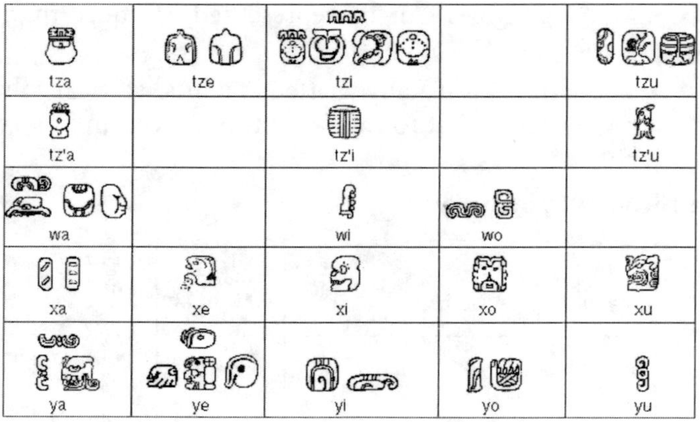

Numerals

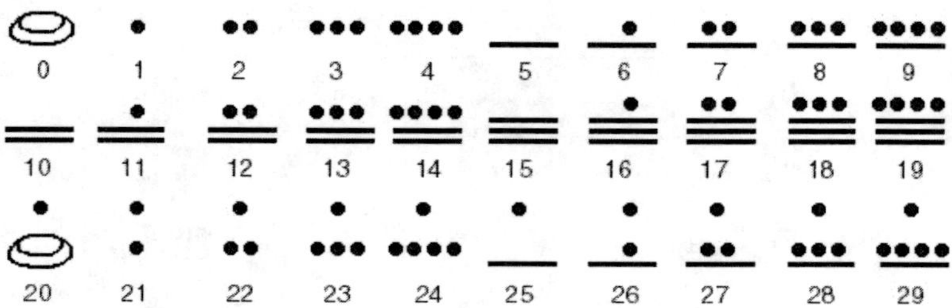

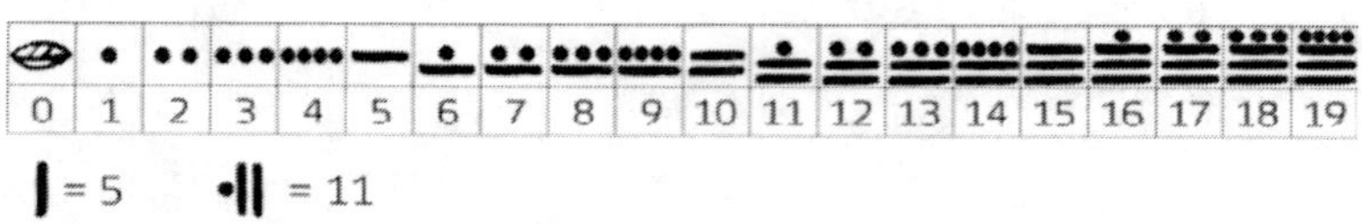

Examples of how to calculate the value of Mayan numerals.gif

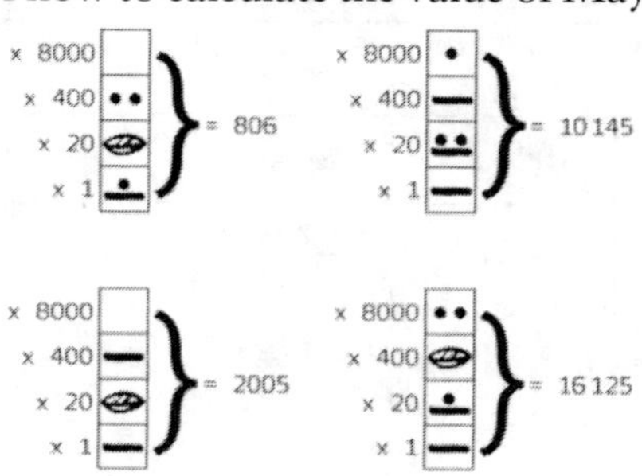

Courtesy: Wikimedia Common

Phoenician/Canaanite

Phoenician was a language originally spoken in the coastal Mediterranean region. It is a Semitic language of the Canaanite subgroup. Its closest living relative is Hebrew. The region where Phoenician was spoken includes modern-day Lebanon, coastal Syria, Palestine, and northern Israel. It was also spoken in the area of Phoenician colonization along the coasts of the South-Western Mediterranean, including modern Tunisia, Morocco and Algeria, Malta, the west of Sicily, Sardinia, Corsica and southernmost Spain.

The Phoenician alphabet developed from the Proto-Canaanite alphabet, during the 1500 BC. Previously, the Phoenicians wrote with a cuneiform[10] script. The earliest known inscriptions in the Phoenician alphabet come from Byblos and date back to 1000 BC. The Phoenicians traded around the Mediterranean and beyond, and set up cities and colonies in parts of southern Europe and North Africa. The origins of most alphabetic writing systems can be traced back to the Phoenician alphabet, including Greek, Etruscan, Latin, Arabic and Hebrew, as well as the scripts of India and East Asia.

Notable Features

- Type of writing system: abjad/consonant alphabet with no vowel indication.
- Direction of writing: right to left in horizontal lines.
- Number of letters: 22.
- The names of the letters are acrophonic, a picture symbol, and their names and shapes can be ultimately traced back to Egyptian Hieroglyphs. For example, the name of the first letter, ˈaleph, means ox and developed

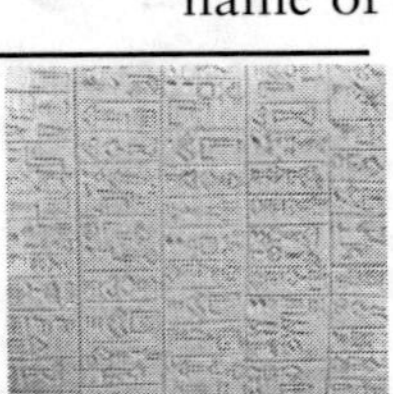

10. Sumerian inscription in monumental archaic style (c. 2600 BC+).

from a picture of an ox's head. Some of the letter names were changed by the Phoenicians, including imel (the third letter of many Semitic alphabets), which meant camel in Phoenician, but was originally a picture of a throwing stick (giml).

The Phoenician Alphabet and Language

Scholars have found that the knowledge of the Phoenician language is based on the few surviving written texts in Phoenician language. Before 1000 BC, Phoenician was written using cuneiform symbols that were common across Mesopotamia. The first signs of the Phoenician alphabet found at Byblos are clearly derived from the Egyptian hieroglyphics, and not from cuneiform. The twenty-two Phoenician letters are simplifications of Egyptian hieroglyphic symbols, which took on a standardized form at the end of the 1200 BC. Like Hebrew and Arabic, Phoenician was written from right to left, and vowels were omitted making the job of deciphering Phoenician very hard.

The earliest Phoenician inscription probably dates from the 1100 BC. The latest inscription from Phoenicia proper is from the 1000 BC when the language was already being superseded by Aramaic.

Phoenician Alphabet

𐤊	𐤉	𐤈	𐤇	𐤆	𐤅	𐤄	𐤃	𐤂	𐤁	𐤀
kaph	yōdh	ṭēth	ḥēth	zayin	wāw	hē	dāleth	gīmel	bēth	'āleph
palm	hand	good	wall	weapon	hook	window	door	camel	house	ox
k	y	ṭ	ḥ	z	w	h	d	g	b	ʾ
[k]	[j]	[tˤ]	[ħ]	[z]	[w]	[e]	[d]	[g]	[b]	[ʔ]

𐤕	𐤔	𐤓	𐤒	𐤑	𐤐	𐤏	𐤎	𐤍	𐤌	𐤋
tāw	šin	rēš	qōph	ṣādē	pē	'ayin	sāmekh	nun	mēm	lāmedh
mark	tooth	head	eye of needle	papyrus	mouth	eye	fish	serpent	water	goad
t	sh	r	q	ṣ	p	ʿ	s	n	m	l
[t]	[ʃ]	[r]	[q]	[sˤ]	[p]	[ʕ]	[s]	[n]	[m]	[l]

5

Language Diffusion and Indo-European Languages

As the communities separate geographically, languages also separate and divide into several new languages by a process like biological speciation. The language changes in different methods in the new communities, and slowly people from detached communities can no longer recognize each other's language. After a passage of time without any contact with original community, a single language could develop into two or more different languages.

Today Indo-European languages are widely spoken by half of the world's population. Around 2000 BC people speaking Indo-European languages begin to spread through Europe, eventually reaching the Atlantic coast and the northern coasts of the Mediterranean region.

Identification of relationships between Indian and European languages began by European visitors to India in the 1600 AD. In 1583, Thomas Stephens, an English Jesuit missionary in Goa, observed relationships between Indian languages like Konkani and Greek and Latin languages.

The observation about the ancient language Sanskrit came from Filippo Sassetti of Florence, Italy, a merchant who traveled to the Indian subcontinent in 1540. He learnt Sanskrit in India. Writing in 1585, he noted some words similarities between Sanskrit and Italian such as devaḥ=dio 'God'; sarpaḥ=serpe 'serpent'; sapta=sette 'seven'; aṣṭa=otto 'eight'; nava=nove 'nine' and so on.

Another missionary Coeurdoux studied Sanskrit from the famous pundits of Nadiya in Bengal. Understanding the enormous wealth of literature in Sanskrit, he asserted that missionaries had no time to copy these studies or money to copy them for circulation in Europe. However, he provided three lists of Sanskrit words with equivalent words closely resembling or identical with Latin and Greek: common with Greek only and common with Latin only. After reviewing theories that might liable for the large number of words common to Sanskrit with Latin and Greek, he concluded that these three languages belonged to a common source, an ancient language which no longer exists.

In 1813, Thomas Young used first time the term Indo-European, which became the standard scientific term through the work of Franz Bopp, whose systematic comparison of these three languages and other old languages supported the theory. Bopp's *Comparative Grammar*, which was published between 1833 and 1852, considered as the starting point of Indo-European Studies as an academic discipline.

Another linguistic group is the Semitic family of languages. These were also supposed to be derived from the language of one tribal group, perhaps nomads in southern Arabia. By about 3000 BC Semitic languages were spoken over a large part of desert territory from southern Arabia to the north of Syria.

6

Some Living Languages

Vulgar Latin

The name Vulgar Latin simply means Latin language spoken by ordinary people in Roman Empire. Classical Latin was always a literary language. It is a hypothetical ancestor of the Romance languages.

During the middle ages, the Vulgar Latin spoken by Roman settlers in early European regions created the foundation of the numerous dialects that developed into modern languages. Vulgar Latin developed separately in the different provinces of the Roman Empire, gradually transforming to modern French, Italian, Spanish, Portuguese, Romanian, Catalan, Romansh, and so on. Vulgar Latin was commonly spoken until the new localized forms deviated very much from Latin. As a consequence, a new standard of languages became important. Vulgar Latin lost its popularity when the local dialects started gathering adequate local characteristics to develop a different language. They changed into Romance languages when an independent characteristic was recognizable in them.

One powerful modification that affected every Romance language was the reorganization of the vowel system of classical Latin. Latin had ten distinct vowels: long and short versions of A, E, I, O, U (Sanskrit too has distinct vowel system: long and short), and three *diphthongs* (with two sounds, or with two tones), AE, OE and AU. There are also long and short versions of the Greek borrowing Y.

The ten vowel system of Classical Latin, which depended on phonemic vowel length, was copied into a system where vowel length distinctions were concealed and variation of vowel quality became phonemic. Due to this change, the stress on accented syllables is widely pronounced in Vulgar Latin than in Classical Latin.

Modern European languages belong to the group of 'Romance' languages. These languages represent living shadows of the ancient Roman Empire, representing the divergent histories of regions previously unified under Roman rule. The reason these languages are called romance language is not because they are romantic, but because they were brought to them by the Romans.

German Language

The Germanic tribes, which probably originated from a combination of peoples along the Baltic Sea coast, populated the northern part of the European continent around 500 BC. By 100 BC, they had proceeded into the central and southern parts of today Germany. Then, there were three major tribal groups: the eastern Germanic peoples lived along the Oder and Vistula rivers; the northern Germanic people settled in the southern part of Scandinavia; and the western Germanic people inhabited the south of Jutland and the area between the North Sea and the Elbe, Rhine, and Main rivers. After the defeat of the Suevian tribe by Julius Caesar about 70 BC, the Rhine River provided a boundary between Germanic and Roman territory.

The frightening presence of hostile tribes beyond the Rhine forced the Romans to wage a campaign of expansion into Germanic province. But the defeat of the regional governor Varus by Arminius at the Battle of the Teutoburg Forest in 9 AD halted Roman expansion.

In Gaul, a mixture of Roman and Germanic societies occurred. Clovis, a Salian Frank belonging to a family supposedly arrived from a mythical idol named Merovech, became the absolute ruler of a Germanic kingdom of mixed Roman-Germanic population in 486.

The period 200 through 600 AD was a period of change and destruction in which eastern and western Germanic tribes left their native lands and settled in newly acquired regions. This period of Germanic history, which afterwards contributed material for heroic epics, included the downfall of the Roman

Empire and resulted in a substantial expansion of habitable area for the Germanic inhabitants. The invasion of Roman Gaul by Frankish tribes in the late 500 AD became a milestone of European history. It was the Franks who became the founders of a civilized German state.

German is the official language of Germany and Austria, one of the official languages of Switzerland and Luxembourg, and is also spoken by minority groups in France, Italy, Hungary, Rumania, and many other countries of the Western Hemisphere. It is a member of Germanic subgroup of the Indo-European family of languages.

Until the middle of the 1400 AD, Latin was the official written language of the Roman Empire, which comprised most of the German-speaking regions of current Europe. During the period, a Roman emperor, Louis IV (1314-47), German language was accepted as the official language of court documents. Between 1480 and 1500 it was introduced for official use in municipalities and courts of Saxony and Meissen and was authorized by the universities of Leipzig and Wittenberg. By 1500, German had become commonly established as the official language of all parts of Saxony and Thuringia and was the written language of the cultured and educated classes.

Standard written German surfaced during the 1600 AD in the eastern midland area of Erfurt, Meissen, Dresden, and Leipzig, where the residents originally from regions farther west and southwest, spoke a dialect based on the Middle and Upper German dialects of High German.

Until about 1800 AD, Standard German was only a written language. At that time, people in urban northern Germany, who spoke dialects different from Standard German, learnt it like a foreign language and tried to pronounce it as close to the spelling as possible. Specific pronunciation guides used to consider that northern German pronunciation to be the standard.

The first dictionary of the Brothers Grimm remains the most comprehensive guide to the words of the German language. In 1860, grammatical and orthographic rules appeared first in the *Duden Handbook*. In 1901, this was declared the standard definition of the German language.

During the 1870s, the German language successfully replaced Latin as the leading language in all major European and North American universities. Most important research work in sciences was published in German and new universities preferred German instead of Greek or Latin.

Generally accepted standard of German pronunciation did not exist. A commission composed of university professors and representatives of the German theater was established in 1898. As a result, certain norms of pronunciation were accepted. These rules and norms have been codified in *Deutsche Buhnenaussprache* (German Stage Pronunciation) and *Deutsche Hochsprache* (Standard German). The speech affected by the pronunciation is even for highly-educated Germans.

German used to be the language of commerce and government, which included a large area of Central and Eastern Europe. Until the mid-1900 AD, it was fundamentally the language of townspeople throughout most of Europe.

The various parts of Germany and other European nations where German was spoken followed different standards of spelling until the 2000 AD. A conference was held in 1901, in which representatives of northern and southern Germany, Austria, and Switzerland participated, and formulated a uniform system of orthography.

Dialects

As a consequence of the colonization methods, the routes for trade and communication through the rivers and of physical separation by high mountains and deep forests, very different regional dialects developed. Sometimes, these dialects were used mutually unintelligent across the Roman Empire.

There was no common German language until lately. Actually, the first common language, Latin, was introduced by the Roman invasion into the Germanic region. It is apparent in German language, the words like *Kaiser* (emperor, from Caesar) and *Student*.

German language belongs to the Netherlandic-German group inside the western branch of the Germanic languages, a subfamily of the Indo-European languages. The language is generally divided into two parts: Hochdeutsch or High German, spoken in the central and southern regions, and Plattdeutsch or Low German, spoken in the north. High German became the standard literary language subsequent to its use by Martin Luther in his translation of the Bible. The difference between High German and other dialects may be seen in such words as das Wasser (the water), which becomes dat Water in Low German.

One way to describe dialects is to compare which words are used for the same thing. In fact, there is no one universal term for some German words. For example, the common word for 'mosquito' in German may mean anything in different German dialects or regions: *Gelse, Moskito, Mugge, Mücke, Schnake,* and *Staunze*. Also, the same word may take a different meaning, depending on the location. *Eine (Stech-) Mücke* in northern Germany is a mosquito. In some parts of Austria, the same word refers to a gnat or house fly, while *Gelsen* are mosquitoes. German has more than one word for 'carrot'—*Karotte, Möhre, Mohrrübe, gelbe Rübe*, and one or another is preferred in different parts of the German-speaking world.

To bring standardization and unification of German language, writers were trying to write in a way that could be understood in the largest possible area. This process went on for several hundred years.

Because of Luther's translation of the Bible into German and his German pamphlets on hymns, catechisms, the High German standard spread throughout the Germany. By 1600 AD, this literary language was strongly established. But its current form was recognized around middle of the 1800 AD.

Main Characteristics

The development of German was influenced by several methodical shifts of certain consonants. The Germanic consonant shift distinguished the ancient Proto-Germanic speech from other Indo-European speech. In this shift, which is described by Grimm's Law, an Indo-European *p, t, k* changed to a Germanic *f, th, h,* respectively; Indo-European *b, d, g* to Germanic *p, t, k;* and similarly Indo-European *bh, dh, gh,* to Germanic *b, d, g.* After the western Germanic dialects had developed their own distinctive behavior, the High German sound shift occurred. During 500-700 AD, it set the High German dialects off from other West Germanic speech. During that period, the Germanic *p,* when it was used initially, or after consonants, or when doubled, became *pf*; when it was used medially or finally after vowels it became *ff* or *f*. Similarly, the Germanic *t* became *z* (pronounced *ts,* as in *Pflanze*) or *ss* (High German *essen,* Low German *eten,* 'to eat'). After vowels, *k* became *ch* (High German *machen,* Low German *maken,* 'to make'). A later change, found also in Low German, is that of the Germanic *th* to *d* (High German *das,* Low German *dat,*). A 'k' in the German word replaces a 'c' in an English word. Words that end in '-c', '-ical' in English tend to end in '-ik' and '-isch' in German.

The first sound shift, affecting both English and German, was from the early phonetic positions documented in the ancient, or classical, Indo-European languages (Sanskrit, Greek, and Latin) to those still evident in the Low German languages, including English; the second shift affected only the High German languages, e.g. standard German. Grimm's law[1] shows that the classical voiceless stops (*k, t, p*) became voiceless aspirates (*h, th, f*) in English and (*h, d, f*) in German, for example the initial sounds of Sanskrit *pitru,* Latin *pater,* English *father,* German *Vater,* and in the middle of Sanskrit *brathru*, Latin *frater,* English *brother,* German *Bruder.*

The German alphabets are the same as that of English, while some consonants have different values. The letter *j* is pronounced *y* (*ja* as in yes), *v* is pronounced *f* (*vier* as in four), *w* is pronounced *v* (*Winter* = winter) and the letters *z* and *c* are pronounced *ts* (*Zoll* as in toll). The letter *c* appears only in foreign words. Among consonant clusters *sch* is pronounced *sh* (*Shule* = school), *st* is pronounced *sht* (*Stern* = star), *sp* is pounced *shp* (*Spass* = joke), and *ch* is pronounced as in the Scottish *loch.* The letter *q* always appears in the sequence *qu.* The letter *y*

1. Known as the First Germanic Sound Shift named after Jakob Grimm.

appears only in loan words in German, although some words have become so common that they are not considered as foreign. The letter *x* occurs only in loan words in German. Words that are pronounced with a *ks* sound are usually written *chs* or *cks*. Nouns are always capitalized.

A peculiar feature of the German language is its long compound words grouping several concepts. Hence, the nouns Bund (republic), Verteidigung (defense), and Minister (minister) may be combined to form the word Bundesverteidigungminister (Federal Defense Minister), and other examples like hochentwickelten (highly developed), Koalitionsregierung (coalition government).

Two types of German script have fought for recognition since the 1900 AD: the old German Gothic script known as Fraktur, and the modern Roman script, as used in English today. The Fraktur was extensively used in printing and writing until World War II, but it is replaced by the Roman. The following verse appears both in Fraktur and in Roman.

Ich weiß nicht, was soll es bedeuten	I am looking in vain for the reason
Daß ich so traurig bin	That I am so sad and distressed
Ein Märchen aus alten Zeiten	A tale known for many a season
Das kommit mir nicht aus dem Sinn.	Does not allow me to rest

Writing System

German is written using the Latin alphabet. In addition to the 26 standard letters, German has three vowels with Umlaut, namely *ä*, *ö* and *ü*, as well as a special symbol for '*ss*', which is used only after long vowels or diphthongs, the Eszett or Scharfes-S ß is used only in the lower case. The only identical mark is the umlaut, which appears over the letters *a*, *o*, and *u* (*ä*, *ö*, *ü*) to indicate a different vowel value. When it is not possible to use the umlauts as *Ä, Ö, Ü, ä, ö* and *ü,* they can be transcribed as *Ae, Oe, Ue, ae, oe* and *ue*, respectively. The ß can be transcribed as *ss*, but it comes from *sz*. Such transcription is not used with names.

The German alphabet consists of the same 26 letters as the modern Roman alphabet:

a, b, c, d, e, f, g, h, i, j, k, l, m, n, o, p, q, r, s, t, u, v, w, x, y, z

A, B, C, D, E, F, G, H, I, J, K, L, M, N, O, P, Q, R, S, T, U, V, W, X, Y, Z

Cognates with English

There are many German words that are cognate to English words. Most of them are easily identifiable and have almost the same meaning.

German	English	German	English	German	English
Adresse	address	*aktiv*	active	*Baby*	baby
Chance	chance	*Club*	club	*Dealer*	dealer
Elefant	elephant	*innovativ*	innovative	*Kapitalist*	capitalist
Kommunist	communist	*Konferenz*	conference	*Konflikt*	conflict
Lyrik	Lyric	*Mechanik*	mechanic	*negativ*	negative
Physik	physique	*plus*	plus	*Service*	service
Wetter	weather	*Sommer*	summer	*Winter*	winter
Bett	Bed	*Finger*	finger	*haben*	to have
Haus	house	*Maus*	mouse	*Katze*	cat
lachen	to laugh	*Nacht*	night	*Pfeife*	pipe
schwimmen	to swim	*schiff*	ship	*singen*	to sing

Because of the turbulent history of both Germany and the German language, the names that other people have chosen to use to refer to it varies.

Erlkönig	Erlking
von J.W. Goethe	Translation by Hyde Flippo
Wer reitet so spät durch Nacht und Wind?	Who rides so late through the night and wind?
Es ist der Vater mit seinem Kind;	It's the father with his child;
Er hat den Knaben wohl in dem Arm,	He has the boy safe in his arm,
Er faßt ihn sicher, er hält ihn warm.	He holds him secure, he holds him warm.
"Mein Sohn, was birgst du so bang dein Gesicht?"—	"My son, what makes you hide your face in fear?"—
Siehst, Vater, du den Erlkönig nicht?	Father, don't you see the Erlking?

Den Erlenkönig mit Kron und Schweif?—	The Erlking with crown and flowing robe?—
"Mein Sohn, es ist ein Nebelstreif."—	"My son, it's a wisp of fog."—
"Du liebes Kind, komm, geh mit mir!	"You dear child, come along with me!
Gar schöne Spiele spiel' ich mit dir;	Such lovely games I'll play with you;
Manch bunte Blumen sind an dem Strand,	Many colorful flowers are at the shore,
"Meine Mutter hat manch gülden Gewand."	"My mother has many a golden garment."
Mein Vater, mein Vater, und hörest du nicht,	My father, my father, and do you not hear
Was Erlenkönig mir leise verspricht?	What the Erlking promises me so softly?
Sei ruhig, bleibe ruhig, mein Kind;	Be quiet, stay quiet, my child;
In dürren Blättern säuselt der Wind.	In the dry leaves the wind is rustling.
Willst, feiner Knabe, du mit mir gehn?	Won't you come along with me, my fine boy?
Meine Töchter sollen dich warten schön.	My daughters shall attend to you so nicely.
Meine Töchter führen den nächtlichen Reihn,	My daughters do their nightly dance,
Und wiegen und tanzen und singen dich ein.	And they'll rock you and dance you and sing you to sleep.
Mein Vater, mein Vater, und siehst du nicht dort	My father, my father, and do you not see over there
Erlkönigs Töchter am düstern Ort?	Erlking's daughters in that dark place?
Mein Sohn, mein Sohn, ich seh es genau:	My son, my son, I see it most definitely:
Es scheinen die alten Weiden so grau.	It's the willow trees looking so grey.
Ich liebe dich, mich reizt deine schöne Gestalt;	I love you; I'm charmed by your beautiful form;
Und bist du nicht willig, so brauch ich Gewalt.	And if you're not willing, then I'll use force.
Mein Vater, mein Vater, jetzt faßt er mich an!	My father, my father, now he's grabbing hold of me!
Erlkönig hat mir ein Leids getan!	Erlking has done me harm!
Dem Vater grausets, er reitet geschwind,	The father shudders, he rides swiftly,
Er hält in Armen das ächzende Kind.	He holds in (his) arms the moaning child.
Erreicht den Hof mit Mühe und Not.	He reaches the farmhouse with effort and urgency.
In seinen Armen das Kind war tot.	In his arms the child was dead.

English Language

English is a member of the Indo-European family of languages. Various branches of the Indo-European family, particularly Germanic and Romance languages, have contributed for the development of English language. Initially, English was a part of the Germanic group of languages. It is assumed that the Germanic group started as a common language in the Elbe river area about 3,000 years ago. By 200 BC, this Germanic language had divided into three separate sub-groups: East Germanic, North Germanic, and West Germanic.

While English was developing separately in British Isles, German was developing in the European continent where Germany is today. Around 500 AD, three large groups from the northern part of present Germany traveled from their homeland to the island of Britain. These three people were the Jutes, the Angles, and the Saxons. They entered the region as invaders and immigrants and exercised a great deal of influence on the culture and language on the regions they occupied. As a result, Germanic language merged with Celtic-English, which was on a developing process, and made English mainly a Germanic language. Because of the geographical distance, German and English developed in two different directions. German was spoken in the northern part of European continent, whereas English was spoken in an island about 500 miles away.

Old English (500-1100 AD)

In 500 and 600 AD, West Germanic invaders from Jutland and southern Denmark, the Angles, Saxons, and Jutes, started to inhabit the British Isles. They spoke a language called Old English. Consequently, four major dialects of Old English emerged, Northumbrian in the north of England, Mercian in the Midlands, West Saxon in the south and west, and Kentish in the Southeast.

These invaders pushed the original inhabitants, Celtic-speaking people from England into Scotland, Wales, Cornwall, and Ireland, retaining a few Celtic words. The Jutes arrived first in 449 and settled in Britain. Around 800 AD invaders from Norse brought many North Germanic words into the English language. Most of the commonly used words in modern English have Old English roots. For example, words like *be*, *water*, and *strong*, derived from Old English roots.

Gradually, Old English further developed from the original form and several regional dialects developed. By the 900 AD, West Saxon became widespread in prose literature. A Mercian mixed dialect used for the poetry.

During the Old English period, a number of Latin words are introduced, many of them from the Greek origin. Typical of these words are *altar, kitchen, mass, priest, psalm, palm, pear* and *temple.* Most of them were brought to Britain by the Germanic invaders, who formerly had come into contact with Roman culture.

The Norsemen or Vikings, who invaded Britain periodically from the late 800 AD onwards and introduced Scandinavian words into Old English. These words were pertaining to the sea and battle, but also the words related to social and administrative system, like the word *law,* entered the language. Also the verb form *are* and words like *take, cut, both, ill,* and *ugly* entered the English Language from Scandinavia.

Middle English (1100-1500 AD)

The Duke of Normandy conquered England in 1066 AD. The new rulers spoke a dialect of Old French known as Anglo-Norman. The Anglo-Norman was a French dialect that had substantial Germanic influences apart from the basic Latin roots.

Linguists believe that the influence of the Normans can be understood by validating two words, beef and cow. The word *Beef* is derived from the Anglo-Norman, while the Anglo-Saxon masses who looked after the cattle, kept the Germanic word *cow.* Many legal terms such as *indict*, *jury*, and *verdict* have Anglo-Norman roots because the Normans controlled the courts.

Occasionally, French words replaced Old English words; *crime* replaced *firen* and *uncle* replaced *eam*. Sometimes French and Old English combined together to form a new word, as the French *gentle* and the Germanic *man* formed *gentleman.*

In 1204 AD, Normandy came under the rule of France. As a result England became the predominant issue for new rulers.

English adopted modified English as their native language. About 150 years later, the Black Death (1349-50) killed about one-third of the English population. Later, the working class people and merchant classes rose in economic and social significance, and along with them English increased its importance compared to Anglo-Norman. This combination of the two languages took form as Middle English. By 1362, the Statute of Pleading was adopted, which made English the language of the courts and it began to be used in Parliament.

In the meantime, several changes in the languages took place. As early as 1200, three or four grammatical case forms of nouns in the singular had been reduced to two, and to indicate the plural the noun ending *-es* had been adopted.

The declension of the noun was made simple by following changes: (a) dropping the final *n* from five cases, (b) neutralizing all vowel endings to *e*, and (c) extending the masculine, nominative, and accusative plural ending *-as*. There are some examples of weak plural ending such as *oxen, man, men,* and *foot, feet,* etc.

Another development in English made was grammatical gender was replaced by natural gender. Furthermore, the Scandinavian *they, them* were substituted for the original *hie, hem* of the third person plural, and *who, which,* and *that* obtained their present qualified functions. The conjugation of verbs was simplified by the exclusion of endings and by the use of a general form.

In the Middle English period, a number of useful words came into the language from Old Norse such as *egg, sky, sister, window,* and *get.*

Midland, the dialect of Middle English derived from the Mercian dialect of Old English, became dominant.

During the 1400 AD, when in districts where Midland dialect was spoken developed, centers of university, economic, and courtly life, the Midland dialect became very popular. The influence of East Midland was reinforced by several events such as by its use in the government offices of London, by its literary propagation in the works of the 1400 AD popular poets, and eventually by its adoption for printed works by William Caxton. These developments contributed to the growth of the East Midland dialect into the Modern English language. The Middle English period ended around 1500 AD with the rise of Modern English.

Modern English (1500-1800 AD)

The next change of improvement in English occurred during Renaissance period. The resurgence of classical scholarship brought many classical Latin and Greek words into the language. It is estimated that Shakespeare recorded around 2,000 familiar words, phrases, and innumerable idioms during this period.

Between 1700 and 1800 AD, certain important grammatical changes occurred. The formal rules of English grammar were established during that period and pronoun *its* came into use replacing the genitive form *his*.

Two other important aspects influenced the language and helped to separate Middle and Modern English. The first was the Vowel Shift. Vowel sounds started to be made further to the front of the mouth and the letter 'e' at the end of words became silent. In Middle English, name was pronounced as *nam-a*, five was pronounced as *feef*, and down was pronounced as *doon*.

The rise of the British Empire and the expansion of global trade not only introduced English to the world, but also to introduced words into English. Hindi, and the other languages of the Indian subcontinent, contributed many words such as *pundit, pajamas*, and *juggernaut*. Practically, every language on Earth has contributed to the development of English.

English travelers and merchants introduced a number of words after their return from journeys on the Continent. From Italian came *cameo, stanza,* and *violin;* from Spanish and Portuguese, *alligator, peccadillo,* and *sombrero*.

In the late 1920s, a simplified form of the English language was developed based on 850 keywords by the English psychologist Charles Kay Ogden. It was called Basic English and it was used to promote English as an international language and to teach English in simple methods.

The primary goal of Basic English was to express any complex idea in simple form by using limited number of day-to-day words. The 850-word primary vocabulary was composed of 600 nouns symbolizing things or events, 150 adjectives for qualities and properties, and 100 general operational words, mostly verbs and prepositions.

Ogden's Rules of Grammar for Basic English

- Make plurals with an 's' on the end of the word. If there are special ways to make a plural word such as 'es' and 'ies', use them.
- There are four word endings to change each of the 600 nouns: -'er' and -'ing', and the two adjective word endings, -'ing' and -'ed'.
- Make qualifiers from adverbs by adding -'ly'.
- Talk about amounts with 'more' and 'most.' Use and know -'er' and -'est'.
- Make opposite adjectives with 'un'.
- Make questions with opposite word order, and 'do'.
- Operators and pronouns conjugate as in normal English.
- Make combined words from two nouns (for example "milkman") or a noun and a directive (sundown).
- Measures, numbers, money, months, days, years, clock time, and international words are in English forms.
- Use the words of an industry or science. [Wikipedia]

An important development of English outside Great Britain occurred with the colonization of North America. Several pronunciations and usages solidified when they reached American border. The most unique dissimilarities between American English and British English are in pronunciation, vocabulary, spelling, pitch, and stress as well.

Old English 450-1150: A Poem by Beowulf

Original

oretmecgas æfter æþelum frægn:
"Hwanon ferigeað ge fætte scyldas,
græge syrcan ond grimhelmas,

heresceafta heap? Ic eom Hroðgares
ar ond ombiht. Ne seah ic elþeodige
þus manige men modiglicran,
Wen ic þæt ge for wlenco, nalles for wræcsiðum,
ac for higeþrymmum Hroðgar sohton."

Him þa ellenrof andswarode,
wlanc Wedera leod, word æfter spræc,
heard under helme: "We synt Higelaces
beodgeneatas; Beowulf is min nama.
Wille ic asecgan sunu Healfdenes,
mærum þeodne, min ærende,
aldre þinum, gif he us geunnan wile
þæt we hine swa godne gretan moton."
Wulfgar maþelode (þæt wæs Wendla leod;
his modsefa manegum gecyðed,
wig ond wisdom): "Ic þæs wine Deniga,
frean Scildinga, frinan wille,
beaga bryttan, swa þu bena eart,
þeoden mærne, ymb þinne sið,
ond þe þa ondsware ædre gecyðan
ðe me se goda agifan þenceð.

Translation

...asked the warriors of their lineage:
"Whence do you carry ornate shields,
Grey mail-shirts and masked helms,
A multitude of spears? I am Hrothgar's
Herald and officer. I have never seen, of foreigners,
So many men, of braver bearing,
I know that out of daring, by no means in exile,
But for greatness of heart, you have sought Hrothgar."
To him, thus, bravely, it was answered,
By the proud Geatish chief, who these words thereafter spoke,
Hard under helm: "We are Hygelac's
Table-companions. Beowulf is my name.

I wish to declare to the son of Healfdene
To the renowned prince, my mission,
To your lord, if he will grant us
That we might be allowed to address him, he who is so good."
Wulfgar spoke—that was a Vendel chief;
His character was to many known
His war-prowess and wisdom—"I, of him, friend of Danes,
The Scyldings' lord, will ask,
Of the ring bestower, as you request,
Of that renowned prince, concerning your venture,
And will swiftly provide you the answer
That the great one sees fit to give me."

Courtesy: Wikipedia

Middle English: 1150-1500

The following is from the first sentence of the Prologue from *The Canterbury Tales* by Geoffrey Chaucer.

Whan that Aprill with his shoures sote The droghte of Marche hath perced to the rote, And bathed euery veyne in swich licour, Of which vertu engendred is the flour; Whan Zephirus eek with his swete breeth Inspired hath in euery holt and heeth The tendre croppes, and the yonge sonne Hath in the Ram his halfe course yronne, And smale fowles maken melodye, That slepen al the niȝt with open ye— So priketh hem Nature in hir corages— Than longen folk to goon on pilgrimages, And palmeres for to seken straunge strondes, To ferne halwes, couthe in sondry londes; And specially, from euery shires ende Of Engelond to Caunterbury they wende, The holy blissful martir for to seke, That hem hath holpen, whan that they were seke.	When April with its sweet showers has pierced the drought of March to the root, and bathed every vein in such liquor from whose power the flower is engendered; when Zephyr [the west wind] also, with his sweet breath has blown [into life] in every wood and heath the tender crops, and the young sun has run his half-course in the sign of the Ram [Aries], and small fowls make melody, who sleep all night with open eye - so Nature stimulates them in their hearts - THEN people long to go on pilgrimages, and palmers [pilgrims carrying palm leaves] to seek strange strands [coastlines], to far [distant] saints [holy places], known in various lands; and specially, from every shire's end [from every county] in England, to Canterbury they wend [go; *went* comes from 'wend'], to seek the holy blissful martyr [Thomas à Becket] who helped them when they were sick.

Courtesy: Wikipedia

Modern English 1500 to the Present

AH, London! London! our delight,
Great flower that opens but at night,

Great City of the midnight sun,
Whose day begins when day is done?
Lamp after lamp against the sky
Opens a sudden beaming eye,
Leaping alight on either hand,
The iron lilies of the Strand.

—*Richard Le Gallienne*

French Language

French Language is a member of the Romance language group of the Italic subfamily of the Indo-European languages. The Gauls, a Celtic people, were the earliest inhabitants of Gaul, or present-day France. They spoke a Celtic language, from which Breton, Irish, Welsh, and other modern Celtic languages derived. After the conquest of Gaul in the 100 BC by the Roman general Gaius Julius Caesar, Celtic lost its control and adapted to the form of Latin used by the illiterate class people in Rome known as the *lingua vulgaris* contrary to the *sermo urbanus* that was used by educated writers and orators.

The history of the French language begins with the invasion of Gaul by Julius Caesar in 59 BC. Then, the land was inhabited by a multitude of different tribes who spoke numerous interrelated Celtic languages. Over the next few centuries Latin, the language of the Romans was slowly adopted by most Gauls. When ancient Gaul (modern France) was conquered by the Romans, its inhabitants spoke a Celtic language called Gaulish, which was rapidly replaced by the Latin of the Roman rulers. The Latin language spoken by the invaders was not the refined form of Latin used in the Roman Senate and in literature, but a completely oral form of the colloquial language, entirely with its own grammar, vocabulary and pronunciation system.

French is descended from Vulgar Latin, vernacular Latin of the Roman Empire. The Franks, a group of Germanic tribes, invaded the Gaul in the 5th cent. AD, but they also were Romanized. Although modern French inherited several hundred words of Celtic origin and from Germanic, its structure and the greater part of its vocabulary has come from Latin.

Due to the emergence of Latin, Gaul became one of the richest and most important provinces of the Roman Empire and Latin replaced the various Celtic (Gaulish) tongues. As a consequence, a number of dialects emerged. When Paris became the capital of France in the 1200 AD, Parisian French attained dominance over the others. In the 17th, 18th, and 19th centuries, French was dominant as an international language. Even though it is partly obscured by English, it remains one of the two working languages of the United Nations.

The invasion of Gaul in the 400s AD by Germanic tribes driving off invaders from Central Asia resulted in a loss of military control by Rome. This move led to the establishment of a new Frankish ruling class whose mother tongue was not Latin. Their adaptation to the speaking of popular Latin by the indigenous population tended to impose a pronunciation that retained a marked Germanic flavor—notably in the vowel sounds. The modern French '*u*' and '*eu*', for example, remain very close to the modern German '*ü*' and '*ö*'—sounds unknown to any other language descended from Latin.

Starting from the 500 AD, France was exposed to numerous invasions—Germanic tribes Franks from the east, and the Vikings from the North. Each language left only minor influences on the language. In 987, Hugues Capet was elected king of Île de France, of the small kingdom in the region of Paris. At this time France was fundamentally composed of small, independent kingdoms. This event became the beginning of political unity as well as of linguistic unity. Capet was the first king in the region to speak the dialect, and as his kingdom grew larger and more powerful, the prestige of the language became popular.

The *lingua vulgaris* was strongly established in Gaul that the later conquerors, the German tribes, Visigoths, Burgundians, and Franks, did not enforce their language upon the occupied region. Instead they adopted the language as they found there. In modern French only about 400 words are found as Germanic origin: for example, *franc* ('free') and *français* ('French'), both from the Germanic word *Franko* ('freeman'); *fauteuil* ('armchair') from the Germanic *faldastol;* and *auberge* ('inn'), from the Germanic *heriberga*. Beginning from the 600 AD, Greek words were also introduced into the *lingua vulgaris*, through Greek colonies through the Mediterranean Sea, especially those at Marseille and Nice. By the 700 AD, the *lingua vulgaris* had been very much modified by the people of France.

By the 900 AD the language spoken in present-day France was sufficiently different from Latin to be a distinct language. It was called Old French and was in progress from the 9th to the 1300 AD. Of the numerous vernaculars of Old French, Francien became the standard form of the language in time because of the growing political and cultural importance of Paris. French language from the 14th through the 1600 AD is known as Middle French. During this period, many words and lexis were borrowed from Latin, Greek, and Italian. A group of French poets persuaded the French to develop and improve their language and literature.

In the 12th and 13th centuries, the *langue d'oïl* was popular throughout Europe. It was the court language of Naples. German princes and barons kept French-born teachers to teach French to their children. After the Norman Conquest of England in 1066, French powerfully competed English as the spoken language and almost replaced it as the literary language. In the middle ages, a large number of Arabic words were added to the language. It was a prestige among French scholars of Arabic science to add Arabic words and also the French brought the words back from Arabic lands that they had occupied.

The Hundred Years' War between France and England in 14th and 15th centuries, gave popular momentum to French nationalism and to acceptance of the court dialect as a national linguistic standard. The 1600 AD produced a great advancement in linguistic development. According to the agreement with the Ordinance of Villers-Cotterêts (1539) of Francis I, French as spoken in Île de France, became the official language throughout the kingdom. In the second half of the 1600 AD, a group of French poets known as the Pléiade, which included Joachim du Bellay and Pierre de Ronsard, declared that French was the appropriate language for prose and poetry. The group came to conclusion that the language required improvement and they approved that this improvement should be brought by modeling French writings on masterpieces of Greek and Latin literature.

The modern period of French began in the 1700 AD. In 1635 AD the French Academy was founded by Cardinal Richelieu to preserve the purity of the language and its literature and to provide a uniform system of approved usage of vocabulary.

By the 1700 AD, the French language had developed into what is essentially its present form. The inflectional endings inherited from Latin had been dropped from most of the part. Instead, the language depended on prepositional phrases and word order to indicate syntactical relationships between words. Publication of the dictionary, widespread literacy, and the extensive use of printing all contributed to the stabilization of the language. In the early 1700 AD, the poet François de Malherbe succeeded in establishing a standard of accuracy in the use of French words through his poetic and critical works. This standard shaped the language into a sophisticated instrument for the clear, concise expression of thought. One of the most important steps toward standardizing and improving the French language was the compilation of a dictionary by the French Academy, a literary society formed in 1635 by the statesman and cardinal Richelieu. The Academy began the compilation of an official French dictionary in 1639 AD, the first edition appeared in 1694 and was followed by seven others, and the eighth appeared in 1932-35. During the reign of Louis XIV, the French language attained the highest point of importance in its history, becoming an international language in Europe for diplomats and scientists.

In the early part of the 1900 AD, the advocates of French literary idealism inaugurated a movement to restore many archaic words to the language. Since the late 1800 AD, the whole tendency has been to enrich the language with words pertaining to new objects and concepts. Most additions to French since the late 1900 AD have come from English language and technological and scientific terms.

French language is one of the world's major languages, competed only by English as the language of international society and diplomacy. Apart from France, it is one of the official languages of Belgium, Switzerland, and Canada. It is also the main language of Haiti and former and present French colonies of Asia and Africa.

Characteristics

The changes made in grammar was very difficult to understand the Latin language used in Christian religious services and in legal documents. As a result, a written modification of the evolving spoken language was found necessary for current legal and political use. The earliest written documents in a distinctly 'French' ('Francien', from 'Frankish') language are the 'Oaths of Strasbourg', sworn by two of Charlemagne's grandsons in 842 AD.

In early medieval times, the spoken languages north and south of the Loire River began to develop separately. By the end of the 1300 AD, they became two distinct languages, the *langue d'oïl* of the north and the *langue d'oc* of the south; the terms were derived from *oïl* and *oc,* the words for 'yes' in both languages. The chief phonetic difference in the two languages was their usage of the free unaccented vowel *a* of Latin. The vowel became *e* in the *langue d'oïl* but remained unchanged in Provençal, the principal dialect of the *langue d'oc.* Thus, the Latin word *mare* ('sea') became *mer* in the *langue d'oïl* and *mar* in Provençal. In each language, several dialects developed. In addition to Provençal, the principal dialects of the *langue d'oc* were the Gascon, Languedocien, Auvergnat, Limousin, and Béarnais. A number of poetry and other literary works were written in the *langue d'oc.*

Changes happening later in French were limited to the gradual modification of pronunciation and addition of new words. In the first half of the 1600 AD, as a result of the wars with Italy, two types of words were introduced: those derived from the arts such as *fugue* and *opéra*; and military terms such as *colonel* and *soldat.* French wars with Spain in the early part of the 1700 AD enriched the French language with about several hundred words, including *cigare* and *nègre.* French wars with Germany in the 1700 AD resulted in the introduction of a small number of words from German such as *blocus* ('blockage') and *cible* ('target'). A section of the newly founded (1795) Institut de France, successor of the Old French Academy, issued an edition of the dictionary in 1798; the appendix of the work included a number of words that had been coined since the outbreak of the French Revolution.

It is said that the grammar of the French language spoken and written today is unaltered from the late 1700 AD. Official efforts to standardize, stabilize, and clarify French grammatical usage were established in the French Academy. The reason of this standardization was political: it is to expand the court's influence and to simplify the processes of law, administration, and commerce throughout and beyond the territory of France.

The Case System

Linguistically, the development of Old French from Vulgar Latin is distinguished by complex phonetic transformations and a simplification of the Latin case system. The trend of change in the Romance languages has been to reduce the Latin case system by removing distinctive endings. The Latin word *porta*, 'door,' for instance, had three singular forms: nominative, vocative, and ablative *porta*; accusative *portam*; and genitive and dative *portae*. Modern Romance languages, however, use only one singular form: French *porte*, Italian and Portuguese *porta*, and Spanish *puerta*. Other modern Romance linguistic features include the elimination of neuter gender, the development of the definite article, larger use of prepositions, firm word order, and the appearance of auxiliary verbs to express tense.

Writing System

The French alphabet is the same as that of English, although the letter *w* appears only in foreign words. Grave (è), acute (é), and circumflex (â) accents are used (*pére*, father; *été*, summer; *élève*, pupil; *âme*, soul); the cedilla (ç) appears under the letter *c* when preceding *a*, *o*, or *u* to indicate as *s* sound rather than *k* (*leçon*, lesson).

A	B	C	D	E	F	G	H	I	J	K	L	M	N	O	P
a	bé	cé	dé	e	effe	gé	ache	i	ji	ka	elle	emme	enne	o	pé

Q	R	S	T	U	V	W	X	Y	Z
qu	erre	esse	té	u	Vé	double	icse	i grec	zède

French spelling commonly reflects the language as it was spoken centuries ago. Silent letters sound, especially at the end of the words (*homes* is pronounced *um*, *aiment* pronounced as *em*) and words are normally divided in the middle, rather than at the end, through a process known as liaison. Here the final consonant of one word is linked with the initial vowel of the word following, so that the sentence *il est assis* (he is seated) is pronounced *ē-lĕ-tă-sē*. Moreover, French pronunciation is governed by consistent rules, which makes easy to learn the language.

ET PEUT-ETRE QUE...	AND MAY BE ALL WAS WRITTEN
Et peut-être que tout était écrit dans le livre mais le livre s'est perdu ou quelqu'un l'a jeté dans les ronces sans le lire n'importe ce qui fut écrit demeure, même obscur, un autre qui n'a pas vécu tout cela et sans connaître la langue du livre, comprendra chaque mot et quand il aura lu, quelque chose de nous se lèvera un souffle, une sorte de sourire entre les pierres.	And maybe all was written in the book but the book got lost or someone threw it in the brambles without reading it no matter, that which was written abides, even hidden, another who has not lived through all that and without knowing the book's language, will understand each word and when he has read it, something of ours will yield a breath, a kind of smile between the stones.

Courtesy: Claude Esteban, © Translation: 2000, John Montague

Spanish Language

Spanish also is a member of the Indo-European family of languages, whose earliest form of language was spoken approximately 5,000 years ago in the area of the Black Sea.

The Spanish language originated in the Southwestern region of Europe known as the Iberian Peninsula. Around the late 600 BC, the territory's first inhabitants of Iberian Peninsula began to mix with the Celts, a nomadic people from central Europe. They were called the Celtiberians, speaking a form of Celtic.

When Iberian Peninsula came under the Roman rule in 19 BC, the region became known as Hispania, and its inhabitants learned spoken language of Latin from Roman traders, settlers, administrators, and soldiers.

Latin remained the official language of government and culture until about 719 AD even after the Visigoths, Germanic tribes of Eastern Europe, invaded Hispania in the 400s AD.

When Arabic-speaking Islamic groups from Northern Africa called Moors conquered the region in around 719, Arabic and an associated dialect called Mozarabic came to be broadly spoken in Islamic Spain. In a few Christian kingdoms in the North such as Asturias, Vulgar Latin continued.

During the following centuries, the Christian kingdoms slowly defeated Moorish Spain, recapturing the country politically, militarily, culturally and linguistically. As the Christians progressed south, their Vulgar Latin dialects became dominant.

The ensuing language was a hybrid since Castilian borrowed numerous words from Mozarabic, and present-day Spanish has an estimated 4,000 words with Arabic roots.

Whereas the majority of Spanish words derived from Latin, many more are derived from other sources like prior Latin languages such as Greek, Celtic, and Basque. Early in the 500 AD, the invasion of the Visigoths introduced some Germanic words. Three centuries later the Muslim invasion introduced a great number of Arabic words, several of which are easily perceived by the prefixed Arabic article *al.* Beginning in the 1100 AD, the influence of French priests, clerics and pilgrims on their way to Santiago de Compostela in northwestern Spain, the Spanish vocabulary was noticeably increased by words and phrases from French. Spanish colonies, possessions and relations led to the introduction of terms from Native American languages and other sources. Due to all these developments, scholarly activities have increased the repository of borrowed words.

In the 1200s, under the guidance of King Alfonso X, who was called the Learned-King of Castile and Leon, the formation of a standardized Spanish language based on the Castilian dialect started. King himself along with a group of scholars in his court made Toledo, a center of culture, as the heart of their activities. There scholars composed original works in Castilian and translated chronicles, histories, scientific, legal, and literary works from other languages (mainly Latin, Greek, and Arabic). This historic attempt of translation was a most important medium for the spreading of knowledge throughout ancient Western Europe. Also Alfonso X adopted Castilian for administrative work and for all official documents and ruling.

During the reign of the Catholic monarchs Isabella of Castile and Ferdinand of Aragón, who reoccupied the Spain from Moors in 1492, the Castilian dialect of Spanish acquired broader recognition. Isabella and Ferdinand made Castilian the official language in their kingdom. In 1492, Antonio de Nebrija's, *Arte de la lengua castellana* (*The Art of the Castilian Language*) book appeared. It was the first book ever produced to study and to define the grammar of a European language. In the same year, the first Latin to Spanish dictionary (*Gramática de la Lengua Castellana*) was written in Salamanca, Spain by Elio Antonie de Negrija.

The Latin dialect that ultimately became Spanish was greatly influenced by the invasion of the Moors, Arabic-speaking people, in 711. For a long time, Latin/Spanish and Arabic existed alongside, and Spanish place names remain Arabic roots even today. Even after the expulsion of Moors in the 1500 AD, thousands of Arabic words have become part of Spanish language. Even though the introduction of Arabic words into Spanish dialect commenced in the 800 AD, several words of Latin and Greek origin had roots in Arabic.

After Latin and English, Arabic is certainly the major contributor of words to the Spanish language, and a big portion of English-Spanish cognates (words that have a common origin or words that the two languages share) come from Arabic, not from Latin. Usually, Arabic origin words are those that start with 'al-,' words, for example, 'algebra,' 'Allah,' 'alkali' and 'alchemy,' and they exist in Spanish as *álgebra*, *Alá*, *álkali* and *alkimia*, respectively.

Characteristics

Characteristic features of Spanish diachronical phonology include *lenition* ('softening' or 'weakening'), *palatization* (palatal consonants are articulated with the body of the tongue raised against the hard palate, the middle part of the roof of the mouth), and *diphthongation* (diphthongs are represented by two vowel symbols intended to indicate roughly the beginning and ending tongue positions). Similar phenomena can be found in most other Romance languages as well.

There are significant variations among the various regions of Spain and Spanish-speaking America. In Spain, the North Castilian dialect pronunciation is normally considered as the national standard.

Pronunciation is administered by strict phonetic rules and the stress follows a steady pattern. The consonants *b* and *v* are pronounced almost alike, the sound falling somewhere between the two sounds in English.

In grammatical structure, Spanish is normally in agreement with French, Italian, Portuguese, and the other Romance languages. However, a pronounced strangeness of Spanish grammar is the use of the preposition *a* as an unchangeable particle before the direct object of a verb if that object is a person; for example, *veo a mi amigo* ("I see [particle] my friend").

Spanish has three second person singular pronouns: *tú* and *usted*. In some parts of Latin America, it is *vos*. Usually, *tú* and *vos* are informal and used with friends and with close relations. *Usted* is generally regarded as the formal form, and is used as a sign of respect, like when addressing elders or strangers. The pronoun 'vosotros' is the plural form of 'tú' in most of Spain. In the Americas, it is replaced with 'ustedes.'

Spanish has a phonemic stress system, where meaning of two words can differ by just changing the stress. For example, the word *camino* (with last but one stress) means 'road' or 'I walk' while *caminó* (with final stress) means 'he/she/it walked'.

Writing System

Spanish is written using the Latin alphabet with an additional letter *ñ*. *Ch* and *ll* are also used in the alphabet (*a, b, c, ch, d, ..., l, ll, m, n, ñ*) and the stressed vowel carries an acute accent (*á*). Beginning about the1200 AD, Spanish writers, who copied documents by hand used the tilde placed over letters to indicate that a letter was doubled (for example, *nn* as *ñ* and *aa* as *ã*). The tilde was used not only with the *n* but with other letters as well. The recognition of the tilde for other letters gradually diminished, and by the 1400 AD the *ñ* was the only letter it was used. The *ñ* does not exist in Latin or in any other Romance languages, but it is the only Spanish letter of Spanish origins.

As the phonetic kind of Spanish became solidified, the *ñ* came to be used for its sound, not only for words with an *nn*. A number of Spanish words such as *señal* and *campaña*, that are English equivalent use the *ñ* where English uses 'gn,' such as in 'signal' and 'campaign,' respectively.

Alphabets

A	B	C	CH	D	E	F	G	H	I	J	K	L	LL
a	be	ce	che	de	e	efe	ge	hache	i	jota	ka	ele	elle

M	N	O	P	Q	R	S	T	U	V	W
eme	ene	o	pe	cu	ere	ese	te	u	ve	dobleue

X	Y	Z
quis	I griega	zeta

The Jewish Spanish Language

Ladino is a Romance language derived from Old Castilian and Hebrew languages. This language was spoken by the Jewish community that existed in 1492 in Spain and then they were expelled from the Spain. Over the centuries, the Spanish language of the late 1500 AD was influenced by different Mediterranean languages spoken where the Jews went to live. Presently, a small number of people speak Ladino, most of them are in Israel. Some activists predict that the Ladino language could extinguish because these speakers adopt the language where they live.

Conventionally, Ladino was written from right to left using the Hebrew alphabet. Nowadays, the Latin alphabet is used, except in some religious writings.

One distinguished grammatical inequality between Spanish and Ladino is that the Ladino does not use the *usted* and *ustedes* forms of the second-person pronoun because their use was developed in Spanish language after the Jews had left Spain.

Similarly, Ladino differentiates the sounds of the *B* and the *V* because it was in the 1500 AD, Spaniards assigned identical sound to those two consonants. Likewise, other features of Spanish, for example, the inverted question mark and the use of the *ñ* are also missing in Ladino.

Pedro Calderón de la Barca (1600-81)

Sueña el rey que es rey, y vive
con este engaño mandando,
disponiendo y gobernando;
y este aplauso, que recibe
prestado, en el viento escribe,
y en cenizas le convierte
la muerte, ¡desdicha fuerte!
¿Que hay quien intente reinar,
viendo que ha de despertar
en el sueño de la muerte?

Sueña el rico en su riqueza,
que más cuidados le ofrece;
sueña el pobre que padece
su miseria y su pobreza;
sueña el que a medrar empieza,
sueña el que afana y pretende,
sueña el que agravia y ofende,
y en el mundo, en conclusión,
todos sueñan lo que son,
aunque ninguno lo entiende.

Yo sueño que estoy aquí
destas prisiones cargado,
y soñé que en otro estado
más lisonjero me vi.
they all thus what they are dream
although no one will so see it.

I dream that I am in here
with these chains and prisons burdened
yet I dreamt that I in other,
more fulsome state saw myself.

¿Qué es la vida? Un frenesí.
¿Qué es la vida? Una ilusión,
una sombra, una ficción,
y el mayor bien es pequeño:
que toda la vida es sueño,
y los sueños, sueños son.

The king dreams he is a king, and lives
in this deception commanding,
disposing of, reigning, ruling,
And the applause, thus on loan received
so gets in the wind written.
And in ashes Death
will turn him - great disgrace!
Who will dare so to govern?
seeing himself come awake
to the sorry dream of Death?

The rich one dreams of his riches
which more care and comfort yields him;
the poor one dreams that he suffers
his sheer misery and poverty.
Dreams he who to live begins,
and he who toils and pretends,
and he who grieves and offends
and in the world, in conclusion,

What is life? A frantic moment,
What is life? But an illusion,
but a shadow, but a fiction,
and the greatest good is small:
for life is all but a dream
and dreams are just that, they're dreams.

Translated by Jorge Solís, 1997

Italian Language

A variety of Italian dialects developed from Vulgar Latin, the spoken language of the Roman Empire. Just like French, the Italian language is derived from Vulgar Latin, a section of the Romance group of the Indo-European ancestors of languages. It is spoken largely in the Italian peninsula, Sicily, San Marino,

Corsica, northern Sardinia, southern Switzerland, and on the northeastern shoreline of the Adriatic Sea, and in North and South America. During the long period of the evolution of Italian language, many dialects emerged. In the north and northwest, the Gallo-Italian dialects dominate; they are Piedmontese, Lombard, Ligurian, and Emilian or Bolognese, all of which demonstrate a close similarity to French in their pronunciation and truncated terminations.

Italian is spoken by about 70 million people mainly in Italy. Standard Italian is based on Tuscan vernaculars and is relatively midway between the languages of the Gallo-Romance languages of the North and Southern Italy. Among all of the Romance languages, Italian language is normally considered to be closely similar to Latin in terms of grammar, pronunciation, and vocabulary.

When the city of Rome lost its control over Western Roman Empire (Western Europe), the Latin-speaking part of the Empire lost its central linguistic political authority. It maintained only the written examples of the old Roman civil law code and the text of the assumed 'Vulgate' bible translated from the Greek by Saint Jerome (AD 385-404) for the use of Latin-speaking parts of the Empire.

The adaptation of the new ruling class language on popular Latin drifted to compel a pronunciation that was unfamiliar to the language passed on from the period of Roman rule.

The grammar of the spoken popular Latin language from which standard Italian descended was simpler than that of the Latin of classical literature. Over the time, regional Italian languages from spoken Latin continued the simplification method much further. A great deal of words that Latin had communicated by inflectional modification was later communicated by separate words or phrases, and particularly by word order. Latin had been enormously flexible since logical relations between words could be identified from word endings only, despite of word order. Most Latin verbs are expressed by one word only. For example, a verb like spectat has three likely descriptions in English: watches, is watching, or does watch.

The history of the Italian language is somewhat intricate but the modern standard of the language was largely formed by recent events. The earliest existing texts are legal procedures from the region of Benevento dating from 960-963 AD. Italian was first formalized in the 1400 AD through the works of Dante Alighieri, who mixed southern Italian dialects, especially Sicilian, with Tuscan in his epic poems known collectively as the Commedia. Dante's much-appreciated works were read throughout Italy and his written dialect became the principle standard that everyone could understand easily. Dante is credited with standardizing the Italian language.

Dante Alighieri (1265-1321): Dante's work *Divina Commedia* was the example that was written in a dialect as against the conventional Latin and it was also proof that in literature the vulgar language could compete with Latin. To prove his point he needed the *Divine Comedy*. Bruno Migliorini wrote about *Divine Comedy* as "the masterpiece in which Italians rediscovered their language in sublime form." The success of his work spread the Florentine dialect, and gave it a status, prestige, acceptance and recognition. For this monumental work, Dante is referred as the father of the Italian Language.

The multiplicity of the dialects and their individual claim upon their local speakers as pure Italian speech presented a strange murkiness in the development of an established form of Italian language that would mirror the cultural unity of the entire Italian peninsula. Even the original popular Italian documents written in the 1000 AD are dialectal in language, and in following three centuries Italian writers wrote in their local dialects, producing numerous challenging regional schools of literature. During the 1400 AD, because of the central position of Tuscany in Italy and aggressive commerce of its most important city, Florence, the Tuscan dialect started to dominate. Besides, of all the Italian dialects, Tuscan departs least in morphology and phonology from classical Latin, and therefore it matches best with the Italian traditions of Latin culture. Florentine culture produced the three literary artists who splendidly summarized Italian thought and feeling of the late middle Ages and early Renaissance: Dante, Petrarch, and Boccaccio.

A passion to introduce linguistic standard and codify the language occupied writers of all subjects. During the 15th and 16th centuries, grammarians attempted to grant the status of a central and classical Italian speech on Tuscan language acknowledging its pronunciation, syntax, and vocabulary. Ultimately, this classicism was extended to include the natural changes unavoidable in a living language. Linguists assume that otherwise it might have made Italian another dead language.

The unification of Italy as a kingdom in 1860 and the spread of railways persuaded the use of standard written Italian as a model for speech that was suitable for commercial and political reasons throughout the region. The stylish model for spoken standard Italian became "la lingua Toscana in bocca romana" ("the Tuscan tongue, in a Roman mouth"—Tuscan dialects spoken with Roman inflection).

During the 1900 AD, the language spoken by educated Tuscans became the language of a new nation. The unification of Italy in 1861 had a deep influence not only on the politics but also on social, economical, and cultural transformation. With compulsory schooling, the literacy rate increased, and many people abandoned their native dialect in support of the national language.

Characteristics

Italian grammar is analogous to other Western Romance languages, particularly similar to the modern French grammar. It demonstrates agreement of adjectives and nouns, loss of noun declension for case, two genders (masculine and feminine), the use of definite and indefinite articles, and an elaborate system of perfect and progressive tenses for the verb. Just like French, the compound tenses are constructed with the verb 'to be' (essere) for the intransitive, with the verb 'to have' (avere) for the transitive verbs. Similar to French, Italian has a partitive article and uses pronominal adverbs.

The important difference between Italian and French or Spanish is that Italian does not use *-s* or *-es* to form the plural of nouns but instead uses *-e* for most feminine words and *-i* for masculine words (and some feminine words). In earliest times,

Italian formed the plural mainly with *-s* as other Romance languages, but a palatalization occurrence caused the passages.

Although the Italian vocabulary is derived mainly from Latin, French contributed largely to the Italian vocabulary: accetta *hatchet* (*F* hachette), cavaliere *knight* (*F* chevalier), *corvetta corvette* (*F* corvette), *dardo* dart (*F* dard), *sciampagna* champagne (*F* champaign), *ventaglio* fan (*F* éventail), etc. The suffix *-aggio* in viaggio voyage, etc. are borrowed from French -age.

There are abundant German borrowings from the late Antiquity and Middle ages, a lot of them were adopted via French: *gaio* gay, *garantire* to guarantee, *guadagnare* to gain, *guerra* war, especially the land directions (nord, sud, est, ovest). The Arabic words (like *arancia* orange) reached Italian mainly via Spanish and French.

The Greek words were inherited from Latin (*ballare* to dance, *governare* to govern), but the development of the scientific literature in Italian during the Renaissance introduced massive Greek words.

There was a tendency not only to borrow new words from Classical Latin, but also to remake the words of the spoken language on Latin pattern: Old Italian *stoggio* study became studio, both from the Latin studium.

Alphabets

Italian is written using the Latin alphabets and it is made up of 21 letters: 5 vowels and 16 consonants. It is a variant of the Latin alphabet used by the Italian language.

A	B	C	D	E	F	G	H	I	L	M	N
a	bi	ci	di	e	effe	gi	acca	I	elle	emme	enne

O	P	Q	R	S	T	U	V	Z
o	pi	cu	erre	esse	tu	u	vu/vi	zeta

The letters *J*, *K*, *W*, *X* and *Y* are not part of the standard Italian alphabet, but they are seen in imported words (such as *jeans*, *whiskey*, *taxi*). *J* may also appear in many words from different dialects.

(a) The consonants *B*, *F*, *M*, *N*, and *V* are pronounced as in English.

(b) *C* before *a*, *o*, *u* and before consonants has a sound similar to the English *k*; before *e* and *i a* sound similar to the English *ch* as in church.

(c) *D* is a bit volatile than in English, with the tongue near the tip of the upper teeth but without target.

(d) *G* before *a*, *o*, and *u* and before consonants has a sound like the *g* in good; before *e* and *i* like the *g* in general.

(e) *Gli* is like *ll* in million, and *Gn* is like the *ny* in canyon.

(f) *H* is silent.

(g) *L* is as in English, but sharper and more forward in the mouth.

(h) *P* is as in English.

(i) *Qu* is pronounced like the English *qu* in quality.

(j) *R* is different from the English *r*; it is pronounced with one flip of the tongue against the gums of the upper teeth. This is the trilled *r*.

(k) Initial *S* before vowels and unvoiced consonants (*c*, *f*, *p*, *q*, *s*, *t*) is pronounced like the *s* in sun.

(l) *S* before voiced consonants (*b*, *d*, *g*, *l*, *m*, *n*, *r*, *v*) is pronounced like the *s* in rose.

(m) *T* is about the same as in English, but no avoidance of breath.

(n) *Z* can be voiced, like *ds* in beds, or voiceless, like *ts* in bets.

Source: http://italian.about.com/cs/pronunciation/ht/pronounceconson.htm

Many Italian words have double consonants. They can never be found as first letters or as last letters. In most circumstances, they are followed by a vowel, as in dubbio = *doubt*, gatto = *cat*, etc.; but in some cases they may be followed by r, as in labbra= *lips*, attrito= *friction*, etc. English also has several words with double consonants. But in Italian, double consonants have a specific sound, whereas in English they are pronounced as if they were single. The Italian sound is identified by breaking the word by the double consonant. For example, if the word *cattle* was spelt *ca - ttle*, i.e. with a very short pause between the two syllables, the *tt* sound is heard more noticeably.

Italian uses two accents to indicate mid-close and mid-open vowels. The acute accent over the letter *E* (as in *perché*, why/because) is to indicate a mid-close vowel, and the grave accent (as in *tè*, tea) is to indicate a mid-open vowel. The grave accent is also used on letters *A*, *I*, *O*, and *U* to indicate the stress position when it is on the last letter of a word (for instance *gioventù*, youth).

The letter *H* is always silent when it begins a word, and is only used to distinguish *ho*, *hai*, *ha*, *hanno;* from *o* (or), *ai* (to the), *a* (to), *anno* (year). *H* is otherwise used for some combinations with other letters, but the '*h*' sound does not exist in Italian.

Dialects

Italian has always had a distinct dialect for each city. The identified dialects of Italian are Tuscan, Piemontese, Abruzzese, Pugliese (Apulian), Umbrian, Laziale, Central Marchigiano, Cicolano-Reatino-Aquilano, and Molisan. Other dialects are Milanese, Brescian, Bergamasc, Modenese, Bolognese, Sicilian and so on, basically one per city. Each region of Italy also has its own dialect, some of which are so distinct from standard Italian that they are mutually unintelligible. The Sicilian dialect for example, is sometimes regarded as a separate language and has a literary tradition older than Italian itself. Many of the so-called dialects of Italian spoken around the country are different from standard Italian to be considered separate languages.

During the 1000 AD, Italian first started to emerge in written documents in the form of notes and short texts inserted into Latin documents like lawsuits and poetry. By the 1400 AD, the Tuscan dialect was being used in political and cultural circles throughout Italy, although Latin remained the most excellent literary language until the 1600 AD.

The first grammar of Italian with the Latin title *Regule lingue florentine* (*Rules of the Florentine Language*) was created by Leon Battista Alberti (1404-72) and published in 1495. During the 15th and 16th centuries both Latin and Italian were used for technical and scientific texts. The Italian used was full of Latin words and over time Latin was used less and less as Italian became increasingly popular.

Dante's Comedia (Henry W. Longfellow translation)

<table>
<tr>
<td>Lo bel pianeto che d'amar conforta
faceva tutto rider l'oriente,
velando i Pesci ch'erano in sua scorta.

I' mi volsi a man destra, e puosi mente
a l'altro polo, e vidi quattro stelle
non viste mai fuor ch'a la prima gente.

Goder pareva 'l ciel di lor fiammelle:
oh settentrional vedovo sito,
of love made all the eastern heavens glad,
veiling the Pisces in the train she led.

Then I turned to the right, setting my mind
upon the other pole, and saw four stars
not seen before except by the first people.

Heaven appeared to revel in their flames:
o northern hemisphere, because you were
denied that sight, you are a widower!</td>
<td>poi che privato se' di mirar quelle!

Com'io da loro sguardo fui partito,
un poco me volgendo a l 'altro polo,
là onde il Carro già era sparito,

vidi presso di me un veglio solo,
degno di tanta reverenza in vista,
che più non dee a padre alcun figliuolo.
The lovely planet that is patroness

After my eyes took leave of those four stars,
turning a little toward the other pole,
from which the Wain had disappeared by now,
I saw a solitary patriarch
near me-his aspect worthy of such reverence
that even son to father owes no more.</td>
</tr>
</table>

Hindi Language

Hindi is the widely-spoken language in the world and an estimated 500-600 million people speak this language. A straight descendant of Sanskrit via Prakrit and Apabhramsha, Hindi pertains to the Indo-Aryan division of languages, a group of the Indo-European family. It has been influenced and enriched by Arabic, Dravidian, Turkish, Farsi, Portuguese, Persian, and English. Hindi is largely identical to Urdu, and is related to Bengali, Gujarati, and Punjabi. Hindi acquired its writing system from Sanskrit.

Development

Without mentioning the Sanskrit, Hindi cannot be understood with its completeness. Hindi not only acquired its writing system from Sanskrit, but also borrowed large amount of vocabulary.

Sanskrit, denoting refined, purified, perfected, is one of the ancient languages and oldest member of the Indo-Aryan language family and the basis of several of the important language in the world.

The enormous amount of Sanskrit literature, most likely the largest collection of literature from the ancient world, offers a unique access to several aspects of Indian culture. The earliest Sanskrit literature is conserved in the Vedas and in the compilation of ancient hymns. Sophisticated scientific literature dealing with linguistics, mathematics, and astronomy evolved to preserve Vedic culture. Gradually, this literature expanded to include works of many other areas.

The wonderful epics and puranas present an inexhaustible source of linguistic works for the study of Indian mythology as well as law and politics. Classical Sanskrit authors composed a rich literature of poetry and drama. Emergence of Buddhism and Jainism created an enormous number of religious and philosophical works together with works on logic and philosophy of language.

The script Sanskrit, also called Devanagari, is exceptionally logical and simple and easy to learn. Unlike English, pronunciation is easy because letters are pronounced exactly the same way.

Sanskrit holds the rank of a classical language, including other languages such as Classical Greek, Latin, Persian, Arabic, and Hebrew. The awarding of the title of a "classical language" needs to fulfill certain requirements from the language in question:

(a) Its origins must be recognized as having taken place over a long period of time.

(b) It should possess a sovereign tradition that arose virtually on its own and not as a derivative of another tradition.

(c) It must have a huge and extremely rich accumulation of ancient literature.

Sanskrit satisfies all these requirements having a tradition going back at least 3,000 years and is the language in which every ancient Hindu text is composed.

Eventually, Sanskrit enabled to emerge the Prakrit (natural) languages, which, enabled to emerge the contemporary Indian languages of today such as Hindi, Bengali, Marathi, Gujarati, Nepali and Singhalese. In fact, Sanskrit is the source language for all of the Indian subcontinent's regional languages. Considered to be the oldest language in human history, Sanskrit is the forefather and inspiration for virtually every language spoken in India. For example, one of the South Indian languages Kannada is filled with 70% of Sanskrit vocabulary. As is the case in Telugu, Malayalam, etc.

Prakrit dialects were spreading and mixing with other various regional languages. Buddhists selected one of these dialects roughly in the 600 BC and developed it into Pali. The simplification of the dialects continued concluding in the Apabhramsha phase in 600 AD. Further modification of the regional Apabhramshas during 600-1000 AD culminated to the New Indo-Aryan languages of today.

Apabhramsha is a term used by Sanskrit grammarians to refer to dialects that deviate from the standard or rules of Sanskrit grammar. The term *apabhramsha* literally means 'corrupt' or non-standard language. This term is used for the dialects developing the transition period between the 6th and 13th centuries.

Apabhramshas evolved into modern languages, which are spoken by millions of people today. Languages such as Hindi, Bengali, Urdu, and Gujarati are all representative languages of contemporary states.

Hindi started to emerge as Apabhramsha in the 700 AD and by the 1000 AD it became stable. Several dialects of Hindi have been used in literature. Braj was the popular literary dialect until it was replaced by khari boli in the 1900 AD. A number of former literary languages with massive number of literature such as Braj, Avadhi, and Maithili, have been effectively merged into the fabric of Hindi. Maithili, spoken in northern Bihar, has huge literature and its own grammar. Advocates of its use maintain that it is a language related closely to eastern Indo-Aryan languages than to Hindi. Other regional languages such as Marwari in Rajasthan and Magadhi in southern Bihar are considered variants of Hindi. Hindi is spoken in northern and central part of India. Linguists think of Hindi and Urdu as the same language, the difference being that Hindi is written in the Devanagari script and derives much of its vocabulary from Sanskrit, while Urdu is written in the Persian script and derives much of its vocabulary from Persian and Arabic languages.

Hindi shares the same ancestral roots as with other European languages. They evolved from a language considered to have been spoken in Central Asia around 5,000 BC, called by linguists the Indo-European parent language. For this reason, many basic words in Hindi are the same as or similar to their correspondent in English. English words of Hindi origin include cot, loot, thug, bandana, bazaar, pundit, coolie, guru, karma, chutney, juggernaut, etc.

Hindi became the official language of India on January 26, 1965, although the Constitution of India recognizes English and 21 other languages as official languages.

After the Independence of India from Britain in 1947, the Government of India started the work on standardization of the language. As a result, the following changes took place:

Standardization of Hindi grammar: In 1954, the Government of India set up a committee for preparing a grammar of Hindi. The committee's report was later released as "A Basic Grammar of Modern Hindi" in 1958.

Standardization of Devanagari script by Central Hindi Directorate, Ministry of Education and Culture to bring uniformity in writing and improve the shape of some of its characters.

Additionally, Hindi spelling was standardized and a system of transcribing the Devanagari alphabet was designed.

The general appearance of the Devanagari script is that letters 'hanging from a line'. The script has no capital letters.

Due to the influence of Hinduism, Hindi derives most of its high-level vocabulary from Sanskrit. Due to the Muslim influence in Northern India, it also has many Persian, Arabic and Turkish loanwords.

Its interesting characteristic is a three levels of reverence, with great sensitivity to match 'formal', 'familiar' and 'intimate' conversational situations. Thus, the polite communication of respect and gratitude is an integral part of the language itself.

Dialects

Hindi has several dialects like Marwari, Braj, Bundeli, Kanauji, Urdu, Chattisgarhi, Bagheli, Avadhi, Bhojpuri, Bundeli, Maithili, and many others.

Hindi Alphabets

Vowels

अ	आ	इ	ई	उ	ऊ	ऋ	ऋ	ए	ऐ
a	*aa*	*e*	*ee*	*u*	*uu*	*Ru*	*RU*	*e*	*E*
ऐ	ओ	ओ	ओ	अं	आ:				
ai	*o*	*O*	*ou*	*am*	*aha*				

Consonants

क	ख	ग	घ	ङ	च	छ	ज	झ	ञ
k	kh	g	gh	G	ch	Ch	ja	Jha	J
ट	ठ	ड	ढ	ण	त	थ	द	ध	न
T	Th	D	Dh	N	t	th	da	dh	n
प	फ	ब	भ	म	य	र	ल	व	श
p	P	ba	bha	ma	ya	ra	la	va	sha
ष	स	ह							
sa	ha								

Numerlas

0	1	2	3	4	5	6	7	8	9	10
shunya	ek	do	tiin	char	paanch	chah	saat	aath	nau	des

A Poem by Mira Bai, 1498-1547

बरसै बदरिया सावन की,	barasai badariyaa saavan kii,
सावन की मन भावन की।	saavan kii man bhaavan kii.
सावन में उमग्यो मेरो मनवा,	saavan mein umagyo mero manavaa,
भनक सुनी हरि आवन की।।	bhanak sunii hari aavan kii.
उमड़ धुमड़ चहुं दिससे आयो,	umad ghumad chahu disase aayo,
दामण दमके झर लावन की।	daaman damake jhar laavan kii
नान्हीं नान्हीं बूंदन मेहा बरसै,	naanhii naanhii bundan mehaa barasai,
सीतल पवन सोहावन की।।	siital pavan sohaavan kii.
मीरा के प्रभु गिरधर नागर,	miiraa ke prabhu giradhar naagar,
आनन्द मंगल गावन की।।	aananda mangal gaavan kii.

It is raining in the month of Savan,
I like the rain coming down.
In Savan, my heart starts to pine,
I hear the sound of Hari coming.
The clouds have rolled in from all sides,
lightening occurs and it pours.
Tiny drops come from the clouds,
and I enjoy the cool breeze.
O lord of Mira, called Giradhar Nagar,
The cloudy season is for singing joyfully.

Courtesy: http://www.cs.colostate.edu/~malaiya/mira.html

Japanese Language

The origin of Japanese language is an extensive debate among academic community. Testimony has been presented for a number of resources: Altaic, Polynesian, Austronesian, Chinese, Korean, Dravidian languages, Malayo-Polynesian languages, and Tibeto-Burmese languages.

Indonesians, Malaysians and Philipinos actually originated from Southern China. Some advocates suggest that these people would have migrated on boats via Taiwan and displace the original inhabitants, who might have been related to Dravidians of Southern India. There has been a lot of migrations from the Asian mainland to the islands of Indonesia, Taiwan, the Philippines and Japan during the ice age.

It seems likely that the Japanese language originated as a mix of languages from Central and Southeast Asia and had fully developed into a distinct language by the time of the Yayoi culture (300 BCE-300 CE).

Because the Japanese language appears to have developed in isolation from other languages, there is no decisive proof connecting Japanese to a single family of languages and to common predecessor language. One theory recognizes Japanese in the family of Altaic language, which include Turkish, Mongolian, and Korean and links Japanese directly to the Korean language. It is said that because some major features and characteristics of the Japanese language do not agree with this hypothesis, some scholars are verifying the possible links to the family of Austronesian languages. This theory is because Austronesian languages influenced Japanese through profound borrowing of vocabulary by the Japanese language. Some scholars also considering the possibility of Southeast Asian languages, including Dravidian languages, because huge number of Southern Indian words are found in the Japanese language.

There are three main theories about the origin of the Japanese language:

(a) Japanese is an Altaic language related to Korean, Mongolian, and Turkish.

(b) Japanese is an Austronesian language related to Papuan, Malayan and other Pacific languages.

(c) Japanese is a Southeast Asian language correlated to Vietnamese, Tibetan, Burmese and/or the Tamil languages of southern India and Ceylon.

Development

Spoken Japanese language evolved in four stages: (1) Old Japanese (up to 800 AD); (2) Late Old Japanese (900-1100 AD); (3) Middle Japanese (1200-1600 AD); and (4) Modern Japanese (from the 1700 AD to the present). Noteworthy modifications from old to modern times have been the gradual decrease of eight vowel sounds to five in addition to phonological, morphological, and vocabulary changes.

When Tokugawa Ieyasu became a military ruler or Shogun in 1603, Japan was completely closed to all outside influence. Christianity, along with Western education and its linguistic control was abandoned. For the next two hundred and fifty years, Japan remained closed to the outside world.

In 1868, Japan's new Meiji leaders decided to westernize Japan and to accept Western technology for the benefit of survival and competition. Soon, the vocabulary of English, German, and other Western languages were introduced into Japanese. Many new Japanese vocabulary terms were also formed to convey new ideas adopted from the West.

After the destruction of World War II, the military forces, which occupied Japan considered Japanese language as cumbersome. They decided to abolish the ancient Chinese characters or Kanji with Romanized symbols, or Romani, based on the roman alphabets in order to simplify the written Japanese language. This much anticipated change never happened. But in 1946, Japan's Education Ministry revised Chinese characters, reducing their numbers to a more manageable number of 1850 characters. Since that time, the Japanese government is managing firm centralized jurisdiction of the language.

Now Japanese is the official language of Japan, and Japan is the only country to have Japanese as an official language.

Dialects

Several diverse regional dialects existed within Japan since ancient times. Japan encompasses numerous hilly islands and this geographical structure restricted communication between the Japanese peoples residing in different areas of the country. Consequently, people in the different regions of Japan developed different dialects of the Japanese language.

Countless number of dialects are spoken all over Japan's four main islands (Hokkaido, Honshu, Shikoku, and Kyushu), in addition to the smaller islands, like the Ryukyu Islands. For example, some dialects spoken in the southern parts of Japan are virtually unintelligible to the speakers of other dialects. Due to this diversity of dialects, the Japanese use a standard dialect to ease the communication throughout the country.

Characteristics

The Japanese language utilizes a broad system of word indicator to convey politeness and respect. This kind of word indicator is visible on verbs, adjectives, and nouns. For example, when talking with someone familiar to the speaker, like a relative or a friend, a person uses the informal form of the verb *to go, iku*. If the person addressed is an outsider or is older than the speaker, the politeness indicator *-masu* is used as *iki-masu*. If the person addressed is superior to the speaker, the respectable form of the verb *to go, irassharu* is used. The respectful form, *irasshai-masu,* and permits the speaker concurrently to be polite to the person addressed and to demonstrate reverence to the person discussed.

Japanese has a widespread grammatical system to express politeness and formality. There are three main levels of politeness in spoken Japanese: the plain form (*kudaketa*), the simple polite form (*teineigo*) and the advanced polite form (*keigo*).

By the addition of *o-* or *go-* as a prefix, a majority of nouns may be made polite in the Japanese language. *o-* is used for words of native Japanese origin, while *go-* is affixed to words of Chinese derivation.

Vocabulary

The original language of Japan was the *yamato kotoba*, which comprise the major category in the Japanese vocabulary. There are also loan words from Chinese and Southeast Asian languages, and growing number of words borrowed from modern times from Western languages such as English. Chinese words entered into the Japanese language from the 500 AD through contact with Chinese culture.

Japanese also borrowed words from Korean and Ainu. It began to borrow words from Portuguese in the 1600 AD followed from Dutch during Japan's segregation period. With the Meiji replacement and the reopening of Japan in the 1900

AD, borrowing of words happened from German, French, and English. Presently, words of English origin are the most commonly used.

By far the majority of foreign words in Japanese are derived from English. When English speakers meet Japanese using English words, they get confused listening to the Japanized English words. This is because in Japanese language every syllable must be in the form 'consonant + vowel'. For example, they pronounce baseball as *besaboru*, strike as *seturoku*. In this way, one can see numerous romaji form of English words in Japanese. Some more examples include '*teburu*' (table), '*biru*' (beer), '*gurasu*' (glass), '*aisu*' (ice), '*takushi*' (taxi) and '*ho*teru' (hotel).

Here are a few examples of words borrowed from Portuguese, Dutch and Spanish, such as '*pan*' (bread) and '*arigato*' (thank you), '*pão*' and '*obrigado*'.

Some linguists think Japanese was initially a language related to Tibetan or to Tamil that was introduced into Japan during the vast migrations of Southeast Asian peoples four or five thousand years ago. This language integrated with Altaic and Austronesian languages to form the current language. Here are some examples of South Indian languages Tamil and Kannada found in Japanese:

English	Japanese	Tamil	Kannada
be	*iru*	*iru*	*iru*
Dark	*kuroppoi*	*karuppu*	*kappu*
earth	*jimen*	*jaminu*	*jaminu*
encumbrance	*jama*	*jama*	*jama*
exist	*iru, aru*	*iru*	*iru*
grass	*kusa*		*kusha*
ground	*jimen*	*jaminu*	*jaminu*
hell	*naraku*	*narakam*	*naraka*
I	*en*	*en*	*en*
place	*tou*	*tavu*	*tavu*

infant	*shouni (soonu)*		*soonu*
refuse	*kasu*	*kasam*	*kasa*
stick	*konbou*	*kombu*	*kombu*
mute	*mogan (mukan)*	*moogan (mukan)*	*mooga (mooka)*
offspring	*shison*	*shishu*	*shishu*
say	*anou, ano*	*annu*	*annu*
spicy	*karai*	*karam*	*kara*
stiff	*katai*	*katu*	*katu*
wear	*haku*		*haku*
you	*temae*	*thamma, tangal*	*Thamma, tavu*

Since all Indian languages are influenced by Sanskrit, we can see Sanskrit origin words also here.

Writing System

Around 1000 years ago, Japanese developed a system of writing from Chinese characters, which contains of syllabaries, or *kana*. Each syllabary is a character that symbolizes a syllable in the language. Unlike a Chinese character, it represents a sound but not a meaning. There are two types of syllabaries, *hiragana* and *katakana,* each containing the same set of sounds. Katakana is used to write words borrowed from Western languages such as French, German, and English. Kanji, Hiragana, and Katakana often appear in the same sentence. Together with Chinese characters and syllabaries, the Roman alphabets are used for names of organizations such as Honda, Toyota, and Sony.

Japanese adapted the Chinese Kanji characters during the sixth to ninth centuries AD to develop their language.

During the 600 AD, along with the introduction of Chinese legislative systems, art styles, manufacturing techniques, and Buddhism, the Chinese writing system was also implemented, giving the Japanese the capability to write for the first time. Japan's first books, the Kojiki (Records of Ancient Matters) and the Nihon Shoki (Chronicles of Japan), both historical compilations containing a large number of myths and legends were written in Chinese characters and a large number of Chinese vocabulary were added to Japanese during this time.

By the 1200 AD, the syllabic writing systems, 'hiragana' and 'katakana', were designed out of 'kanji', providing the Japanese a new devise to write their native language. Now, Japanese is written with a combination of the three: 'kanji', 'hiragana', and 'katakana'.

Conventionally, Japanese is written vertically with lines starting at the right side of the page. As this writing method even now dominates, a different method uses horizontal lines and starts from the top left-hand side of the page like in English.

The structure of Chinese characters is considered as the very difficult system to learn because of the large number of characters and the complication involved both in writing and in reading each character. Each character has a related meaning, but individually has no meaning at all. There are thousands of characters in the Japanese language. In 1946, the Japanese government recognized 1850 characters for everyday use. In 1981, the government extended the list to 1945 characters and conferred the name Joyo Kanji List (kanji for everyday use).

Toyotomi Hideyoshi, a Japanese warrior brought wooden moveable type of printing device from Korea into Japan. This printing system significantly expanded the literacy rate of the public, and increased the status of the Edo (Tokyo) Dialect as the primary dialect of Japanese.

Pronunciation

Nearly all Japanese syllables end with a vowel, and a syllable may be made of a single vowel. There are five vowels in the language: *a, i, u, e,* and *o*. Vowel length distinguishes words, as in *to* for door and *too* for ten. The fundamental Japanese consonants are *p, b, t, d, k, g, s, z, h, m, n, r, y, w,* as well as the nasal consonant that happens at the end of a syllable, as in *hon* (book). When preceding the vowels *a, o,* or *u,* several of these consonants can be *palatalized*. For example, a palatalized *k* before each of these vowels creates a sound like *kya, kyu,* and *kyo*. The consonant *t* is pronounced as *ts* and *d* as *dz* in front of the vowel *u*. When the consonants *t, d, s,* and *z* precede the vowel *i,* they are pronounced as *chi, ji, shi,* and *ji,* correspondingly.

Heike is a war tale from the 1300 AD

祇園精舎の鐘の聲、
諸行無常の響あり。
娑羅雙樹の花の色、
盛者必衰のことわりをあらはす。
おごれる人も久しからず、
唯春の夜の夢のごとし。
たけき者も遂にほろびぬ、
偏に風の前の塵に同じ。

Gion shouja no kane no koe
shogyou mujou no hibiki ari.
Shara souju no hana no iro
jousha hissui no kotowari o arawasu.
Ogoreru hito mo hisashikarazu,
Tada haru no yo no yume no gotoshi.
Takeki mono mo tsui ni horobinu.
Hitoe ni kaze no mae no chiri ni onaji.

The knell of the bells at the Gion temple
Echoes the impermanence of all things.
The color of the flowers on its double-trunked tree
Reveals the truth that to flourish is to fall.
He who is proud is not so for long,
Like a passing dream on a night in spring.
He who is brave is finally destroyed,
To be no more than dust before the wind.

Translated by P.G.O'Neill
Courtesy: http://www.classical-japanese.net/Poetry/heike.html

7

Basic Grammar

A brief introduction to basic grammar for some living languages is given in this section. For more detail understanding of the grammar, it is recommended to refer to the regular grammar books.

GERMAN GRAMMAR

Articles

In German, gender does not depend completely on sex. The noun for a male is usually masculine and takes the definite article *der*, the noun for a female is generally feminine and takes the definite article *die*. Things are not always neuter. Some are masculine, some are feminine, and some are neuter and take the definite article das.

The Indefinite Article: *a, an*

Masculine	Feminine	Neuter	Plural
ein	eine	ein	keine

The Definite Article: *the*

Masculine	Feminine	Neuter	Plural
der	die	das	die

In German, the articles are the main indicators of grammatical case. Here are the examples of definite and indefinite articles.

Definite Article—Singular

	Masculine (Father)	Feminine (Mother)	Neuter (Child)
Nominative	*der Vater*	*die Mutter*	*das Kind*
Genitive	*des Vaters*	*der Mutter*	*des Kindes*
Dative	*dem Vater*	*der Mutter*	*dem Kind(e)*
Accusative	*den Vater*	*die Mutter*	*das Kind*

Definite Article—Plural

	Masculine (Father)	Feminine (Mother)	Neuter (Child)
Nominative	*die Väter*	*die Mütter*	*die Kinder*
Genitive	*der Väter*	*der Mütter*	*der Kinder*
Dative	*den Vätern*	*den Müttern*	*den Kindern*
Accusative	*die Väter*	*die Mütter*	*die Kinder*

Indefinite Article—Singular

	Masculine (Father)	Feminine (Mother)	Neuter (Child)
Nominative	*ein Vater*	*eine Mutter*	*ein Kind*
Genitive	*eines Vaters*	*einer Mutter*	*eines Kindes*
Dative	*einem Vater*	*einer Mutter*	*einem Kind(e)*
Accusative	*einen Vater*	*eine Mutter*	*ein Kind*

There is no plural indefinite article. The adjective *kein* (meaning 'no') is used to show the pattern.

	Masculine (Father)	Feminine (Mother)	Neuter (Child)
Nominative	*keine Väter*	*keine Mütter*	*keine Kinder*
Genitive	*keiner Väter*	*keiner Mütter*	*keiner Kinder*
Dative	*keinen Vätern*	*keinen Mütern*	*keinen Kindern*
Accusative	*keine Väter*	*keine Mütter*	*keine Kinder*

Nouns and Gender

All nouns like a person, place, thing, animal, idea or event have a grammatical gender in German. They are either masculine (**der**), feminine (**die**), or neuter (**das**).

Masculine	the man	*der mann*	the table	*der Tisch*
Feminine	the woman	*die Frau*	the shower	*die Dusche*
Neuter	the child	*das Kind*	the money	*das Geld*

The German noun is easily recognized in writing because it is capitalized. All German nouns belong to one of three grammatical genders: masculine, feminine, or neuter. The gender is most easily identified by the noun's definite article in the nominative case: *der* (masculine), *die* (feminine and plural), and *das* (neuter).

Names of professions ending in *-er* can be made feminine by adding *-in*. For example: *Lehrer/Leherin* (teacher). Names of weekdays, months, seasons, and basic directions are all masculine. Nouns ending in *-er* (particularly professions) are usually masculine, but there are many exceptions to this rule. Names of trees, flowers, are usually feminine. Nouns ending in *-age, -ei, -heit, -keit, -schaft, -ie, -ik, --ion, -tät, -ur, -in,* and *-ung* are almost always feminine. Young people and young animals are often neuter. Names of many metals are neuter. Names of many animals are neuter. Nouns ending in *-tum, -ment, -ium,* and *-um* are usually neuter.

Many nouns are made plural by adding *-e*. Many monosyllabic neuter and a few masculine nouns are made plural by adding *-er*.

Most feminine nouns are made plural by adding *-en* or simply *-n*; *Frau/Frauen* (woman), *Tante/Tanten* (aunt). All nouns ending in *-ung* are feminine and made plural with *-en*. Nouns made feminine by adding *-in* and can be made plural by adding *-nen*; *Studentin/Studentinnen* (female student). Only a few neuter nouns are made plural by adding *-en*: *Bett/Betten* (bed). Many foreign words recently adopted into German are made plural simply by adding an *-s*: *Job/Jobs* (job), *Park/Parks* (park). Proper names are made plural by adding *-s*. For examples: *die Schillers* means 'the *Schillers*'.

Subject Pronouns

	Singular		Plural	
1st person	I	*ich*	we	*wir*
2nd person	you (familiar)	*du*	you (all)	*ihr*
3rd person	he, she, it, one	*er, sie, es, man*	they , you (formal)	*sie, Sie*

Verbs

To conjugate the verb in German language, appropriate ending to the stem is added. Each verb has a stem form, the basic part of the verb. Many commonly used German verbs are not regular verbs

Conjugating the verb to go: *gehen*

Person		Singular	Example		Plural	Example
1st	I go	*-e*	ich gehe	we go	*-en*	*wir gehen*
2nd	you go (familiar)	*-st*	du gehst	You (all) go	*-t*	*ihr geht*
2nd				You (formal)	*-en*	*Sie gehen*
3rd	he, she, it, one goes	*-t*	er, sie, es geht	they go	*-en*	*sie gehen*

Conjugating the verb to have: *haben*

Person		Singular		Plural
1st person	I have	*ich habe*	we have	*wir haben*
2nd person	you have (familiar)	*du hast*	you have	*ihr habt*

3rd person	he has	*er hat*	they have	*sie haben*
	she has	*sie hat*	you have (formal, both S and P)	*Sie haben*
	it has	*es hat*		

Verb stems ending in *-t* or *-d*

Person		Singular		Plural
1st	I wait	*ich warte*	we wait	*wir warten*
2nd	you wait (familiar)	*du wartest*	you (all) wait	*ihr wartet*
2nd			you (formal) wait	*Sie warten*
3rd	he, she, it, one waits	*er, sie, es wartet*	they wait	*sie warten*

Verb that change *e* to *i*:

		Conjugath with *ich*, *du*, and *er*		
to give	*geben*	*ich gebe*	*du gibst*	*er gibt*
to take	*nehmen*	*ich nehme*	*du nimmst*	*er nimmt*
to help	*helfen*	*ich helfe*	*du hilfst*	*er hilft*

Verb that change *e* to *ie*

		Conjugath with *ich*, *du*, and *er*		
to read	*lessen*	*ich lese*	*du liest*	*er liest*
to see	*sehen*	*ich sehe*	*du siehst*	*er sieht*

Verb that change *a* to *ä*

		Conjugath with *ich*, *du*, and *er*		
to sleep	*schlafen*	*ich schlafe*	*du schläfst*	*er schläft*
to wash	*waschen*	*ich wasche*	*du wäschst*	*er wäscht*

Regular verbs that end in *-ieren* do not require a change to the stem in conjugations.

Prepositions: Some common prepositions.

In German, the object of the preposition is not always in the accusative case. The case of the object is decided by the preposition and how it has been used.

	Acc		Dative		Genitive		Acc/Dat
through	*durch*	out, from	*aus*	during	*während*	at, to, on	*an*
against	*gegen*	with	*mit*	in spite of	*trotz*	onto, on to	*auf*
around	*um*	from, by	*von*	instead of	*anstatt*	behind	*hinter*
for	*für*	since, for	*seit*	because	*wegen*	in, into	*in*
without	*ohne*	near, at	*bei*			beside, next to	*neben*

		after, to	*nach*			over, above	*über*
		to	*zu*			under	*unter*
		across from	*gegenüber*			in front of, before	*vor*
		besides	*außer*			between	*zwischen*

Adjectives

Example of Possessive Adjectives

	Masculine	Faminine	Neutral	Plural
Nominative	*mein*	*meine*	*mein*	*meine*
Accusative	*meinen*	*meine*	*mein*	*meine*
Dative	*meinem*	*meiner*	*meinem*	*meinen*
Genetive	*meines*	*meiner*	*meines*	*meiner*

Question Words: Common German question words:

What?	was?
When?	Wann?
Where?	Wo?
Who?	Wer?
Where to?	Wohin?
How?	Wie?
How much?	Wie viel?
Why?	Warum?
Which?	Welch?
Whom?	When?

Where is your father?	*Wo ist dein Vater?*	Who is he?	*Wer ist er?*
What do you have?	*Was hast du?*	Why is he tired?	*Warum ist er müde?*
When are you coming home?	*Wann kommst du nach Hause?*	How does he play tennis?	*Wie spielt er Tennis?*
Why did he go home?	*Warum geht er nach Hause?*	Whom are you visiting?	*Wen besuchen Sie?*

Negatives

Nicht and *kein* are forms of negation, but *nicht* means not, and *kein* means no, not a, not any. *NICHT* (not) is used when a definite article precedes the noun:

not ever again	*nie mehr*	never	*nie*
no more, no longer, any more	*nicht mehr*	not yet	*noch nicht*
not at all	*gar nicht, überhaupt nicht*	not ever	*noch nie*
nothing, not...anything	*nichts*	nobody, not...anybody	*niemand*

German Alphabets and Pronunciation

Letter	Pronunciation	Examples
A a	ah	as in f**a**ther (long), **cup** (short)
Ä ä	ay	as in g**e**t
B b	bay	as in **b**all or as in **p**ay at the end of a syllable
C c	tsay	as in **k**ey, **c**at
D d	day	as in **d**ay or as in **t**ea at the end of a syllable
E e	ay	as in **ge**t, **s**ay
F f	eff	as in **f**air
G g	gay	as in **g**o
H h	ha	as in **h**ouse
I i	ee	as in h**i**t
J j	yawt	as in **y**es
K k	kah	as in **k**ey
L l	ell	as in **l**eaf
M m	emm	as in **m**other
N n	enn	as in **n**umber
O o	oh	as in h**o**t, g**o**t
Ö ö	ooh Umlaut	as in h**e**r (short) or as in **eu**ro (long)
P p	pay	as in **p**ay
Q q	kv	as in bac**k** **v**ent, **kv**etch
R r	air	as in **r**ain
S s	ess	as in **sis**ter (middle)
Ss	ess	as in **z**oo
ß	ss	as in **s**ound, **stress**
T t	tay	as in **t**ea
U u	oo	as in p**u**re, f**oo**l
Ü ü	oo Umlaut	as in d**oo**r
V v	fow	as in **f**it, **f**air
W w	vay	as in **V**i**v**ian
X x	ix	as in fa**x**, wa**x**
Z z	tset	as in bi**ts**, nu**ts**

German Phrases

English	German
How are you?	*Wie geht es Ihnen?*
Fine, and you?	*Danke, gut. Und Ihnen?*
What is your name?	*Wie ist Ihr Name? Wie heißt du?*
My name is...	*Mein Name is .. Ich heiße ...*
I would like to introduce you to ...	*Darf ich Ihnen... vorstellen.*
I am pleased to meet you.	*Angenehem.*
Do you live here	*Wohnen Sie hier? Wohnst du hier?*
Where are you going?	*Wohin fahren Sie? Wohin fährst du?*
What are you doing?	*Was machen Sie? Was machst du?*
Warm greetings	*Herzliche Grüße*
Thank you	*Danke*
Thank you very much.	*Vielen Dank*
You are welcome	*Bitte*
Yes	*Ja*
No	*Nein*
Excuse me.	*Entschuldigung*
Sorry	*Entschuldigung*
Don't worry	*Macht nichts*
Hello	*Guten Tag*
Hi	*Hallo*
Good day	*Guten Tag*
Good morning	*Guten Morgan*
Good afternoon	*Guten Tag*
Good evening	*Guten Abend*
Goodbye	*Auf Wiedersehen*
See you later	*Bis später*
Bye	*Tschüss/Tschau*
Keep in touch.	*melden Sie sich doch mal!; Melde dich mal!*
Bless you!	*Gesundheit!*
Bon voyage!	*Gute Reise!*
Cheers!	*Prost!*

Good luck!	*Viel Glück!*
Happy Birthday	*herzlichen Glückwunsch zum Geburtstag!*
What is the weather?	*Wie ist das Wetter?*
It is cloudy	*Es ist wolking.*
It is cold	*Es ist kalt.*
It is freezing	*Es ist eiskalt*
It is hot	*Es ist heiß*
It is raining	*Es ist regnerisch*
It is sunny	*Es ist sonnig*
It is warm	*Es ist warm*
It is windy	*Es ist windig*
Who?	*Wer?*
Who is that?	*Wer ist das?*
What?	*Was?*
What is that?	*Was ist das?*
Which?	*Welcher?*
Which station is that?	*Welcher Bahnhof ist das?*
When?	*Wann?*
When does it open?	*Wann öffnet es?*
Where?	*Wo?*
Where is the station?	*Wo ist der Bahnhof?*
How?	*Wie?*
How do you say it in English?	*Wie sagt man das auf Englisch?*
How much?	*Wieviel?*
How many?	*Wie viele?*
Why?	*Warum?*
Do you speak English?	*Sprechen Sie Englisch?*
Yes, I speak a little English.	*Ja, ich spreche ein bisschen Englisch.*
Do you understand me?	*Verstehen Sie mich?*
Yes, I understand you.	*Ja, ich verstehe Sie.*
No, I don't understand you.	*Nein, ich verstehe Sie nicht.*
What time is it?	*Wie spät ist es?*
It is ten o'clock.	*Es ist zehn Uhr.*

It is half past one.	*Es ist halb zwei.*
It is quarter past one.	*Es ist viertel nach eins.*
It is twenty past one.	*Es ist zwanzig nach eins.*
How much is it?	*Wie viel kostet es?*
Can you write down the price?	*Können Sie den Preis aufschreiben?*
Do you accept credit cards?	*Nehmen Sie Kriditkarten?*
Where is the bank?	*Wo ist der Bank?*
What is your phone number?	*Wie ist Ihre Telefonnummer?*
The number is...	*Die Nummer ist...*
Hello	*Hallo!*
Can I speak to...?	*Kann ich mit...sprechen?*
Can I leave a message?	*Kann ich eine Nachricht hinterlassen?*
Please tell him/her I called.	*Bitte sagen Sie ihm/ihr, dass ich angerufen habe.*
I will call back later.	*Ich rufe später nochmal an*
What time should I call?	*Wann kann ich am besten anrufen?*
It is getting cold.	*Es wird kalt.*
It is getting hot	*Es wird heiß*
It is getting warm	*Es wird warm*
It is getting cool	*Es wird kühl*
It is getting dark.	*Es wird kunkel.*
It is getting bright.	*Es wird hell.*
It is getting loud.	*Es wird laut*
It is getting quiet.	*Es wird leise.*
Do you like it?	*Gefällt es dir?*
He likes that.	*Das gefällt ihm.*
He likes the books.	*Das Bücher gefällt uns.*
Do you like the play?	*Gefällt euch das Schauspiel?*
Don't you like it?	*Gefällt es Ihnen nicht?*
They Don't like the play.	*Der Schauspiel gefällt ihnen nicht.*
Did you play Tennis?	*Spieltest du Tennis?*
Did you need money?	*Brauchten Sie Geld?*
Did you listen to the radio?	*Hörten Sie Radio?*
Did you learn English?	*Lerntest du Englisch?*

Where did he live?	*Wo wohnte er?*
Who worked here?	*Wer arbeitete hier?*
Whom did he visit?	*Wen besuchte er?*
Where does he live?	*Wo wohnt er?*
Who works here?	*Wer arbeitet hier?*
Whom is he visiting?	*Wen besucht hier?*
He will read the newspaper.	*Er wird die Zeitung lesen.*
She will run to school.	*Sie wird in die Schule laufen.*
Sabine will wear a new dress.	*Sabine wird einen neuen Kleid tragen.*
Andreas will catch the ball.	*Andreas wird den Ball fangen.*
Where will she meet the tourists?	*Wo wird sie die Touristen treffen?*
I have stayed	*ich bin geblieben*
She has driven	*sie ist gefahren*
You have fallen	*Sie sind gefallen*
He has gone.	*er ist gegangen.*
You have come	*du bist gekommen*
It has happened	*es ist passiert*
I have been	*ich bin gewesen*
He has died	*er ist gestorben*
She has become	*Sie ist geworden*
The nice man's daughter is a teacher.	*Die Tochter des netten Mannes ist Lehrerin.*
A child's voice is always sweet.	*Die Stimme eines Kindes is immer süß.*
My children's bedroom is too little.	*Das Schlafzimmer meiner Kinder ist zu klein.*
Our house is bigger than your house.	*Unser Haus ist größer als euer Haus.*
Anna speaks slower than Heidi.	*Anna spricht langsamer als Heidi.*
The coffee is warmer than the tea.	*Der Kaffee ist wärmer als der Tee.*
He plays better than me.	*Er spielt besser als ich.*
His sister is the youngest.	*Seine Schwester ist am kleinsten.*
The white horse runs the fastest.	*Das weiße Pferd läuft am schnellesten.*
That is a good idea.	*Das ist eine gute Idee.*
That is a better idea.	*Das ist eine bessere Idee.*
That is the best idea.	*Das ist die beste Idee.*

There is a dark room.	*Es gibt ein dunkles Zimmer.*
There is a darker room.	*Es gibt ein dunkleres Zimmer.*
The darkest room.	*Das dunkelste Zimmer.*
I did not know that you are an Austrian.	*Ich wußte nicht, daß du Österreicher bist.*
She is sad because her father died.	*Sie ist traurig, weil ihr Vater gestorben ist.*
Whenever I am in Berlin, I visit my uncle.	*Wenn ich in Berlin bin, besuche ich meinen Onkel.*
The city is destroyed.	*Die Stadt wird zerstört.*
The city was destroyed.	*Die Stadt wurde zerstört.*
The city has been destroyed.	*Die Stadt ist zerstört worden.*
The city will be destroyed.	*Die stadt wird zerstört werden.*
What number do you want?	*Welche Nummer wünschen Sie?*
Where are you calling from?	*Woher rufen Sie an?*
Would you repeat the number, please?	*Können Sie die Nummer bitte Wiederholen?*
Replace the receiver and dial again.	*Legen Sie auf und wählen Sie noch einmal.*
I will try to reconnect you.	*Ich versuche es noch einmal.*
Hold the line, caller.	*Bitte bleiben Sie am Apparat*
All lines to Munich are engaged. Please try later.	*Alle Leitungen nach Munich sind besetzt, bitte rufen Sie später noch einmal an.*
The line is engaged or busy.	*Die Leitung is besetzt.*
Could I have extension 999?	*Können Sie mich bitte mit Apparat 999 verbinden?*
Could I speak to Mr. Henderson, please?	*Kann ich bitte mit Herrn Graupner sprechen?*
Who is speaking?	*Wer ist am Apparat?*
I am calling from England.	*Ich rufe aus England an.*
Marriot Hotel, can I help you?	*Hotel Marriot, guten Tag.*
Who is calling please?	*Wer ist am Apparat, bitte?*
Who shall I say calling?	*Wen darf ich melden?*
Do you know his extension number?	*Wissen Sie, welchen Apparat er hat?*
There is no reply?	*Es meldet sich niemand?*

Mr. Roy is talking on the other line.	*Herr Roy spricht gerade auf der anderen Leitung.*
Sorry to keep you waiting.	*Bitte bleiben Sie am Apparat.*
Hello, this is Anne speaking.	*Hallo, Anne hier.*
Would you like to leave a message?	*Möchen Sie eine Nachricht hinterlassen?*
Can I take a message for him?	*Kann ich ihm etwas ausrichten?*
Put the phone down and I will call you back.	*Legen Sie bitte auf, ich rufe Sie zurück.*
This is a recorded message.	*Hier spricht der automatische Anrufbeantworter.*
The number is not ringing.	*Ich bekomme kein Rufzeichen.*
I cannot get through.	*Ich komme nicht durch.*
Their phone is out of order.	*Das Telefon ist gestört.*
I must have dialed the wrong number.	*Ich muß mich verwählt haben.*
You gave me a wrong number.	*Sie haben mir die falsche Nummer gegeben.*
What are you going to do with it?	*Was machst du damit?*
Did you read the article in the newspaper?	*Lasen Sie den Artikel in der Zeitung?*
Yes. I read the article in it.	*Ja, ich las den Artikel darin.*
Have you spoken to him about it?	*Haben Sie mit ihm darüber gespochen?*
Are you going with her?	*Gehst du mit ihr?*
No. I'm not going with her.	*Nein. Ich gehe nicht mit ihr.*
The house is gray.	*Das Haus ist grau.*
The gray house is on the right.	*Das graue Haus ist rechts.*
What do you think about that?	*Was denken Sie darüber?*
What do you think of the movie?	*Wie finden Sie den Film?*
I'll take you to the airport.	*Ich bringe Sie zum Flughafen.*
What can I get for you?	*Was bekommen Sie?*
That tastes good!	*Das schmeckt!*
What are you looking for?	*Was suchst du?*
She's waiting for the bus.	*Sie wartet auf den Bus.*
When do you eat lunch?	*Wann isst du zu Mittag?*
I'd rather drink coffee.	*Ich trinke lieber Kaffee.*

FRENCH GRAMMAR

Articles

Articles are adjectives and therefore they have to agree in number and gender with the nouns they modify.

The Definite Article: *the* The Indefinite Article: *a*

	Singular	Plural		Singular	Plural
masculine	*le*	*les*	masculine	*un*	*des*
feminine	*la*	*les*	feminine	*une*	*des*
l'-masculine or feminine singular before a vowel or vowel sound			*de* or *d'* is used after a negative verb other than *être*		

Nouns and Gender

In French language, gender is a characteristic of a noun. Each noun has a gender associated with it and it is a part of that word's characteristics. In French, there are two genders—masculine and feminine. Each noun in the French language is either masculine or feminine.

	Masculine	Feminine
dancer	*le danseur*	*la danseuse*
singer	*le chanteur*	*la chanteuse*
actor/actoress	*l'acteur*	*l'actrice*
director	*le directeur*	*la directrice*

Subject Pronouns

	Singular Personal Pronouns		Plural Personal Pronouns	
1st person	I	*je*	we	*nous*
2nd person	you	*tu*	you	*vous*
3rd person	he, it	*il*	they	*els*
	she, it	*elle*	they	*elles*
	one	*on*		

tu and *vous* both mean 'you'. *Tu* is used in referring to one person of equal status. *Vous* is used when more than one person or elders or strangers are there.

Verbs

There are three types' regular verbs in French: *-er* ending, *-re* ending, and *-ir* ending verbs. To conjugate a verb, take off the ending to give stem or root word, and add the following verb endings:

To talk, speak = *Parler*

Present	Singular		Plural	Subjunctive	Singular		Singular
je	*parle*	*nous*	*parlons*	*je*	*parle*	*nous*	*parlions*
tu	*parles*	*vous*	*parlez*	*tu*	*parles*	*vous*	*parliez*
il *elle* *on*	*parle*	*ils* *elles*	*parlent*	*il* *elle* *on*	*parle*	*ils* *elles*	*parlent*
Imperfect				Past			
je	*parlais*	*nous*	*parlions*	*je*	*parlai*	*nous*	*parlâmes*
tu	*parlais*	*vous*	*parliez*	*tu*	*parlas*	*vous*	*parlâtes*
il *elle* *on*	*parlait*	*ils* *elles*	*parlaient*	*il* *elle* *on*	*parla*	*ils* *elles*	*parlèrent*

Present indicative endings of regular *-re* verbs

I	*je*	s	we	*nous*	*ons*
you	*tu*	s	you	*vous*	*ez*
he	*il*	no ending	they	*ils*	*ent*

An example of an *-re* verb is *descendre*. To obtain the root, take off the '*re*' to get *descend* and put the root with the endings.

to descend = *descendre*

I descend	*je descends*	we descend	*nous descendons*
you descend	*tu descends*	you descend	*vous descendez*
he descends	*il descend*	they descend	*ils descendent*

Most regular *-re* verbs end their stems with '*d*' or '*p*.' An example of an *-re* verb is *descendre*. To obtain the root, take off the '*re*' to get *descend* and put the root with the endings.

Present indicative endings of regular: to finish = *finir*

I finish	*je finis*	we finish	*nousfinissons*
you finish	*tu finis*	you finish	*vous finnissez*
he finishes	*il finit*	they finish	*ils finissent*

Irregular verbs

The two very important irregular verbs are 'to be' and 'to have.'

to be = *être*		to have = *avoir*	
I am	*je suis*	I have	*j'ai*
you are	*tu es*	you have	*tu as*
he is	*il est*	he has	*il a*
we are	*nous sommes*	we have	*nous avons*

you are	*vous êtes*	you have	*vous avez*
they are	*ils sont*	they have	*ils ont*

Even though this verb ends in *-er*, it is not regular. to go = *aller*

I go	*je vais*	wego	*nous allons*
you go	*tu vas*	you go	*vous allez*
he goes	*il va*	they go	*ils vont*

faire = to do; to make

I do	*je fais*	we do	*nous faisons*
you do	*tu fais*	you do	*vous faites*
he does	*il fait*	they do	*ils font*

Present indicative: to take = *prendre*

I take	*je prends*	we take	*nous prenons*
you take	*tu prends*	you take	*vous prenez*
he takes	*il prend*	they take	*ils prennent*

Prepositions: Some common prepositions.

at the bottom	*en bas*	in front of	*devant*
at the top	*en haut*	in the	*sur*
above	*au-dessus de*	near	*près de*
across	*en face de*	next to	*à cóté de*
between	*entre*	toward	*envers*
behind	*derrière*	toward, about	*vers*
far from	*loin de*	under	*sous, au-dessous de*

Adjectives

Adjectives agree in number and gender with the noun they modify. Most adjectives add an *e* for feminine and an *s* for plural:

	singular	plural
masculine	*vert*	*verts*
feminine	*verte*	*vertes*

There is no difference between the masculine and feminine forms when the unmodified adjective ends in *e*.

	singular	plural
masculine	*rouge*	*rouges*
feminine	*rouge*	*rouges*

There is no difference between the singular and plural masculine forms when the unmodified adjective ends in *s* or *x*.

	singular	plural
masculine	*gris*	*gris*
feminine	*grise*	*grises*

Some irregular gender patterns:

Ending	masculine	feminine
-en	*canadien*	*canadienne*
-on	*bon*	*bonne*
-et	*complet*	*complète*
-f	*naïf*	*naïve*
-er	*cher*	*chère*
-eux	*heureux*	*heureuse*
-eur	*flatteur*	*flatteuse*
-il *-el* *-ul*	*gentil* *actuel* *nul*	*gentille* *actuelle* *nulle*

Irregular plural patterns:

Ending	masculine singular	masculine plural
-eau	*beau*	*beaux*
-al	*idéal*	*idéaux*

Completely irregular:

	Singular		Plural	
Adjective	Masculine	Feminine	Masculine	Feminine
beautiful	*beau*	*belle*	*beaux*	*belles*
new	*nouveau*	*nouvelle*	*nouveaux*	*nouvelles*
crazy	*fou*	*folle*	*fous*	*folles*

Possessive Adjectives

English	Masculine	Feminine	Before vowel	Plural
my	*mon*	*ma*	*mon*	*mes*
your (sing., fam.)	*ton*	*ta*	*ton*	*tes*
his, her, its	*son*	*sa*	*son*	*ses*
our	*notre*	*notre*	*notre*	*nos*
your (plur., form)	*votre*	*votre*	*votre*	*vos*
their	*leur*	*leur*	*leur*	*leurs*

Question Words

Most common French question words:

how?	*comment?*	how much?	*combine?*
when?	*quand?*	why?	*pourquoi?*
what?	*que?*	where?	*où?*

How are you doing?	*Comment allez-vous?*	What would you like?	*Que désirez-vous?*
How much do you want to change?	*Combien voulez-vous changer?*	Where are you going?	*Vous allez où?*
When do we leave?	*Quand partons-nous?*	What must I do?	*Que dois-je faire?*
Why is he going out?	*Pourquoi sort-il?*	May I help you?	*Puis-je vous aider?*

Beginning a sentence with *est-ce que* is common in both formal and informal circumstance.

Est-ce que je pourrais parler avec Bob?
May I speak with Bob?

Est-ce que je suis fou?
Am I crazy?

Negatives

In French, negatives are formed using *-ne* and the proper negative expression. Usually, the *-ne* precedes the verb with the negative term. The most common negative expressions are *ne... pas, ne... plus, ne... rien, ne... personne, ne... jamais, ne... aucun, ne... que, ne... ni... ni..., ne... nulle.*

No one	=	*ne...personne,*
Nothing	=	*ne...rien,*
None/not any	=	*ne...aucun(e),*
Nowhere	=	*ne...nulle part,*
Neither...*nor*	=	*ni...ni.*

Here are some examples:

They are not dusting the living room.	*Ils n'époussettent pas la salle de séjour.*
I am not doing what I have to.	*Je ne fais pas ce qu'il me faut.*
We don't live in Canada.	*Nous n'habitons pas en Canada.*
That's my friend. He would never do that.	*C'est mon ami. Il ne ferait jamais cela.*
She doesn't want to speak to him anymore.	*Elle ne veut plus lui parler.*

She didn't want to go anywhere.	*Elle ne voulait aller nulle part.*
He didn't do anything interesting.	*Il n'a rien fait d'intéressant.*
We had never seen this film.	*Nous n'avions jamais vu ce film.*
Nobody came to the party.	*Personne n'est venu à la fête.*
Don't speak to me any more!	*Ne me parlez plus!*
Haven't you seen it?	*Ne l'avez-vous pas vu?*
He never wants to do it again.	*Il ne veut plus jamais le refaire.*
I never told it to him.	*Je ne le lui ai jamais dit.*

French Alphabets and Pronunciation

Letter	Pronunciation	Examples
A a	ah	as in h**ea**rt
B b	bay	as in **b**all, **b**oy
C c	say	as in **c**ylinder
D d	day	as in **d**ay, **d**og
E e	ew	as in g**e**t, go
F f	ef	as in **f**air, fish
G g	jay	as in **gem**
gn	ni	as in oni**on**
H h	ash	silent
I i	ie	as in h**i**t
J j	gee	as **g**em
K k	kah	as in **k**ey, **k**ing
L l	el	as in **l**eaf
M m	em	as in **m**other
N n	en	as in **n**umber (usually silent at the end of the word)
O o	oh	as in h**o**t, g**o**t
P p	pay	as in **p**ay (usually silent at the end of the word)
Q q	cue	as in **qu**ick
R r	air	as in **r**ain (usually silent at the end of the word)
S s	es	as in **s**i**s**ter sit (usually silent at the end of the word)
T t	tay	as in **t**ea (usually silent at the end of the word)
U u	you	as in p**u**re, f**oo**l
V v	vay	as in **v**ase
W w	double-vay	as in **w**inter
X x	ix	as in fa**x**, wa**x**
Y y	iegrec	as in yes
Z z	zed	as in **z**oo

è (grave)		*élève*
é (acute)		*été, pére*
â (circumflex		*âme*
ç (cedilla)	s	*leçon*. ç when preceding *a*, *o*, or *u* indicates as *s* sound (*leçon*, lesson).

French Phrases

English	French
At what time does the game end?	*Á quelle heure finit le match?*
They choose a carrot cake.	*Ils choisissent un gâteau au carrotte.*
I choose a chocolate cake.	*Je choisis un gâteau au chocolat.*
You choose a carrot cake.	*Tu choisis un gâteau au carrotte*
They make great cakes.	*Elles réussissent les gâteaux.*
I am going out Saturday night.	*Je sors samedi soir.*
She is leaving the sports stadium.	*Elle sort du stade.*
We leave on the 19th.	*Nous partons le dix-neuf.*
Are you leaving for France?	*Tu pars pour la France?*
He sleeps during the game.	*Il dort pendant le match.*
They sleep after the party.	*Ils dorment après la soirée.*
Are you free?	*Est-ce que vous ètes libre?*
Are you free?	*Êtes-vous libre?*
Do you like opera?	*Est-ce que vous aimez l'opéra?*
Do you like opera?	*Aimez-vous l'opéra?*
Is she buying a present?	*Achète-t-elle un cadeau?*
Is he going to the festival?	*Va-t-il au festival?*
Is he organizing a party?	*Organize-t-il une soirée?*
I am not free	*je ne suis pas libre.*
He does not speak English.	*Il ne parle pas anglais.*
We are not finishing the dessert.	*Nous ne finissons pas le dessert.*
You are not looking for Robert.	*Vous ne cherchez pas la Robert.*
He does not live in Berlin.	*Il n'habite pas á Berlin.*
You don't study music.	*Vous n'étudiez pas la musique.*
She is not Swiss.	*Elle n'est pas suisse.*
We don't have time.	*Nous n'avons pas le temps.*
I am going to Straubrug on Monday.	*Je vais à Stragu lundi.*
He is arriving on Saturday.	*Il arrive samedi.*

We are going to Paris on the first of October.	*Nous allons à Paris le premier octobre.*
You are going to London on the third of December.	*Vous allez à London le trois décembre.*
Let us meet in Paris on the fifteenth of September.	*Randez-vous à Paris le quinze septembre.*
Do you know the answer?	*Savez-vous la réponse?*
He knows how to dance.	*Il sait danser*
Do you know her name?	*Sais-tu comment elle s'appelle?*
The weather is nice.	*Il fait beau.*
The weather is sunny.	*Il fait du soleil.*
The weather is windy.	*Il fait du vent.*
The weather is cool.	*Il fait frais.*
The weather is cold.	*Il fait froid.*
The weather is hot.	*Il fait chaud.*
The weather is mild.	*Il fait doux.*
I am going to travel to Rome.	*Je vais partir à Rome.*
We are going to buy a house.	*Nous allons acheter une maison.*
You are going to be cold.	*Tu vas avoir froid.*
It is going to be hot this summer.	*Il va faire chaud ce été.*
Is it going to rain?	*Est-ce qu'il va pleuvoir?*
There is a train at 9 A.M.	*Il y a un train à 9 heures.*
Is there any champagne?	*Est-ce qu'il y a du champagne?*
How many months are there in a year?	*Combien de mois y a t-il dans l'année?*
What day is it?	*Quel jour sommes-nous?*
At what time are you leaving?	*À quelle heure partez-vous?*
What a wonderful evening!	*Quelle soirée magnifique!*
How hot it is!	*Quelle chaleur!*
What is it?	*Qu'est-ce que c'est?*
What time is it?	*Quelle heure est-il?*
It is two o'clock.	*Il est deux heurs.*
It is ten past two.	*Il est deux heurs dix.*
It is five past two.	*Il est deux heurs cinq.*
It is quarter past two.	*Il est deux heurs et quart.*
It is half past two.	*Il est deux heurs et demie.*
It is twenty five to three.	*Il est trois heurs moins vingt-cinq.*

It is quarter to three.	*Il est trois herus moins le quart.*
It is twenty to three.	*Il est trois heurs moins vingt.*
It is noon.	*Il est midi.*
It is twelve thirty.	*Il est midi et demi.*
It is midnight.	*Il est minuit.*
Are you having coffee? Yes.	*Vous prenez du coffee? Oui.*
You don't drink coffee? Yes, I do.	*Vous ne buvez pas de coffee? Si.*
He does not need to loose weight? Oh yes.	*Il n'a pas besoin de maigrir? Mois si!*
She never runs in the marathon.	*Ille ne participe jamais au marathon.*
He never works on Sundays.	*Il ne travaille jamaise le dimanche.*
I eat nothing in the morning.	*Je ne mange rien le matin.*
How old are you?	*Quel âge avez-vous?*
I am twenty two.	*J'ai vingt-deux ans.*
How old is she?	*Quel âge a-t-elle?*
She is twelve.	*Ele a douze ans.*
How far...?	*À quelle distance...?*
What is the shortest way?	*Quel est le chemin le plus court?*
Do you have a road map?	*Avez-vous une carte routière?*
What an evening!	*Quelle soirée!*
What a pleasure!	*Quel plaisir!*
What beautiful children!	*Quels beaux enfants!*
What strange habits!	*Quelles habitudes étranges!*
I have been working for this company for 3 months.	*Je travaille pour cette société depuis trois mois.*
He has been living in Munch for a year.	*Il habite à Munich depuis un an.*
Since when have you been sick?	*Depuis quand es-tu malade?*
I have been sick since yesterday.	*Je suis malade depuis hier.*
I am going to buy this dress.	*Je vais acheter cette robe.*
I am going to buy it.	*Je vais l'acheter.*
You want to buy this tie?	*Tu veux acheter cette cravate?*
You want to buy it?	*Tu veux l'acheter.*
Good morning.	*bonjour.*
I would like to speak to Mr. Roy	*Je voudrais parler à monsieur Roy.*
Who should I say is calling?	*C'est de la part de qui, s'il vous plait?*
It is Peter Brown speaking.	*C'est Peter Brown à l'appareil.*

His line is busy. Do you want to leave a message?	*La ligne est occupée. Voulez-vous lui laisser un message?*
Could you tell him to call me this afternoon?	*Pourriez-vous lui dire de m'appeler cet après-midi?*
Certainly. What is your telephone number?	*Bien sûr, quel est votre numéro de téléphone?*
He can reach me at 9999999	*Il peu me joindre au 9999999*
How are you doing?	*Comment allez-vous?*
How much do you want to change?	*Combien voulez-vous changer?*
When do we leave?	*Quand partons-nous?*
Why is he going out?	*Pourquoi sort-il?*
What would you like?	*Que désirez-vous?*
Where is the cashier's window?	*Qú se trouve la caisse?*
The kitchen is larger than the living room.	*La cuisine est plus grande que le salon.*
This apartment is more expensive than the other one.	*Cet appartement est plus cher que l'autre.*
The kitchen is smaller than the living room.	*La cuisine est moins grande que le salon.*
This one is less spacious than that one.	*Celle-ci est moins spacieuse que celle-là.*
The kitchen is as large as the living room.	*La cuisine est aussi grande que le salon.*
He is as bright as his brother.	*Il est aussi intelligent que son frère.*
He likes the hotel and the room.	*Il aime l'hôtel et la chambre.*
There is heat and hot water.	*Il y a du chauffage et de l'eau chaude.*
He likes neither the hotel nor the room.	*Il n'aime ni l'hôtel ni la chambre.*
There is neither heat nor hot water.	*il n'y a ni chauffage ni eau chaude.*
Who is that player?	*Qui est ce joueur?*
What is happening?	*Qu'est-ce qui se passe?*
Whom do you prefer?	*Qui préfères-tu?*
What are you doing?	*Qu'est-ce que tu fais?*
What are you talking about?	*De quoi parles-tu?*
Excuse me. Or I am sorry.	*Excusez-moi.*

I am sorry to be late.	*Excusez-moi d'arriver en retard.*
Excuse me. Or pardon me.	*Pardon.*
My apologies.	*Toutes mes excuses.*
I am terribly sorry.	*Je suis navré/Je suis désolé.*
It is not serious.	*Ce n'est pas grave.*
Somebody called you.	*Quelqu'un t'a téléphoné.*
I am five minutes late.	*Je suis en retard de cinq minutes.*
She is always on time.	*Elle est toujours à l'heure.*
He arrived late.	*Il est arrivé regard.*
She is early.	*Elle est en avance.*
Our flight is late.	*Notre vol a du retard.*
My watch is on time.	*Ma montre est à l'heure.*
Better late than never.	*Mieux vout tard que jamais.*
Sooner or later.	*Tôt ou tard.*
As soon as possible.	*Le plus tôt possible.*
He does no go to the movies on Sundays.	*Il ne va pas au cinéma le dimanche.*
Did you make some reservations before leaving?	*Aviez-vous fait des réservations avant de partir?*
Before taking this trip, buy a guide book.	*Avant de faire ce voyage, achetez un guide.*
Before going to England, buy an umbrella.	*Avant d'aller en England, archetez un parapluie.*
Before going to bed, read this book.	*Avant de vous coucher, lisez de ce livre.*
After exploring Florence, did you go to Sicily?	*Après avoir exploré la Florence, êtes-vous allé en Sicily?*
After eating all those crepes, were you still hungry?	*Après avoir mangé toutes ces crépes, aviez-vous encore faim?*
After stopping an hour, they kept driving on.	*Après s'êtés une heure, ils ont continué leur route.*
He would like to visit the museum.	*Il voudrait visiter le musée.*
I would be delighted.	*Cela me ferait très plaisir.*
I would like to see the Mona Lisa.	*J'aimerais voir la Joconde.*
Could you help us?	*Pourriez-vous nous aider?*
You should come and see us.	*Vous devriez venir nous voir.*
You should see this exhibit.	*Tu devrais voir cette exposition.*

If I had the time, I would go to the museum.	*Si j'avais le temps, j'irais au musée.*
If you changed careers, what would you do?	*Si tu changeais de carrière, qu'est-ce que tu ferais?*
If it rains, I am staying home.	*S'il pleut, je reste à la maison.*
If you want, we could go to Kennedy Center.	*Si tu veux, on pourrait aller au Centre Kennedy.*
I am happy to see you again.	*Cela me fait plaisir de vous revoir.*
I will be delighted to meet them.	*Cela me fera plaisir de faire leur connaissance.*
I liked your gift very much.	*Votre cadeau m'a fait très plaisir.*
What would you like for your birthday?	*Qu'est-ce qui vous ferait plaisir pour votre anniversaire?*
I am pleased to meet you.	*Cela m'a fait plaisir de vour recontrer.*
You should have gone there.	*Tu aurais dû y aller.*
They should have exercised more.	*Ils auraient dû faire plus d'exercice.*
I think he is reading the news paper.	*Je pense qu'il lit le journal.*
I think she is in London.	*Je crois qu'elle est à London.*
He thinks he will come.	*Il pense qu'il viendra.*
I thought he was in Paris.	*J'ai pensé qu'il était à Paris.*
He thought you were on vacation.	*Il a cru que vous étiez en vacances.*
We thought he had gone.	*Nous croyions qu'il était parti.*
You have to put this down on paper.	*Tu dois le mettre por écrit.*
The students hand in their papers to the teacher.	*Les étudionts remettent leurs copies au professeur.*
Please give me a piece of paper.	*Donne-moi une feuille de papier, s'il te plaît.*
Whatever he says, I don't believe him.	*Quoi qu'il dise, je ne le crois pas.*
Whatever you do, you will succeed.	*Quoi que tu fasses, tu réussiras.*
Whatever your degrees, you have to speak English.	*Quels que soient vos diplômes, il faut que vous parliez anglais.*
Wherever she goes, she will find work.	*Oú qu'elle aille, elle trouvera du travail.*
Whoever you are, you can apply for a job.	*Qui que vous soyez, vous pouvez faire une demande d'emploi.*
Whether you are in Munich or Keil, the meetings will be in English.	*Que vous soyez à Munich ou à Keil, les réunions seront en anglais.*
Although I study this language, I am not fluent.	*Quoique j'étudie cette langue, je ne la parle pas couramment.*

Although it is cold, we will go for a walk.	*Quoiqu'il fasse froid, nous irons faire une promenode.*
How is your brother doing?	*Ton frère, comment va-t-il?*
It is nice weather outside during the month of May.	*Il fait beau temps au mois de mai.*
That gets people thinking.	*Ça fait penser.*
They are making a decision today.	*Ils prennent une décision aujourd'hui.*
I hurt myself often.	*Je me fais mal souvent.*
We talk to each other as much as possible.	*Nous nous parlons autant que possible.*
They help each other do their homework.	*Elles s'aident à finir les devoirs.*
French <u>is</u> spoken in numerous countries.	*Le français <u>se parle</u> dans de nombreux pays.*
I am not doing what I have to.	*Je <u>ne</u> fais <u>pas</u> ce qu'il me faut.*
Are you going to school today?	*Tu vas à l'école aujourd'hui?*
You wanted to speak to me?	*Vous vouliez me parler?*
We believe you.	*Nous te croyons.*
They are going to hurt me	*Ils vont me blesser*
They tell you the truth	*Ils vous disent la verité*
I doubt that you are doing your homework.	*Je doute que vous <u>fassiez</u> vos devoirs.*
It is doutful that you will arrive on time.	*Il est douteux que vous <u>arriviez</u> à l'heure.*
It seems that the school is producing intelligent students.	*Il semble que l'école <u>produise</u> d'élèves intelligents.*
It doesn't seem that winter will be leaving soon.	*Il ne paraît pas que l'hiver <u>parte</u> bientôt.*
It is important that you vote for the better candidate.	*Il est important que vous <u>votiez</u> pour le meilleur candidat.*
My mother wants me to do my homework.	*Ma mère veut que je <u>fasse</u> mes devoirs.*
You insist that the work be done well.	*Vous tenez à ce que le travail <u>soit</u> bien fait.*

SPANISH GRAMMAR

Subject Pronouns

	Singular Personal Pronouns	Plural Personal Pronouns
1st	*Yo* I	*nosotros* we
2nd	*tú* you (informal/familiar)	*vosotros* you (in Spain only) (informal/familiar)

3rd	*él* he	*ellos* they (all male or mix of men and women)
3rd	*ella* she	*ellas* they (all female)
2nd	*usted* you (formal/polite)	*ustedes* you (formal/polite)

Verbs

There are three basic types of verbs in Spanish: *-ar*, *-er*, and *-ir*. They are classified by their ending in the infinitive form.

Present Tense -AR Verb Endings

To conjugate *-ar* verbs, drop the ending and add:	To conjugate *-er* verbs, drop the ending and add:	To conjugate *-ir* verbs, drop the ending and add:
-o -as -a -amos -áis -an	-o -es -e -emos -éis -en	-o -es -e -imos -ís -en

Examples for each type of verbs:

	-AR	Example	-ER	Example	-IR	Example
subject pronouns	verb endings	hablar (to speak)	verb endings	comer (to eat)	verb endings	vivir (to live)
yo	*-o*	*hablo*	*-o*	*como*	*-o*	*Vivo*
tú	*-as*	*hablas*	*-es*	*comes*	*-es*	*Vuves*
él/ella/usted	*-a*	*habla*	*-e*	*come*	*-e*	*vive*
nosotros	*-amos*	*hablamos*	*-emos*	*comemos*	*-imos*	*vivimos*
vosotros	*-áis*	*habláis*	*-éis*	*coméis*	*-ís*	*vivis*
ellos/ellas/ustedes	*-an*	*hablan*	*-en*	*comen*	*-en*	*viven*

There are two forms of the verb 'to be' in Spanish.

SER		ESTAR	
yo	*soy*	*yo*	*estoy*
tú	*eres*	*tú*	*estás*
él/ella/usted	*es*	*él/ella/usted*	*está*
nosotros	*somos*	*nosotros*	*estamos*
vosotros	sois	vosotros	estáis
ellos/ellas/ustedes	son	ellos/ella/ustedes	están

SER is used for permanent conditions such as occupation, physical characteristic, and material as well as to tell time.

ESTAR is used for temporary conditions such as happy, sad, sick tired as well as physical location.

Other important irregular verbs:

IR (to go)		TENER (to have)	
yo	*voy*	*yo*	*tengo*
tú	*vas*	*tú*	*tienes*
él/ella/usted	*va*	*él/ella/usted*	*tiene*
nosotros	*vamos*	*nosotros*	*tenemos*
vosotros	*vais*	*vosotros*	*tenéis*
ellos/ellas/ustedes	*van*	*ellos/ella/ustedes*	*tienen*
QUERER (to want)	*e > ie stem* changing verb	PODER (to be able)	*o > ue stem* changing verb
yo	*quiero*	*yo*	*puedo*
tú	*quieres*	*tú*	*puedes*
él/ella/usted	*quiere*	*él/ella/usted*	*puede*
nosotros	*queremos*	*nosotros*	*podemos*
vosotros	*queries*	*vosotros*	*podéis*
ellos/ellas/ustedes	*quieren*	*ellos/ella/ustedes*	*pueden*

Adjectives

- Adjectives that end in *-o* have four forms: Ex: *alto, alta, altos, altas.*
- Adjectives that end in *-e* have two forms: Ex: *inteligente, inteligentes.*
- Most adjectives that end in a consonant have two forms: Ex: *popular, populares* (form plural by adding *-es*).

Possessive Adjective

mine	*mío, mía, míos, mías*
yours (singular familiar)	*tuyo, tuya, tuyos, tuyas*
its, his, her, their, yours, his, hers, theirs (singular or plural formal)	*suyo, suya, suyos, suyas*
our, ours	*nuestro, nuestra, nuestros, nuestras*
yours (plural familiar)	*vuestro, vuestra, vuestros, vuestras*

Prepositions

The Spanish language has a number of prepositions. Most common prepositions are listed below along with some examples:

a, ante, bajo, cabe, con, contra, de, besde, durante, en, entre, hacia, hasta, mediante, para, por, según, sin, so, sobre, tras. All of the above prepositions are derived from Latin excluding *hasta*.

after, behind	*tras*	They walked one after the other.	*Caminaban uno tras otro.*
after	*después de*	We are eating after class.	*Comemos después de la clase.*
according to	*según*	According to the newspaper, it is going to snow.	*Según el periódico, va a nevar.*
against	*contra*	I am against the strike.	*Estoy contra la huelga.*
before	*antes de*	I read before going to sleep.	*Leo antes de dormirme.*
behind	*detrás de*	The dog is behind the table.	*El perro está detrás de la mesa.*
beween	*entre*	The dog is between the table and the sofa.	*El perro está entre le mesa y el sofá.*
by	*por*	It's faster by the motorway.	*Es más rápido por la autopista.*
during	*durante*	We slept during the class.	*Dormimos durante la clase.*
for	*para*	These flowers are for you.	*Estas flores son para tí.*
for	*por*	I exchanged my euros for dollars	*Cambié mis euros por dólares.*
of,	*de*	The hat is made of paper.	*El sombrero es hecho de papel.*
from,	*de*	I am from New York.	*Soy de Nueva York*
inside	*dentro de*	The dog is inside the cage.	*El perro está dentro de la jaula.*
in, on	*en*	She is in New York. The dog is on the table.	*Ella está en Nueva York.* *El perro está en la mesa.*
near	*cerca de*	The dog is near the table.	*El perro está cerca de la mesa.*
over, about	*sobre*	He fell over the chair. It's a program about the president.	*Se cayó sobre la silla.* *Es un programa sobre el presidente.*
to, at, by	*a*	We are going to the city. I am coming at three. We are traveling by foot.	*Vamos a la ciudad.* *Vengo a las tres.* *Viajamos a pie.*
toward	*hacia*	We are walking toward the school.	*Caminamos hacia la escuela.*
since, from	*desde*	I haven't eaten since yesterday. He threw the baseball from the car.	*No comí desde ayer.* *Tiró el béisbol desde el carro.*
under	*bajo*	The dog is under the table.	*El perro está bajo la mesa.*
until	*hasta*	I'm sleeping until six.	*Duermo hasta las seis.*

with	*con*	I'll come to the party with you girls	*Iré a la fiesta con vosotras*
without	*sin*	A tea without milk, please	*Un té sin leche, por favor*

Question Words

¿cómo?	how? what?	¿dónde?	where?
¿cuál es?	what is? which is?	¿para qué?	for what purpose?
¿cuáles son?	what are? which are?	¿por qué?	why?
¿cuándo?	when?	¿qué?	what?
¿cuánto/a?	how much?	¿quién?	who?
¿cuántos/as?	how many?	¿quiénes?	who? (plural)

Negatives

To make a sentence negative, the word *no* before the verb is placed. Other key Spanish negatives are

none, not any	*ninguno /a/os/as*
no one, nobody	*nadie*
nothing, not anything	*nada*
neither, not either	***tampoco***
never	***nunca***
neither, nor	***ni***

No one has it	*Nadie lo tiene*	He doesn't buy anything either.	**Él no compra nada tampoco.**
Nothing is going to happen	*Nada va a pasar.*	He never eats.	**Él nunca come.**
None of the children are here	*Ninguno de los niños está aquí*	I didn't eat any of the soup	**No comí ninguna de la sopa.**

Spanish Alphabets and Pronunciation

Alphabets	**Pronunciation**	**Examples**
A a	a	as in f**a**ther
B b	be	as in **b**all, **b**oy
C c	ce	as in **c**ylinder, **c**igar
ch	che	as in **n**acho, **n**acho
D d	de	as in **d**ay, **d**og
E e	e	as in **e**gg
F f	efe	as in **f**air, **f**ish

G g	ge	as in **g**old, **g**overnment
H h	hache	as in **h**onor (h is always silent)
I i	I	as in h**i**t, pol**i**ce
J j	jota	as the English letter **'h'**
K k	ka	as in **k**ey, **k**ing
L l	ele	as in **l**eaf, **l**egal
LL ll	elle	as in **y**awn, **y**ummy, **y**oke
M m	eme	as in **m**other
N n	ene	as in **n**umber
Ñ ñ	eñe	as in ca**n**yon, o**n**ion, uni**o**n
O o	o	as in h**o**t, g**o**
P p	pe	as in **p**ay
Q q	cu	as in **ch**emical
R r	ere	as in ladde**r**
rr	erre	as in **r**adio
S s	ese	as in **s**i**s**ter, **s**oup
T t	te	as in **t**ea
U u	u	as in p**u**re, t**u**tor
V v	ve, uve	as in **b**everage
X x	equis	as in fa**x**, wa**x**
Y y	I griega	as in **y**ellow
Z z	zeta	as in **s**ocks

Spanish Phrases

English	**Spanish**
How much is it?	*¿Cuánto es él?*
This one.	*éste.*
That one over there.	*aquél allá.*
I want something like this.	*Deseo algo similar.*
Thank you, sir.	*Gracias, sir.*
Who? Whom?	*¿Quién? ¿Quién?*
Who is it?	*¿Quién es él?*
What is that?	*¿Cuál es ése?*
What did you say?	*¿Qué usted dijo?*

When does the train leave?	*¿Cuándo el tren se va?*
Where is the subway?	*¿Dónde está el subterráneo?* *¿Dónde está el metro?*
How are you?	*¿Cómo es usted?*
My name is...	*Mi nombre es...*
From which country are you?	*¿De qué país es usted?*
I am from the United States.	*Soy de los Estados Unidos.*
Where do you leave?	*¿Adónde usted se va?*
What does that mean?	*¿Qué ese medio?*
It is OK.	*Está bien.*
It is good.	*Está bueno.*
Are you warm?	*¿Es usted caliente?*
How is the weather over there?	*¿Cómo está el tiempo allá?*
It is very cold.	*Hace mucho frío.*
It is hot/It is warm	*Hace calor*
It is very cool.	*Hace mucho fresco.*
It is very sunny.	*Hace mucho sol.*
It is very windy.	*Hace mucho viento.*
It is raining.	*Está lloviendo.*
It is snowing.	*Está nevando.*
Execuse me sir, where is the nearest post office?	*Disculpe, senõr, ¿dónde está la oficina de correos más cercana?*
It is very far from here.	*Está muy lejos de aquí.*
How many kilometers from here?	*¿A Cuántos kilómetros de aquí?*
Execuse me sir, I am looking for this address?	*Disculpe, senõr, yo busco esta dirección.*
You follow this street.	*Siga usted esta calle.*
Then, turn to the left at G street.	*Después, doble a la izquierda en la calle G.*
Then, turn right at the police station.	*Después, doble a la derecha en la estación de policía.*
Go straight ahead for 50 meters.	*Vaya derecho por cincuenta metros.*
It is near the bakery.	*Está cerca de la pandería.*
It is next to the hospital	*Está al lado del hospital*
Can you make me a map?	*¿Puede usted hacerme un mapa?*
Certainly.	*Por cierto./ Ciertamente.*
Good morning, John, how are you?	*Buenos días, Juan, ¿cómo es usted? (está)*
Fine, and you?	*¿Bien, y usted?*
Not bad. Whar are you doing today?	*Más o menos. ¿Qué hace usted hoy?*

I am going to my parent's house.	*Yo voy a la casa de mis padres.*
Are you going by car?	*¿Va usted por coche?*
No, I am going by bus.	*No. Voy en autobús.*
Now it is late. I should go.	*Ya es tarde. Debo irme.*
Yes, of course, see you soon.	*Sí, claro, hasta luego.*
I speak Spanish.	*Yo hablo español.*
You speak English very well.	*Tú hablas inglés muy bien.*
She speaks with an accent.	*Ella habla con acento.*
You talk too much.	*Ustedes hablan demasiado.*
They speak Spanish.	*Ellos hablan español.*
You speak too quickly for me.	*Ustedes hablan demasiado rápido para mi.*
I am sick.	*Yo estoy enfermo.*
You are tired.	*Tú estás cansado.*
I am busy.	*Estoy ocupado.*
We are happy.	*Nosotros estamos felices.*
You are unhappy.	*Usted está infeliz.*
I am going to go to the beach.	*Yo voy a ir a la playa.*
It is going to rain.	*Va a llover.*
You are going to leave next week.	*Ustedes van a salir la semana próxima.*
I would like to go there.	*Quisiera ir allí.*
I would like to leave this evening.	*Quisiera salir esta tarde.*
You can start now.	*Tú puedes comenzar ahora.*
She should rent a car.	*Ella debe alquilar un coche.*
We can arrive tomorrow.	*Podemos llegar mañana.*
They can sell their house.	*Ellos pueden vender su casa.*
I must sleep tonight.	*Tengo que dormir esta noche.*
I sell news papers.	*Yo vendo periódicos.*
You sell magazines.	*Tú vendes revistas.*
She sells vegetables.	*Ella vende legumbres.*
He sells meat.	*El vende carne.*
We sell our tickets.	*Nosotros vendemos neustros boletos.*
They sell nice things.	*Ellos venden cosas finas.*
I bought the book.	*Yo compré el libro.*
You bought your car.	*Tú compraste tu coche.*
He bought a car last week.	*El compró un coche la semana pasada.*
We bought something for my mother.	*Ustedes compraron also para mi madre.*

They bought things for their friends.	*Ellos compraron cosas para sus amigos.*
What is today's date?	*¿Cuál es fecha de hoy?*
Today is Friday, June 3.	*Hoy es viernes, tres de junio.*
Tomorrow is Saturday, June 4.	*La mañana es sábado, cuarto de junio.*
In your country, is the weather good or bad in the four seasons: winter, spring, summer, and fall?	*¿En su país, hace bueno tiempo o mal tiempo en las cuatro estaciones: el invierno, la primavera, el verano, y otoño?*
In the winter it snows and it is cold, and in the summer it is hot and sunny.	*En el invierno nieva y hace frio, y en el verno hace calor y sol.*
In the spring and the fall it is cool or it rains very much.	*En la primavera y en el otoño está fresco o llueve mucho.*
I invite friends to read my novel.	*Invito a los amigos a leer mi novela.*
Hi, friend.	*Hola, amigo.*
Good morning, Sir	*Buenos dias, señor.*
Good day, Sir	*Buenos dias, señor.*
Come in, please.	*Pasen Uds., por favor!*
Please come in. miss.	*!Haga Ud. el favor de pasar, señorita!*
Thank you.	*gracias / muchas gracias.*
Welcome.	*Bienvenido, Bienvenida, Bienvenidos.*
What is your name?	*¿Cuál es su nombre?*
My name is Roy.	*Me llamo es Roy. / Mi nombre es Roy.*
Great pleasure.	*Mucho gusto.*
How are you?	*How are you?*
I am very well. And how are you Sir?	*Estoy muy bien. ¿Y cómo es usted señor?*
So, so. I am not sick.	*Asi, asi. No estoy enfermo.*
Not very well. I am ill.	*No estoy muy bien. Estoy enferma.*
Excuse me.	*Excúseme.*
Until tomorrow.	*Hasta mañana.*
Until later.	*Hasta luego. / Hasta la vista.*
Good-bye.	*Adiós.*
How old are you?	*¿Cómo viejo es usted?*
I am twenty years old.	*Soy veinte años.*
What is the matter with you?	*¿Cuál es la materia con usted?*
I have a bad headache.	*Tengo un mal dolor de cabeza.*
What time is it?	*¿Cuándo es?*
It is one o'clock.	*Es la una.*
What time is it now?	*¿Qué hora es ahora?*
It is two o'clock. It is not one.	*Son las dos. No es la una.*

It is half past five.	*Son las cinco y media.*
It is a quarter past eight.	*Son las ocho y cuarto.*
It is four minutes to one.	*Es la una menos cuatro.*
What day is it today?	*¿Qué dia es hoy?*
Today is Friday.	*Hoy es viernes.*
What is the date?	*¿A cuántos estamos?*
It is September 7.	*Estamos siete de septiembre.*
July 4 is the United States' Independence Day.	*El cuatro de julio es el Día de la Independencia de los Estados Unidos.*
Where are you going?	*¿Adónde usted va?*
I am going to the park.	*Voy al parque.*
Why are you going to the park?	*¿Por qué vas al parque?*
I am going for a walk there.	*Voy de paseo alli.*
He is my best friend. She is also my best friend.	*Él es mi mejor amigo. Ella también es mi mejor amiga.*
I have the best friends in the world.	*Tengo los mejores amigos del mundo.*
My sister is older than I	*Mi hermana es mayor que yo.*
I am the youngest in the family.	*Soy la menor de la familia.*
You and I are the worst in the team.	*Tú y yo somos los peores del equipo.*
She speaks Spanish and I speak English.	*Ella habla español y yo hablo inglés.*
I eat bread and you eat rice.	*Yo como pan y tú comes arroz.*
You wish to live in Spain.	*Deseas vivir en España.*
I don't work on Monday.	*No trabajo el lunes.*
I don't work on Tuesdays.	*No trabajo los martes.*
There is a party on Wednesday.	*Hay una fiesta el miércoles.*
What day is today?	*¿Qué día es hoy?*
Today is Monday.	*Hoy es lunes.*
Tomorrow is Tuesday.	*Mañana es martes.*
What's the table made of?	*¿De qué material es la mesa?*
It's made of wood.	*Es de madera.*
It's important to practice every day.	*Es importante practicar cada día.*
It's necessary to speak a lot.	*Es necesario hablar mucho.*
What are you eating?	*¿Qué estás comiendo?*
I am eating rice and beans.	*Estoy comiendo arroz y frijoles.*
How much does the tie cost?	*¿Cuánto cuesta la corbata?*

What (Which) are your favorite books?	*¿Cuáles son tus libros favoritos?*
With whom am I speaking?	*¿Con quién hablo?*
For what reason do you study Spanish?	*¿Por qué estudias español?*
Because it's required.	*Porque es un requisito.*
For what purpose do you study Spanish?	*¿Para qué estudias español?*
I have to eat the vegetables.	*Tengo que comer las verduras.*
One must study a lot.	*Hay que estudiar mucho.*
It's pouring.	*Hay lluvias torrenciales.*
There's a windstorm.	*Hay un vendaval.*
It's hailing.	*Hay granizo.*
It's sprinkling.	*Hay lloviznas.*
The dog chases the cat.	*El perro persigue <u>a</u> la gata.*
I drink the milk.	*Bebo la leche.*
He doesn't like to smoke.	*A él no le gusta fumar.*

ITALIAN GRAMMAR

Articles

Articles are adjectives and therefore they have to agree in number and gender with the nouns they modify.

The Definite Article: *the*

		Singular		Plural
Masculine	*il*	before consonants	*i*	before consonants
	lo	before *z*, *gn*, or *s* and consonants.	*gli*	before vowels, *z*, *gn*, or *s* and consonants.
	l'	before vowels		
Feminine	*la*	before consonants	*le*	before consonants and vowels
	l'	before vowels		

The Indefinite Article: *a, an*

Masculine		Feminine	
un	before consonant or vowel	*una*	before consonants
uno	before z, gn, or s and consonants.	*un'*	before vowels

Some or Any:

	Singular	Plural
Masculine	*del*	*dei*
Masculine (before a vowel)	*dell'*	*degli*
Masculine (before the ltters z, x + consonant, and gn)	*dello*	*degli*
Feminine	*della*	*delle*
Feminine (before a vowel)	*dell'*	*delle*

Nouns and Gender

In Italian, nouns can be masculine or feminine, singular or plural. There is no neuter gender in Italian.

- Nouns that end in '*o*' are masculine and form the plural with '*i*.'
- Nouns that end in '*a*' are feminine and form the plural with '*e*.'
- Nouns that end in '*e*' can be masculine or feminine and form the plural with '*i*.'
- Some nouns have both masculine and feminine forms.
- Some nouns simply change the ending to '*a*' to form the feminine:

  ragazzo/ragazza, amico/amica, nonno/nonna
- Others, particularly professions and titles, change the ending to '*-essa*':

  professore/professoressa, studente/studentessa, dottore/dottoressa, poeta/poetessa
- Nouns that end in '*-tore*' in the masculine change to '*-trice*' in the feminine:

  pittore/pittrice, attore/attrice, autore/autrice, scrittore/scrittrice
- Most Italian nouns end in a vowel. Those nouns that end in a consonant are of foreign origin and all nouns have a gender, even those that refer to things, ideas or qualities.

Usually, nouns ending in *-o* are masculine, nouns ending in *-a* are feminine.

Masculine	*amico, treno, fratello, libro, nonno, ragazzo, dollaro, panino, vino*
Feminine	*amica, casa, ragazza, sorella, bicicletta, lira, studentessa*

Nouns ending in *-e* may be masculine or feminine.

Masculine	*studente, ristorante, giornale, mare, nome, pane, ponte, caffè*
Feminine	*automobile, frase, nave, notte, classe, canzone, arte*

Nouns ending *-ione* are generally feminine, while nouns ending in *-ore* are almost always masculine.

Feminine		Masculine	
television	*televis**ione***	actor	*att**ore***
nation	*naz**ione***	author	*aut**ore***
opinion	*opin**ione***	professor	*profess**ore***

Nouns ending in a consonant are usually masculine: bar, autobus, film, sport.

Subject Pronouns

	Singular		Plural	
1st person	I	*io*	we	*noi*
2nd person	you (familiar)	*tu*	you (familiar)	*voi*
3rd person	he	*lui (egli/esso)*	they (m)	*loro (essi)*
	she	*lei (ella/essa)*	they (f)	*loro (esse)*
	you (formal)	*Lei*	you (formal)	*Loro*

The *tu* and its plural form *voi* are used in addressing members of the family, friends, children, and animals. In all other cases, *Lei* and its plural *Loro* are used.

Verbs

Italian verbs are divided into three categories: *-are*, *-ere*, and *-ire*. Some infinitives end in *rre,* such as *trarre, porre.*

Conjugating Essere (to be)

Person		Singular		Plural
1st person	I am	*io sono*	we are	*noi siamo*
2nd person	you are (familiar)	*tu sei*	you are (familiar)	*voi siete*
3rd person	you are (formal)	*Lei è*	you are (formal)	*Loro sono*
	he/she is	*lui/lei*	they are	*loro sono*

Conjugating Andare (to go)

Person		Singular		Plural
1st person	I go	*io vado*	we go	*noi andiamo*
2nd person	you go (familiar)	*tu vai*	you go (familiar)	*voi andate*
	you go (formal)	*va'*	you go (formal)	*Loro sono*
3rd person	he/she goes	*lui/lei/Lei va'*	they go	*loro/Loro vanno*

Conjugating Venire (to come)

Person		Singular		Plural
1st person	I come	*io vengo*	we come	*noi veniamo*
2nd person	you come (familiar)	*tu vieni*	you come (familiar)	*voi venite*
3rd person	he/she comes	*lui/lei/Lei viene*	they come	*loro/Loro vengono*

Prepositions

di (of), a (at, to), da (from), in (in, to, into), con (with), su (on, over, on top of), per (for), tra/fra (between), (by). The prepositions *di, a, da, in, and su* always contract with the article to form a single word. Examples:

a+il	*al*	a+l'	*all'*
a+lo	*allo*	a+i	*ai*
a+gli	*agli*	a+la	*alla*
a+le	*alle*	da+il	*dal*
da+l'	*dall'*	da+lo	*dallo*
da+i	*dai*	da+gli	*dagli*
da+la	*dalla*	da+le	*dalle*
di+il	*del*	di+i	*dei*
di+l'	*dell'*	di+la	*della*
di+lo	*dello*	di+le	*delle*
di+gli	*degli*	in+il	*nel*
in+l'	*nell'*	in+lo	*nello*
in+i	*nei*	in+gli	*negli*
in+la	*nella*	in+le	*nelle*

Adjectives

Adjectives, which modify nouns, usually come after the noun in Italian. Adjectives can be feminine or masculine, singular or plural, depending on the gender and number of the noun to which they refer. Adjectives that end in *-a* are feminine and form the plural with *-e*. Adjectives that end in *-o* are masculine and form the plural with *-i*. Adjectives that end in *-e* can be masculine or feminine and in both cases form the plural with *-i*.

Possessive Adjectives

	Masculine Singular	Plural	Femine Singular	Plural
my	*il mio*	*i miei*	*la mia*	*le mie*
your (of *tu*)	*il tuo*	*i tuoi*	*la tua*	*le tue*
your (of *Lei*)	*il Suo*	*i Suoi*	*la Sua*	*le Sue*
his, her, its	*il suo*	*i suoi*	*la sua*	*le sue*
our	*il nostro*	*i nostri*	*la nostra*	*le nostre*
your (of *voi*)	*il vostro*	*i vostri*	*la vostra*	*le vostre*
your (of *Loro*)	*il Loro*	*i Loro*	*la Loro*	*le Loro*
their	*il loro*	*i loro*	*la loro*	*le loro*

Question Words

how?	*come?*	what?	*che, che cosa, cosa?*
how much/how many?	*quanto, quanta, quanti, quante?*	where?	*dove?*
when?	*quando?*	which?	*quale/qual?*
why?	*perché?*	who?	*chi?*
whose?	*di chi?*		

What are you doing?	*Che cosa fai?*	When are you free?	*Quando è libero?*
How is Nicolitta?	*Come sta Nicolitta?*	How much is a ticket to Rome?	*Quanto costa un biglietto per Roma?*
Where is the child?	*Dov'è il bambino?*	Are there discounts?	*Ci sono delle riduzion?*
Why do you smoke so much?	*Perché fumi tnato?*	Which platform does the train leave from?	*Da quale binario parte il treno?*

Negatives

Non means no in Italian. A negative sentence is created by adding *non* in front of the verb. Also there are other ways of expressing negation. Here is a chart with negative expressions in English and their Italian equivalent:

not	*non*	no one, nobody	*non…nessuno*
never	*non…mai*	not yet	*non…ancora*
nothing	*non…niente,*	nothing	*non…nulla*
not anymore, no long, no more	*non…piú*	neither…nor	*non…n'e…n'e*

not even	*non…neanche*	not even	*non…nemmeno*
not even	*non…neppure*	not at all	*non…affatto*
not at all	*non…mica*	not at all	*non…punto*
not any	*non…nessun/o*	not any	*non..nessuna*
only	*non…che*		

Italian Alphabets and Pronunciation

Alphabets	**Pronunciation**	**Examples**
A a	a	as in f**a**ther, car
B b	bi	as in **b**all, **b**oy
C c	ca	as in **cane**, **care**
	ci	as in **ch**urch, **ch**est
D d	di	as in **d**ay, **d**og
E e	e	as in **e**gg, s**e**t
F f	effe	as in **f**air, **f**ish
G g	gi	as in **g**old, **g**overnment
	ge	as in **g**em, **g**eneral
H h	acca	silent
I i	i	as in h**i**t, pol**i**ce
L l	elle	as in **l**eaf, **l**egal
M m	emme	as in **m**other, **m**ath
N n	enne	as in **n**umber
O o	o	as in h**o**t, g**o**, b**o**ld
P p	pi	as in **p**ay, **p**arty
Q q	qu	as in **q**uality, **q**uantity
R r	erre	as in **r**un, **r**ain
S s	esse	as in **s**teal, **s**oup
T t	ti	as in **t**ea
U u	u	as in s**oo**n, n**oo**n
V v	vi/vu	as in **V**irginia, vase
Z z	zeta	as in se**ts**, re**ds**
è (grave accent)		as in **tea** tè
Foreign Letters	**Italian Name**	**Example**
j	i lunga, lungo	as in **j**oy, **j**og, **j**am, **j**ungle
k	cappa	as in **k**ilogram, **k**ettle
w	vu dopio	as in **w**ater, **w**eather
x	ics	as in bo**x**, fo**x**
y	i greco, ipsilion	as in **y**oga, **y**ard

Italian Phrases

English	Italian
Good morning. Do you speak English?	*Boon giorno. Parla inglese?*
No. I am sorry, I don't speak English.	*No, mi dispiace, a non lo parlo inglese.*
I am afraid I speak only a little Italian.	*Purtroppo so soltanto un po' di italiano.*
That is alright. I understand you.	*Non fa niente. Riesco a capirla.*
I understand you very well.	*La capisco benissimo.*
Hi, may I sit next to you?	*Ciao, posso sedermi vicino a te?*
Sure. It is open.	*Certo. É libero.*
My name is Roy, what is yours?	*Mi chiamo Roy e tu?*
My name is Nicolitta.	*Mi chiamo Nicolitta.*
Hello?	*Pronto?*
Who is speaking?	*Chi parla?*
Is Carol in please?	*C'é Carol, per favore?*
May I leave a message?	*Posso lasciare un messaggio?*
Goodbye.	*Arrivederla.*
Happy birthday, Roy.	*Buon compleanno, Roy.*
Thank you.	*Grazie.*
How old are you today?	*Quanti anni compi?*
Twelve, like you?	*Dodici, come te?*
What time is it?	*Che ora é? / Che ore sono?*
It is one o'clock.	*É l'una.*
It is noon.	*É mezzogiorno.*
It is midnight.	*É mezzanotte.*
It is 3:15.	*Sono le tre e quindici.*
It is 12:10.	*É mezzo giorno e dieci.*
Hi Nicolitta, it is me. I wanted to invite you over for dinner this evening.	*Hi Nicolitta. Sono io. Volevo invitarvi a cena questa sera.*
I must ask Robert. All right, we will come with pleasure.	*Devo chiedere a Roberto. Allora, verremo molto volentieri.*
Then see you this evening.	*Allora, a questa sera.*
Hello. What are you doing? Are you working?	*Ciao. Che cosa fai? Lavori?*
No. I am reading.	*No. Sto leggendo.*
What are you reading?	*Che cosa stai leggendo?*
A book. What are you doing now?	*Un libro. E che cosa stai facendo allora?*

I am writing.	*Scrivo. / Sono estorco.*
What are you writing?	*Che cosa stai scrivendo?*
I am writing a letter to my parents.	*Sto scrivendo una lettera ai miei genitori.*
What is that noise?	*Che cos'é quale rumore?*
I don't know.	*Non so.*
Great idea.	*Bella idea.*
I phoned a few days ago to book a table.	*Ho telefonato qualche qiorno fa per prenatare un tavolo.*
What name please?	*A quale name, per favore?*
My name is Roy.	*Il mio name Roy.*
How many people is it for?	*Per quante persone?*
Two of us.	*Noi siamo due. / due di noi.*
Come this way please. Is it all right here?	*Prego, da questa parte. Vi piace qui?*
That is fine.	*Va benissimo.*
What are you looking for?	*Chi cerchi? Che cosa state cercando?*
I am looking for my boy friend?	*Cerco il mio ragazzo.*
I have been looking for him for half an hour.	*Lo cerco già da mezz'ora.*
Where there is a will, there is a way.	*Volere è potere.*
There is no getting away from it.	*Volere o volare.*
How is the weather?	*Che tempo fa?*
The weather is nice.	*Fa bel tempo.*
The weather is bad.	*Fa cattivo tempo.*
It is warm.	*È caldo.*
It is cold.	*È freddo.*
It is cool.	*È fresco.*
What day is today?	*Che giorno è oggi?*
Today is Tuesday.	*Oggi è martedì.*
Yesterday was Monday.	*Ieri è stato lunedi.*
How are you today?	*Come stai oggi?*
I am fine. Thanks.	*Sto bene. Grazie.*
Are you Italian?	*Sei italiano?*
Of course not. I am French.	*Certo che no, sono francese.*
Where do you live?	*Dove vivi?*
In Paris, and you?	*In Paris, e tu?*
I live in London. Do you have a house?	*Io vivo in London. Hai una casa?*
Yes, with a garden.	*Si con un giardino.*

See you tomorrow.	*A domani.*
See you soon.	*A presto.*
Goodbye.	*Arrivederci.*
Good morning.	*Boon giorno.*
Good afternoon.	*Boon pomeriggio.*
Good evening.	*Buona sera.*
Good night.	*Buona notte.*
Hi./Bye	*Ciao.*
Pleased to meet you.	*Piacere di conoscerla.*
He barks more than he bites.	*Abbaia più che non morde.*
I promise less than I give.	*Prometto meno di quel che do.*
The more I study, the more I learn.	*Più studio, più imparo.*
Rather death, than dishonour.	*Piuttosto la morte che il disonore.*
It is half past two.	*Sono le due a mezzo.*
It is ten minutes past three.	*Sono le tre e dieci.*
It is twenty minutes to four.	*Ci manacano venti minuti alle quattro.*
It is a quarter to five.	*Sono le cinque meno un quarto.*
How many times I have told you.	*Quante volte te l'ho detto.*
I am glad you are well.	*Sono lieto che Lei stia bene.*
You are too kind.	*È troppo gentile.*
How do you do?	*Come stanno?*
I promise to visit you.	*Le prometto di visitarla.*
I was looking for you.	*Stavo cercandoli / Le cercava.*
I should like to see him.	*Vorrei verderlo.*
I should like to know.	*Vorrei sapere.*
I have seen many things.	*Ho veduto molte cose.*
Are you enjoying yourselves, young gentemen?	*Si divertono, signorini?*
I was just going out.	*Stava per uscire.*
It may be true.	*Può essere vero.*
If it were true, I should believe it.	*Se fosse vero lo crederei.*
If I had it, I should give it to you.	*Se l' avessi te lo darei.*
If he came, we should go.	*Se venisse noi ce ne andremmo.*
If he did it, he will be punished.	*Se lo fece sarà punito.*
Be seated.	*Si accomodi.*
Be quiet.	*Stiano zitti.*
Be it so.	*Sia pure.*
It is true that I have been there.	*È vero che ci sono stato.*

It is necessary to look out for it.	*È necessario da osservare fuori per esso.*
In three days it will be finished.	*Fra tre giorno sarà finito.*
It is far from here.	*È lontano di qua.*
I promise as a man of honor.	*Prometto da uomo d' onore.*
Do you like it?	*voi lo gradiscono? / Le piace?*
He is not well.	*Non sta bene.*
Whether it is true or not.	*Sia vero o no.*
It is very beautiful.	*È molto bello / è bellissimo.*
How are you?	*Come stai? / Come sta?*
How is it going?	*Come va?*
I am fine.	*Sto bene.*
I am terrific.	*Sto benone.*
I am very well.	*Sto benissimo.*
I am very well.	*Sto molto bene.*
I am quite well.	*Sto abbastanza bene.*
I am so so.	*Sto così così.*
I am sick.	*Sto ammalato*
I am not well.	*Non sto bene.*
Not too bad.	*Non c'è male.*
Fine, thank, and you?	*Bene, grazie, e tu? / Bene, grazie, e Lei?*
In Rome there are seven hills.	*A Roma ci sono sette colli.*
I have a thousand dollars in the bank.	*Ho mille dollari in banca.*
She won a million dollars.	*Lei ha vinto un milione di dollari.*
I would like to win a billion dollars.	*Vorrei vincere un miliardo di dollari.*
How many friends do you have here?	*Quanti amici voi hanno qui?*
I want to talk to you about it.	*Voglio parlarne con te.*
How many apples did you buy?	*Quanti mele hai comprato?*
What is the date today?	*Qunti ne abbiamo oggi?*
It is the ninth.	*È il nono / oggi ne abbiamo nono.*
How old is your father?	*Quanti anni ha tuo padre?*
He is seventy eight.	*Ne ha settantotto.*
What do you know about the situation?	*Cosa sai della situazione?*
I don't know anything.	*Non ne so niente.*
Will you give it to me?	*Lo darete me? / Me la dai?*
Luciano Pavarotti sings well.	*Luciano Pavarotti canta bene.*

I went to the beach every summer when I was young.	*Io andavo all mare ogni estate quando ero giovane.*
The players were tall and strong.	*I giocatori erano alti e forti.*
Did you go for a walk today?	*Avete fatto la passeggiata oggi?*
No, but will go tomorrow.	*No, ma la feremo domani.*
Are you going to London this year?	*Andate in Londra quest'anno?*
Yes, next month we will go to London.	*Sì, il mese prossimo andremo a Londra.*
Nicolitta eats very slowly.	*Nicolitta mangia molto lengamente.*
Ice cream is good, but cake is better.	*Il gelato è buono, ma la torta è migliore.*
Roy is bigger than I am and he is my older brother.	*Roy è più grande di sono ed è il mio fratello più anziano.*
Milan is bigger than Brescia.	*Milano è più grande di Brescia.*
The project on which you are working is interesting.	*Il progetto su cui siete funzionamento è interessante.*
I like the job that I found.	*Mi piace il lavoro che ho trovato.*
Serenity is what counts in life.	*La serenità è ciò che conta nella vita.*
I told you everything I know.	*Ti ho detto tutto quello che so.*
If I had the money, I would go to Europe.	*Se avessi I soldi, andrei a Europa.*
If it is nice tomorrow, I am going to beach.	*Se fa bello domani, vado al mare.*
I am happy you can come to dinner.	*Sono contenta che voi possa venire a cena.*
It is raining and it is cold. What an awful weather!	*Piove e fa freddo. Che tempaccio!*
Where do you come from?	*Da dove vieni tu?*
I come from Londra.	*Vengo dal Londra.*
I would like something to eat.	*Vorrei qualcosa da mangiare.*
I would like something hot to drink. I am cold.	*Vorrei qualcosa di caldo da bere. Ho freddo.*
How long have you known Richard?	*Quanto tempo avete conosciuto Riccardo?*
Dante wrote the Divine Comedy.	*Dante scrisse la Divina Commedia.*
What kind of books do you read usually?	*Che tipo di libri leggi di solito?*
What is your favorine magazine?	*Qual è la tua rivista preferita?*
What a beautiful film!	*Che bel film!*
What a horrible day!	*Che giornataccia!*
How ugly!	*Che brutto!*
Which ones are mine?	*Quali sono I miei?*

Checks are not accepted.	*Non si accettano assegni.*
Foreign languages are studied at the university.	*Le lingue straniere sono studiate all'università.*

HINDI GRAMMAR

There is **no** definite article (*the*) in Hindi. The numeral '*ek*' (one) may be used for the singular indefinite article if it needs to be stressed.

Noun and Gender

There are two genders in Hindi: masculine and feminine. All words indicating male like people, animals, and plants are considered to be masculine. All words indicating female like females, female animals, plants, are considered to be feminine. Words indicating things, inanimate articles and abstract nouns are either masculine or feminine according to agreement. Sanskrit neuter nouns become masculine in Hindi. Generally, nouns ending in *-a* are masculine, and nouns ending in *-i* or *in* are feminine. There are exceptions.

		Singular	Plural
Masculine	boy	*Ladaka*	*ladake*
Feminine	daughter	*beti*	*betiyah*

Subject Pronouns

	Singular		Plural	
1st person	I	*main*	We	*hum*
2nd person	you (familiar)	*tu*	you	*tum, aap*
	you (formal)	*aap*		
3rd person	he, she, it	*vah, ve*	they	*ve*

Verbs

Verbs are referred to in their infinitive noun form which ends in *na*. The infinitive form of any verb ends with *na*. Examples: *karna* (to do), *dena* (to give), *ana* (to come).

Conjugation for the verb *to do, karna*—

Person	Singular	Plural
Masculine		
1st	*karta hun*	*karte hai*
2nd	*karte ho*	*karte ho*
3rd	*karta hai*	*karte hain*
Feminine		
1st	*karti hu*	*karte hain*
2nd	*kartii ho*	*karti ho*
3rd	*kartii hai*	*karti hain*

The root of any verb can be made by removing the suffix *-na* from the matching infinitive form.

Present Imperfect

I speak	*main bolta hun*
you speak (intimate)	*tu bolta hai*
this, he, it speaks	*yah bolta hai*
that, he, it speaks	*vah bolta hai*
we speak	*ham bolte hain*
you speak (familiar)	*tum bolte ho*
you speak (respect)	*ap bolte hain*
these, they speak	*ye bolte hain*
those, they speak	*ve bolte hain*

Same with the following tenses:

Present Continuous	I am speaking	main bolta hun
Past Tense	I used to speak	main bolta tha
Past Continuous	I was speaking	main bol raha tha
Future Imperfect	I will speak	main bolunga
Future Continuous	I will be speaking	main bolta rahunga

Postpositions

Hindi uses postpositions instead of prepositions that follow the noun. Some postpositions are compound ones and some of them, normally the pronouns, can be incorporated within the noun.

	Postpositions
Subject case	*ne*
to	*ko*
of	*ka*
of	*ki*
of	*ke*
from, of, with, by	*se*
with	*ke saath*
for	*ke liye*
in, on	*Me*
on, in	*Par*
near	*ke paas*

Adjectives

There are two kinds of adjectives in Hindi for morphological purposes.

The feminine form for the adjectives are made by dropping the ending vowel *-a* and adding long *-i* instead. Example: small = *chota* (Masculine), *choti* (Feminine).

Person	Example	Singular	Plural
Masculine	small room	*chota kamra*	*chote kamre*
	small house	*chota ghar*	*chote ghar*
Feminine	small orange	*choti narangi*	*choti narangiyan*
	small table	*choti mez*	*choti mezen*

Some long *-a* ending adjectives do not change any inflection relating to gender or number.

Question Words

Questions can also be formed by modifying intonation. Some question words are provided below.

who?	*kaun?*	which?	*kaunsa?*
what?	*kya?*	how many?	*kitne?*
why?	*kyon?*	how much?	*kitna?*
when?	*kab?*	where?	*kahan?*
how?	*kaise?*		

What is your name?	*Aapka naam kya hai?*	How are you?	*Aap kaise hain?*
How much is this?	*Ye kitne ka hai?*	Where can I find?	*Kahan milenge?*

Is this very far?	*Kya ye bahut door hai?*	Why? What is the matter?	*Kyò? Kya bath hai?*
Who is Sharmaji?	*Sharma ji kaun hai?*	He is a boy, isn't he?	*vah ladaka hai, na?*

Negatives

Negation is formed by adding the words, *mat*, *na* or *nahin* in the appropriate place in the sentence.

mat	don't go there	*vaha mat ja*
mat or *na*	don't go there (familiar)	*vaha na jao*
na or *nahin*	don't go there (formal)	*vaha nahi jayiye*

Hindi Alphabets and Pronunciation

Alphabets	Pronunciation	Examples
अ	A	as in **a**pproximate
आ	Aa	as in **A**rt
इ	e	as in **e**ar
ई	ee	as in k**ee**p
उ	u	as in p**u**t
ऊ	oo	ase in s**oo**n, n**oo**n
ऋ	Ri	as in **ri**shi
ए	ai	as in cl**i**mate
ऐ	Ai	as in cl**ai**m
ओ	o	as in **o**ver
औ	ou	as in ab**ou**t
अं	um	as in b**um**per
अ:	aha	not used
क	ka	as in **k**ey, **k**ing
ख	kha	as in **kh**an
ग	ga	as in **g**old, **g**overnment
घ	gha	as in **Gh**ana
ङ	iana	rarely used
च	ch (soft)	as in **ch**ubby
छ	chha	as in **ch**ase
ज	ja	as in **ja**smine
झ	jha	
ञ	jna	rarely used
ट	ta (soft)	as in **t**ea

ठ	th	as in **t**able
ड	da (soft)	as in Bay, **d**og
ढ	dh	
ण	Na	
त	ta (soft)	as in **th**ink
थ	tha	
द	da (soft)	as in **th**at
ध	dha	
न	na	as in **n**umber
प	pa	as in **p**ay, **p**arty
फ	pha	as in **ph**ilidel**ph**ia
ब	ba	as in **b**all, **b**oy
भ	bha	as in **Bh**uthan
म	ma	as in **m**other, **m**ath
य	ya	as in **y**ellow
र	ra	as in **r**un, **r**ain
ल	la	as in **l**eaf, **l**egal,
व	va	as in **V**irginia, **v**ase

Hindi Phrases

English	*Hindi*
What places did you go in the U.S.A.	*Aap U.S.A. mein kaha kaha gaye?*
We went to Washington DC, New York, and Florida.	*Hum Washington DC, New York, aur Florida gaye.*
Now tell me what did you do in Washington DC?	*Yah bataayiye ki aapnay Washington mein kya kiya?*
We went to see White House and Monument, and we went to shopping.	*Hum White House aur Monument dekhay, aur shopping karne gaye.*
And how did you like Washington?	*Aur kaisaa laga Washington?*
It was beautiful. We saw the Potomac river also.	*Bahuth sundar. Hum Potomac nadi bhi dekhy.*
And how did you like New York?	*Aur New York aapko kaisa laga?*
It was very crowded and it was very cold.	*Bahuth bheer thee aur bahuth cold tha.*
All right. Talk to you later.	*Acchha, aapsay phir baath hogee.*
The book is on the table.	*pusthak mez par hai.*
Stephanie and I are both old.	*Stephani aur mai donoh bude hai.*

This house belongs to that woman.	*yah makaan vus sthree ka hai.*
How is your son?	*aapka beta kaise hai.*
How is your daughter?	*aapki beti kaisi hai.*
How are you?	*aap kaise hai?*
I speak Hindi.	*Mai Hindi bolta hu.*
Those women don't speak Hindi.	*Ve auratheh Hindi nahi boltih.*
I am going.	*Mai chaltha hu.*
I always speak in Hindi with him.	*Mai hamesha usase Hindi bolta hu.*
My brother and his wife live in Delhi.	*Mere bayi aur unki pathni Delhi me rahathe hai.*
The girl and her mother are going to Japan tomorrow.	*yah ladaki aur uski mah kal Japan ja rahi haih.*
I am going to London.	*mai London ja raha hu.*
I was in America during the attack.	*Akraman ke samay mai America me tha.*
I have just come.	*mai abhi aaya hu.*
I came yesterday.	*Mai kal aaya tha.*
I came yesterday.	*mai kal aaya.*
May I go?	*mai chalooh?*
Perhaps I will go to California tomorrow.	*Shayad kal mai California jauooh.*
Shall we go?	*chaleh?*
Probably they are coming now.	*abhi aathe honge.*
They must have come just now.	*abhi aaya honge.*
I was there too.	*Mai bhi vahah tha.*
Hello.	*Namasthe.*
How much is this?	*Yah kithne kaa hai?*
Thank you.	*Dhanyavaad.*
Happy birthday.	*Janmadinka mubarak.*
What is the time?	*Kithane baje hai?*
This room is very big. Are the other rooms small?	*Yah kamara bahuth bada hai. Kya dusre kamare chote hai?*
No. only one room is small, the others are big.	*Nahi. Sirf ek kamra chota hai. Dusre bade hai.*
Very good. The room is clean and very airy.	*Bahut accha. Kamara saaf aur bahuth havadar hai.*
Hello Gupta, how are things? Everything is OK?	*Halo Gupta. Kya hal hai? Sab teek hai?*

Yes, everyting is OK. And how are you?	*Ha. Sab teek hai. Aur aap kaise hai?*
I am well too. Thank you.	*Main bhi accha hu. Sukriya.*
Raju, where are you?	*Raju, tum kaha ho?*
I am in my room now father. Why?	*Main mera kamare me hu pitaji. Kya bath hai?*
Where is my pen?	*Mera pen kaha hai?*
Is it not on the big table?	*Bari mez par nahai hai?*
Oh. Here it is.	*Oh. Yaha hai.*
The food was hot, but the tea was completely cold.	*Khana to garam tha, par chai ekdam thandi thi.*
Rekha is taller than Gupta.	*Rekha Gupta se lumbhi hai.*
Gupta is fatter than Rekha.	*Gupta Rekha se mota hai.*
Son, do you know where Uncle Gupta's keys are?	*Beta, thumhe malum hai ki Gupta chacha ki chabiyah kahah hai?*
Which keys? The car keys or house keys?	*Kaunsi chabiyah? Gaadi ki chabiyah ya ghar ki chabiyah?*
The house keys?	*Ghar ki chabiyah?*
I am sorry that you have a cold.	*Mujhe afsos hai ki tumko zukam hai.*
It is not good that the boy stays alone at home.	*Yah acchi baat nahi hai ki ladka ghar par akela reh raha hai.*
I speak pure Hindi.	*Mai shuddha Hindi bolta hu.*
Does Rajiv understand English?	*Kya Rajiv angreji samajtha hai?*
Where do you live?	*Tum kaha rahathe hun?*
I never smoke.	*Mai cigrate kabhi nahi peetha.*
Rajiv does not eat meat.	*Rajiv goshth nahi khata.*
He thinks that your pronunciation is good.	*Vah sochtha hai ki thumhara ucchaaran accha hai.*
How many languages do you know?	*Thumko kitani bhashayeh aathi hai?*
What do they call this script?	*Is lipi ko kya kahathe hai?*
They call it Sanskrit.	*Isko Sanskrit kahathe hai.*
Take care of yourself.	*Apana khayal rakhna.*
Do anyone speak English in your home?	*Aapke ghar me koyi angreji bolta hai?*
Yes, father knows five languages. But we mostly speak Hindi.	*Ha. Pitaji ko paanch bhashayeh aathi hai. Par ham log jyadathar Hindi bolte hai.*
Is there any cinema near your house?	*Kya aapke ghar ke najadeek koyi cinema hai?*
Tell me something about your friends.	*Apani saheliyon ke baare me kuch bathayiye.*

What do you want?	*Aapko khya chahiye?*
We want coffee, not tea.	*Hame coffee chahiye, tea nahi.*
Rajiv, what are you doing here in the narrow lanes of Delhi?	*Rajiv, thum yaha Delhi ki thang galiyo me kya kar rahe ho?*
I am doing some work with a friend.	*ek mithra ke saath main ne kuch kaam kar raha hu.*
So are you staying in Delhi nowadays?	*Tho kya thum aajkal Delhi main thehar rahe ho?*
Yes.	*Ha.*
We are learning Hindi.	*Ham Hindi seek rahe hai.*
Which story you are reading?	*Tum kaunsi kahani pad rahe/rahi ho?*
You were ringing the wrong number.	*Tum galat number dial kar rahe the.*
This is Nita speaking.	*Main Nita bol rahi hu.*
I will come to New York sometime.	*Mai kabhi New York aavoonga.*
Rajiv will phone you.	*Rajiv thumko phone karenge.*
He is going.	*Vah ja raha hai.*
He was going.	*Vah ja raha tha.*
He will be going.	*Vah ja raha hoga.*
Smoking is prohibited.	*Cigaratte peena mana hai.*
To be or not to be.	*Hona ya na hona.*
On arriving home, phone us.	*Ghar pahunchane par hame phone kariye.*
There is no need to shout.	*Chillane ki jaroorath nahi hai.*
Hello. This is Rajiv speaking. Is Guptaji there?	*Helo, mai Rajiv bol raha hu. Kya Gupta ji hai?*
No Rajiv. He is out. He will come in half an hour. Should I give him some message?	*Nahi Rajiv. Vah bahar hai. aadhe gante me aayenge. Mai unhe koyi message doo?*
Yes. Please tell him that Nita wants to talk to him.	*Ji. Aap unhe yah bathayiyi ki Nita unse baat karna chahthi hai.*
Is it something urgent?	*Koyi jaroori baat hai?*
Madam, it is very important that Guptaji phone Nita himself.	*Madam, bahuth avashyak hai ki Guptaji khud Nita se baath kare.*
I will tell him.	*Bathavoongi unko.*
If it rains, we will stay inside.	*Agar barasat hoti hai tho ham andar rahenge.*
We used to meet our friends and chat.	*Ham apane dosthon se milkar gapshap karthe the.*
She called a taxi and went straight home.	*Vah taxi bulakar seedhe ghar gayi.*
You should read this book.	*Thumhe is kithab ko padna chahiye.*
The weather should be good.	*Mausam accha hona chahiye.*

It is ten to seven.	*Saath bajane me das minute hai.*
It is twenty past eight.	*Aat bajkar bees minute hai.*
It is nearly ten o'clock in the morning.	*Subah ke lagbag das baje hai.*
How do you like California?	*California aapko kaisi lagati hai?*
I like this city very much.	*Yah nagar muje bahut accha lagtha hai.*
I feel at home here.	*Yaha mera dil lagta hai.*
This sentence does not seem right.	*Yah vakhya teek nahi lagta.*
The Taj Mahal was built by Shahjahan.	*Taj Mahal Shahajahan ke dwara banaya gaya tha.*
Sanskrit is read just as it is written.	*Sanskrit jaisi likhi jaati vaisi hi padi bhi jaati hai.*
Take as much as you want.	*Jithana thumko chahiye, utha lo.*
Tell us plainly.	*Hame saaf saaf bathao.*
Thank you very much indeed.	*Bahuth bahuth dhanyavad.*
Sanjay is neither lazy nor stupid.	*Sanjay na aalasi hai na bevakoof.*
We eat neither onions nor garlic.	*Ham na pyaj khathe hai na lahasun.*
Immediately after receiving the letter, I wrote a reply.	*Pathr paathe he maine utthar likh dala.*
Don't do anything without thinking.	*Bina soche kuch math karna.*
Please don't smoke here.	*Yaha cigaratte na peejiye.*
Just wait here please.	*Zara yaha tahariye.*
We will have to learn at least two languages.	*Hame kam se kam do bhashaye seekhni padengi.*
When you are free, come and eat at our place.	*Jab aapko purasath ho to hamare yaha khana khane ana.*
Photographs should not be taken in the temple.	*Mandir me photo nahi kheencha jana chahiye.*
Life should be made a little simpler.	*Jindagi ko thoda aur saral banaya jana chahiye.*
The harder you study, the more you will learn.	*Thum jithane dhyan se padonge, uthana seekhoge.*
In the evening grandmother always go to the temple.	*Shaam ko dadiji hamesha mandir jaya karthi hai.*
It happened just as you had said.	*Jaisa apane kaha tha, vaisa hi ho gaya.*

JAPANESE GRAMMAR

Particles

In Japanese, grammatical parts of the sentence are shown very clearly by particles. These particles are placed after the word or phrase they modify. Most particles are multi-functional and also they act as prepositions.

The particles are *de, ga, ka, kashira, kana, na, naa, ne, ni, no, o, sa, wa, yo, ze, zo,* etc.

de	Let's play in Japan!	*nihon* ***de*** *asobimashou!*
ga	The cat is strange.	*neko* ***ga*** *hen.*
ka	Are you Japanese?	*Nihon-jin desu* ***ka****.*
kashira	I wonder who that person is.	*Ano hito wa dare* ***kashira****.*
kana	I wonder if Mr. Hakes will come tomorrow.	*Hakes-san wa ashita kuru* ***kana****.*
na	Don't do such a thing!	*Sonna koto o suru* ***na****!*
naa	How great it is!	*Sugoi* ***naa****.*
ne	It's a beautiful day, isn't it?	*Ii tenki desu* ***ne****.*
ni	Let's go to Japan!	*nihon* ***ni*** *ikimashou!*
no	I made this myself.	*Kore jibunde tsukutta* ***no****.*
o	I read a book.	*hon* ***o*** *yomimashita.*
sa	I definitely know of such a thing.	*Sonna koto wa wakatteiru* ***sa****.*
wa	I am a student.	*Watashi* ***wa*** *gakusei desu.*
yo	Don't get so angry with me!	*Okoranaide* ***yo****!*
ze	Let's go for a drink!	*Nomi ni ikou* ***ze****.*
zo	I'm going!	*Iku* ***zo****.*

Subject Pronouns

Pronouns are not used in Japanese as much as they are in English. Often the pronoun is used once in the beginning and when the subject changes to something else, the pronoun is dropped.

	Singular		Plural	
1st person	I/me	*watashi*	we/us	*watashi tachi*
2nd person	you	*anata*	you	*anata tachi*
3rd person	he/him she/her it	*kare* *kanojo* it is not used, instead sore (that) is used	they/them	*kare ra*

Nouns and Genders

Japanese language has no gender, number, or articles and the nouns are non-inflecting. For example, *neko* can be interpreted as cat, cats, a cat, the cat, some cats, etc., depending on the context. Usually, the prefix *o-* for Japanese native nouns, and *go-* for Sino-Japanese nouns are used to translate the noun to polite form. Instead of replacing pronouns for nouns, Japanese eliminates words from the sentence to avoid reiterating them.

Verbs

In Japanese language, the verb generally comes at the end of the sentence. Since Japanese's sentences often omit the subject, the verb is probably the most important part in understanding the sentence. Japanese verbs are divided into three groups: (a) *-u* ending verbs, (b) *Iru* and *Eru*, ending verbs, and (c) Irregular verbs.

-u ending verbs

to speak	*hanasu*
to write	*kaku*
to listen	*kiku*
to wait	*matsu*
to drink	*nomu*

-iru and *-eru* ending verbs.

	Iru		*Eru*
to wear	*kiru*	to open	*akeru*
to see	*miru*	to give	*ageru*
to get up	*okiru*	to go out	*deru*
to get off	*oriru*	to sleep	*neru*
to believe	*shinjiru*	to eat	*taberu*

Irregular verbs *-suru* ending verbs.

to study	*benkyousuru*
to travel	*ryokousuru*
to export	*yushutsusuru*
to dance	*dansusuru*
to shampoo	*shanpuusuru*

Adjectives

There are two kinds of adjectives in Japanese: *i-* and *na-*adjectives. All *i*-adjectives end in *-i,* but they never end in *-ei.* Here are some examples of adjectives.

-i Adjectives

big	*ookii*	dark	*kurai*	good	*ii*	small	*chiisai*
cool	*suzushii*	difficult	*muzukashii*	hot	*atsui*	short	*mijikai*
cold	*samui*	early	*hayai*	far	*tooi*	bad	*warui*
delicious	*oishii*	easy	*yasashii*	near	*chikai*	warm	*atatakai*

-na Adjectives

convenient	*benrina*	favorite	*sukina*	lively	*nigiyakana*	pretty	*kireina*
dangerous	*kikenna*	honest	*shoujikina*	mean	*ijiwaruna*	safe	*anzenna*
distasteful	*kiraina*	healthy	*genkina*	polite	*teineina*	showy	*hadena*
famous	*yuumeina*	kind	*shinsetsuna*	quiet	*shizukana*	skillful	*jouzuna*

Question Words

Questions can be made by adding a *ka* to the end of the sentence. In Japanese the question mark (?) is not required. Just like in English, the last syllable is raised up in intonation.

Where is it?	*doko desu ka?*	Who is he?	*kare wa dare desu ka?*
What time is it?	*nan ji desu ka?*	When is it?	*itsu desu ka?*
Who is it?	*dare desu ka?*	Are you Japanese?	*Nihon-jin desu ka?*

Negatives

Negatives are formed by inflecting the verb. To make sentence negative, verb endings are changed into negative forms *-nai.*

For verbs ending in *-ru*, the polite negatives form is made by dropping *-masu* from the polite form of the verb and adding *-nai* or *-masen.*

For verbs not ending in *-ru*, drop *-masu* from the polite form and change the last vowel sound to

-a, and then add *-nai*. For polite form, drop the *-masu* and add *-masen.*

Please do not run here	*Otosanai de kudasai*	My husband and I do not fight.	*Uchi no danna to kenka shinai.*
It is not hot	*atsuku nai*	I don't go.	*Watashi wa ikanai.*
I don't read the newspaper	*Watashi wa shinbun o yomanail*	I do not understand English	*Eigo ga wakarimasen.*

Japanese Alphabets and Pronunciation—Hiragana, Katakana, Kanji

The characters *rōmaji* appear on the left, the *hiragana* symbols appear in the middle, and the *kanji* symbols appear on the right.

平仮名（ひらがな） hiragana

a	あ	安	i	い	以	u	う	宇	e	え	衣	o	お	於
ka	か	加	ki	き	幾	ku	く	久	ke	け	計	ko	こ	己
sa	さ	左	shi	し	之	su	す	寸	se	せ	世	so	そ	曽
ta	た	太	chi	ち	知	tsu	つ	川	te	て	天	to	と	止
na	な	奈	ni	に	仁	nu	ぬ	奴	ne	ね	祢	no	の	乃
ha	は	波	hi	ひ	比	fu	ふ	不	he	へ	部	ho	ほ	保
ma	ま	末	mi	み	美	mu	む	武	me	め	女	mo	も	毛
ya	や	也				yu	ゆ	由				yo	よ	与
ra	ら	良	ri	り	利	ru	る	留	re	れ	礼	ro	ろ	呂
wa	わ	和	wi	ゐ	為				we	ゑ	恵	wo	を	遠
												n	ん	无

片仮名（カタカナ） katakana

a	ア	阿	i	イ	伊	u	ウ	宇	e	エ	江	o	オ	於
ka	カ	加	ki	キ	幾	ku	ク	久	ke	ケ	介	ko	コ	己
sa	サ	散	shi	シ	之	su	ス	須	se	セ	世	so	ソ	曽
ta	タ	多	chi	チ	千	tsu	ツ	川	te	テ	天	to	ト	止
na	ナ	奈	ni	ニ	二	nu	ヌ	奴	ne	ネ	祢	no	ノ	乃
ha	ハ	八	hi	ヒ	比	fu	フ	不	he	ヘ	部	ho	ホ	保
ma	マ	万	mi	ミ	ミ	mu	ム	牟	me	メ	女	mo	モ	毛
ya	ヤ	也				yu	ユ	由				yo	ヨ	輿
ra	ラ	良	ri	リ	利	ru	ル	流	re	レ	礼	ro	ロ	呂
wa	ワ	和	wi	ヰ	井				we	ヱ	恵	wo	ヲ	乎
												n	ン	无

Kanji

水	雨水	海水	水素	恐水病	水族館	水車
mizu	amamizu	kaisui	suiso	kyōsuibyō	suizokukan	suisha
water	rainwater	seawater	hydrogen	hydrophobia	aquarium	waterwheel
			(water element)	(fear water illness)	(water tribe building)	(water vehicle)

Source: http://www.omniglot.com/writing/japanese_hiragana.htm

Japanese Phrases

English	*Japanese*
Hello, Good afternoon.	*Konnichi wa.*
Good morning	*Ohayoo gozaimasu.*
Good evening.	*Konban wa.*
Good night.	*Oyasumi nasail*
Thank you.	*Arigatoo gozaimasu.*
How are you?	*Ogenki desu ka?*
Very well, thanks.	*Okagesama de genki desu.*
And you?	*Anata wa?*
Not bad. Thanks.	*Okagesama de doo ni ka yatte orimasu.*
What is your name?	*Onamae wa nan to osshaimasu ka? or Onamae wa?*
What is the weather today?	*Kyoo no tenki wa doo desu ka?*
It is nice weather.	*Ii tenki desu.*
The weather is bad today.	*Kyoo was tenki ga warui desu.*
It is raining.	*Ame ga futte imasu.*
It is snowing.	*Yuki ga futte imasu.*
It is hot.	*Atsui desu.*
It is cold.	*Samui desu.*
It is cool.	*Suzushii desu.*
Where is a restaurant?	*Resutoran wa doko ni arimasu ka?*
Where is a hotel?	*Hoteru wa doko ni arimasu ka?*
Where is station?	*Eki wa doko ni arimasu ka?*
Where is the post office?	*Yuubinkyoku wa doko ni arimasu ka?*
Where is he?	*Doko ni imasu ka?*
Where is it?	*Doko desu ka?*
When is it?	*Itsu desu ka?*
Is he here?	*Koko ni imasu ka?*
Is he over there?	*Asoko ni imasu ka?*

Where is it?	*Doko desu ka?*
Who is it?	*Dare desu ka?*
Who is it? (with respect)	*Donata desu ka?*
Why is it?	*Naze desu ka?*
Why is it?	*Dooshite desu ka? (less formal)*
How much is it?	*Ikura desu ka?*
How many?	*Ikutsu desu ka?*
Which building is it?	*Dono tatemono desu ka?*
Which person is it?	*Dono hito desu ka?*
Did you go?	*Ikimashita ka?*
Why did you go?	*Naze ikimashita ka?*
How did you go?	*Nan de ikimashita ka?*

8

Some Indian Languages

BENGALI ALPHABETS

Bengali Vowels

অ	আ	ই	ঈ	উ	ঊ	ঋ	এ	ঐ	ও	ঔ
a	ā	i	ī	u	ū	ṛ	e	ai	o	au
[ɔ, o]	[ɑː]	[i, e]	[i]	[u, o]	[u]	[ri]	[e, æ]	[oj]	[o]	[ow]
ক	কা	কি	কী	কু	কূ	কৃ	কে	কৈ	কো	কৌ
ka	kā	ki	kī	ku	kū	kṛ	ke	kai	ko	kau

Consonants

চ	ca	[ʧɔ]	ছ	cha	[ʧʰɔ]	জ	ja	[ʤɔ]	ঝ	jha	[ʤʰɔ]	ঞ	ña	[nɔ]
ট	ṭa	[ʈɔ]	ঠ	ṭha	[ʈʰɔ]	ড	ḍa	[ɖɔ]	ঢ	ḍha	[ɖʰɔ]	ণ	ṇa	[nɔ]
ত	ta	[t̪ɔ]	থ	tha	[t̪ʰɔ]	দ	da	[d̪ɔ]	ধ	dha	[d̪ʰɔ]	ন	na	[nɔ]
প	pa	[pɔ]	ফ	pha	[pʰɔ]	ব	ba	[bɔ]	ভ	bha	[bʰɔ]	ম	ma	[mɔ]
য	ya	[ʤɔ]	র	ra	[rɔ]	ল	la	[lɔ]						
শ	śa	[ʃɔ/sɔ]	ষ	ṣa	[ʃɔ]	স	sa	[ʃɔ/sɔ]	হ	ha	[ɦɔ]			
য়	ya	[jɔ]	ড়	ṛa	[ɽɔ]	ঢ়	ṛha	[ɽʰɔ]						

Numerals

০	১	২	৩	৪	৫	৬	৭	৮	৯	১০
শূন্য	এক	দুই	তিন	চার	পাঁচ	ছয়	সাত	আট	নয়	দশ
śūnya	ek	dui	tin	cār	pñāc	chay	sāt	āṭ	nay	daś
0	1	2	3	4	5	6	7	8	9	10

BENGALI LANGUAGE

Brief History of Bengali Language

Bengali language is a member of the Indo-European language family. According to some linguistic researchers, in ancient times a combination of Oriya, Assamese, and Bengali languages started as a single branch. After sometime Oriya and Assamese split and became separate languages. Some scholars suggest that Bengali had its origin in the 1000 AD stemming from Magadhi Apabhramsha.

Writing

Bengali script is believed to have evolved from a revised Brahmi script between 1000 and 1100 AD.

Bengali is written from left to right. The script is characterized by many conjuncts, upstrokes, down strokes and other features that hang from a horizontal line. The standard Bengali consists of 35 consonants depending on the sound and 11 vowels. Bengali has a wide variety of diphthongs, combinations of vowels occurring within the identical syllable.

Unlike English and other European languages, Bengali features the use of postpositions instead of prepositions.

Postpositions in Bangla, occur after the nominal or the pronominal where the nominal or the pronominal function as their object.

For example: Rama tomara pashe baseche (Ram sat near you.)

Dialects

There are two standard styles in Bengali: the Sadhubhasha and the Chaltibhasha. Sadhubhasa is refined language used by scholars and the Chaltibhasa is a colloquial language used by common people.

Linguist Suniti Kumar Chatterjee grouped the Bengali dialects into four large clusters of spoken language known as Radha (West Bengal proper); Varendra (the northern parts of West Bengal and Bangladesh); Kamarupa (northeastern Bangladesh); and Bangla (the dialects of the rest of Bangladesh) along with several minor dialects.

Influence of Other Languages

Even though Bengali is an Indo-European language, it has been influenced by several well-known languages in South Asia such as Dravidian, Austroasiatic, and Tibeto-Burman families. Pali and Prakrit also contributed to the Bengali. All these languages added a wealth of vocabulary to Bengali and provided specific structure to the language.

Its status increased by Sanskrit with several literary works during the time of Chaitanya Mahaprabhu and also during the Bengali Renaissance.[1]

Development of Language by Literary Works

Three periods are identified in the history of Bengali language: Old Bengali, Middle Bengali, and New Bengali.

1. Old Bengali (900 to 1400 AD): Charyapada, a collection of poems from the tantric tradition in Kalinga was written between 10th and 12th centuries. They are mystic songs composed by various Buddhist monks: Bhusukupada, Chatilpada, Dhendhanpada, Kanhapada, Kukkuripada, Kamlipada, Luipada, Shantipada, Shabarapada, etc. Pronouns *Ami*, *tumi*, etc. appeared. The scripts and languages during this period were mainly influenced by the Kamarupa Prakrit.

---

1. The **Bengal Renaissance** refers to a socioal, cultural and religious reform movement during the 1900 and early 2000 AD in undivided India's Bengal province. The Bengal Renaissance began with Raja Ram Mohan Roy (1775-1833) and continued until the time of Rabindranath Tagore. The Renaissance was a revitalization of the positives of India's past and appreciation of the impact of the Modern West. Hence, the Bengal Renaissance incorporated the teachings of the Upanishad in order to create public opinion against Hindu superstitions including caste-division, child marriage, Sati, infanticide, polygamy, inter-caste hatred, dowry, untouchability, etc.

Krittibas Ojha (1381-1461) was a medieval period Bengali poet. The translation of the Indian epic Ramayana to Bengali is his major contribution to Bengali literature and culture.

Vidyapati (1352-1448) was a Maithili poet and a Sanskrit scholar. Generally, Vidyapati is known for his love songs and prayers for Shiva. But he also wrote on other topics including ethics, history, geography, and law. His works include:

(a) Puruṣa Parīkṣā: deals with moral teachings.

(b) Likhanabali: On writing

(c) Bhu-Parikrama: On local geography

(d) Vibhāgasāra: On nature

(e) Dānavākyāvalī: On charity

(f) Gangāvākyāvalī: On Ganges river

(g) Varṣakṛtya: about works completed in a year

(h) Durgābhaktitaraṅgiṇī: On devotion to Durga

(i) Śaivasarvasvahāra: on Shaivas

(j) Kīrttipatākā: On glorification of fame

(k) Kīrttilatā: On fame

2. **Middle Bengali (1400 to 1800 AD):** Major text of this period is Boru Chandidas's Shrikrishna Kirtana, which illustrates a new kind of language style. Persian influence also occurred in this period.

Mangal-Kāvya is a group of Bengali Hindu religious texts, composed between 1300 and 1800 AD consisting of narratives of native deities of rural Bengal in the social settings of the middle ages. The Mangal-Kāvyas are usually written in the form of verses. The Chaitanya Bhagavata is a biography of Chaitanya Mahaprabhu (1486 AD), the famous Vaishnava saint, written by Vrindavana Dasa Thakura (1507-89 AD).

3. **New Bengali since 1800 AD:** Several changes to verbs and pronouns happened during this period. Bengal has produced a large group of literates who were responsible for social reforms through their writing in India since 1800 AD. Notable poet and writer is Rabindranath Tagore.

Rabindranath Tagore (7 May 1861-7 August 1941) was a Bengali poet who reformed Bengali literature and music. He was an author of *Gitanjali*, which won the Nobel Prize for literature for its sublime, sensitive, fresh and beautiful verses. Tagore introduced new prose and verse forms and the use of colloquial language into Bengali literature thus releasing it from traditional classical Sanskrit models. He was highly influential to introduce the best of Indian culture to the West and Western culture to India. Apart from *Gitanjali*, he has written several books on poetry, fictions, and dramas contributing a wealth of literature to Bengali language.

MARATHI ALPHABETS (DEVANĀGARĀ)

Vowels and Vowel Diacritics

अ	आ	इ	ई	उ	ऊ	ऋ	ए	ऐ	ओ	औ	अं	अः	अँ	ऑ
a	ā	i	ī	u	ū	ṛ	e	ai	o	au	aṅ	aḥ		
[ə]	[a]	[i]	[i]	[u]	[u]	[ru]	[e]	[əi]	[o]	[əu]	[$ə^{n}$]	[əh]	[æ]	[ɔ]
प	पा	पि	पी	पु	पू	पृ	पे	पै	पो	पौ	पं	पः		
pa	pā	pi	pī	pu	pū	pṛ	pe	pai	po	pau	paṅ	paḥ		

Consonants

क	ka	[kə]	ख	kha	[k^{h}ə]	ग	ga	[gə]	घ	gha	[$g^{ɦ}$ə]	ङ	ṅa	[ŋə]
च	ca	[tsə/tʃə]	छ	cha	[ts^{h}ə]	ज	ja	[ʥə/zə]	झ	jha	[$ʥ^{ɦ}$ə/$z^{ɦ}$ə]	ञ	ña	[ɲə]
ट	ṭa	[ʈə]	ठ	ṭha	[$ʈ^{h}$ə]	ड	ḍa	[ɖə]	ढ	ḍha	[$ɖ^{ɦ}$ə]	ण	ṇa	[ɳə]
त	ta	[t̪ə]	थ	tha	[$t̪^{h}$ə]	द	da	[d̪ə]	ध	dha	[$d̪^{ɦ}$ə]	न	na	[n̪ə]
प	pa	[pə]	फ	pha	[p^{h}ə/fə]	ब	ba	[bə]	भ	bha	[$b^{ɦ}$ə]	म	ma	[mə]
य	ya	[jə]	र	ra	[rə]	ऱ	ṟa	[ɽə]	ल	la	[lə]	व	va	[və/wə]
श	śa	[ʃə]	ष	ṣa	[ʂə]	स	sa	[sə]						
ह	ha	[ɦə]	ळ	ḷa	[ɭə]	क्ष	kṣa	[kʃə]	ज्ञ	jña	[ʥɲə]	श्र	śra	[ʃrə]

Notes

च [ç] ज [ʝ] झ [$ʝ^{ɦ}$] when followed by front vowels (i, e, etc) and in loanwords

०	१	२	३	४	५	६	७	८	९	१०
संढया	एक	दोन	तीन	चार	पाच	सहा	सात	आठ	नऊ	दहा
sańdhyā	ek	don	tin	chār	pāc	sahā	sāt	āṭh	nū	dahā
0	1	2	3	4	5	6	7	8	9	10

Modi Consonants

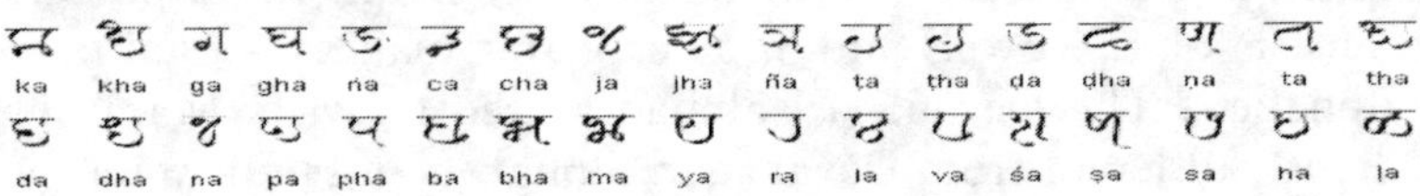

Modi Vowels and Vowel Diacritics

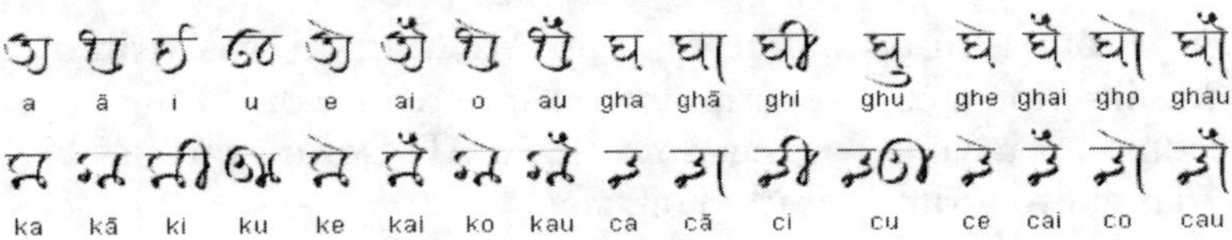

Modi Numerals

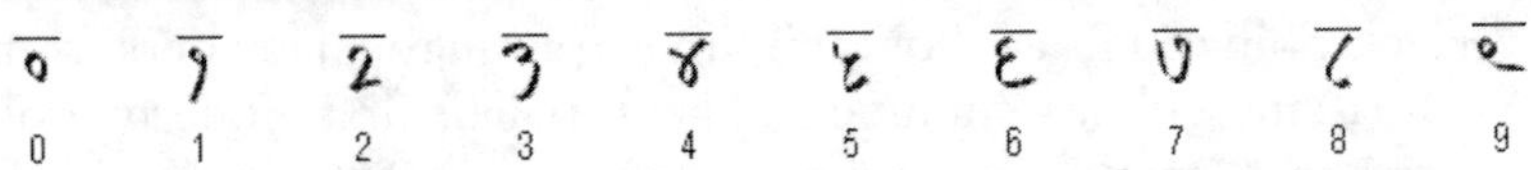

MARATHI LANGUAGE

Brief History of Marathi Language

Marathi language belongs to the group of Indo-Aryan languages which are a part of the Indo-European languages. Marathi is originated from Prakrit[2] Maharashtri which was spoken by people living in the territory of Maharashtra.

The earliest reference of spoken Marathi is discovered in the 800 AD poem "Kuvalaymala" of Udyotansuri. Kuvalayamala is a Jain literature in the form of manuscripts during the 800 AD. The book explains the social, religious, cultural, political and economic condition of the people during that period.

The history of written Marathi is recorded from 1100 AD on stone inscriptions and copper plates. There are various stone inscriptions in Marathi found at Akashi in Raigad district, Patan,

2. Any vernacular languages of North and Central India recorded from the 300 BC to the 400 AD.

Pandharpur, etc. Marathi was the court language during the rule of the Yadava kings.

Writing

The script presently used in Marathi is called Balbodh, which is a modified form of Devanagari script. Marathi script consists of 15 vowels and 38 consonants making a total of 53 alphabets. The Devanagari alphabet used to write Marathi is slightly different from Devanagari alphabets of Hindi and other languages. There are a couple of additional letters in the Marathi alphabet. It is written from left to right.

From 13th to middle of 2000 AD Marathi was written in Modi script, a cursive script intended to reduce the lifting of pen from paper while writing. Since 1950 AD Devanagari has been adapted to write Marathi language.

Marathi grammar is same as other modern Indo-Aryan languages. The primary word order of Marathi is subject-object-verb combination. It follows all three grammatical genders from Sanskrit: masculine, feminine and neutral. The first modern book related to Marathi Grammar was printed in 1805 by William Carey.

Dialects

The major dialects are Ahirani, Khandeshi, Varhadi, Zadi Boli, Vadvali, Samavedi and Are Marathi. Also Deshastha Marathi is spoken in Tanjore in Tamil Nadu.

Majority of words discovered in Marathi are Sanskrit based because it is derived from ancient Sanskrit language. Apart from Sanskrit, Marathi has been influenced by other languages of its adjacent states such as Karnataka (Kannada) and Andhra Pradesh (Telugu).

Influence of Other Languages

Marathi has immersed words from different languages of different rulers who occupied India at different times. During the Mughal period, a huge number of words from Persian, Arabic and Turkish sources entered Marathi. These include *baajaar* (market), *darvajaa* (door), *dukaan* (shop), *hushaar* (clever), *jamin* (land), *kaagad* (paper), *meherbaani*, *maafii*, *shahar* (city), and so on. The words entered from Portuguese are *bataataa* (potato), *bashii* (saucer), *pagaar* (salary), *istrii* (iron) and so on.

Development of Marathi Language by Literary Works

Marathi literature began and developed under the Yadava dynasty of Devagir from (850-1334 AD). Yadavas adopted Marathi as the court language and supported Marathi scholars. Also religious sects such as Mahanubhav Panth and Warkari Panth enriched the Marathi language through their religious songs and literature. During the period of Yadava kings, a great amount of literature on astrology, medicine, Puranas, Vedanta, kings and courtiers were created. Nalopakhyan, Rukmini Swayamvar and Shripati's Jyotish Ratnamala (1039) are notable contributions to Marathi language. The oldest book *Vivekasindu*, which is in prose form was written by Mukundaraj. His another work *Paramamrita* explains the Vedanta in a systematic form in Marathi language.

A notable example of Marathi literary work is *Leelacharitra* of Mahima Bhatta about Chakradhar Swami's spiritual experiences written in 1238 AD.

Commentary on *Bhagwad Gita* (*Jnaneshwari*) and *Amritanubhava* were written by Sant Jnaneshwar, a 1300 AD poet and philosopher. He composed devotional songs called Abhangas also. *Jnaneshwar* brought a higher status to Marathi by translating Bhagavad Gita from Sanskrit to Marathi.

Social reformers like Sant Tukaram, Samartha Ramadas transformed Marathi into a rich literary language. Tukaram wrote over 3000 Abhangas and Samartha Ramadas wrote Manache Shlok, Dasabodh, etc. Jainism also boosted Marathi language during Bahamani period. Marathi Keertan developed a type of art to educate mass through a stage performance act, which was for mainly glorification of God.

In the modern period Christian missionary William Carey standardized Marathi grammar and played an important role in the production of scientific dictionaries and grammars. In 1831 an all-inclusive Marathi-English (Murathee and English) dictionary was compiled by Captain James Thomas Molesworth.

9

Indo-Dravidian Languages

Introduction to Dravidian Languages

Dravidian languages are a language family conversed largely in southern India and parts of eastern and central India including northeastern Sri Lanka, Pakistan, Nepal, Bangladesh, and in other countries like Malaysia and Singapore. Among Dravidian languages, Telugu, Tamil, Kannada, and Malayalam are spoken by majority of people. There are also small bands of Dravidian-speaking scheduled tribes, who live outside the conventional communities. Only two Dravidian languages are exclusively spoken outside India; Brahui in Pakistan and Dhangar,[1] a dialect of Kurukh[2] in Nepal and a few other northern districts.

Some studies indicate that Dravidian languages were once spoken much widely across the Indian subcontinent. They provide examples such as Dravidian place names along the northwest coast, in Maharashtra, Goa, Gujarat, and a small number in Sindh. Also they provide examples of Dravidian grammatical influence such as clusivity[3] in Marathi, Konkani, Gujarati, Marwari, and to a small number in Sindhi languages.

---

1. The word *Dhangar* is considered to be related to a term for cattle wealth and Dhangar people were a herding caste of mass mainly located in the Indian state of Maharashtra. Their original home is assumed to be Gokul, Vrindavan, near Mathura. From Gokul they might have moved to Mewar, and then have spread into Gujarat and Maharashtra.
2. Kurukh belongs to the Northern Dravidian group of the Dravidian family of languages.
3. Clusivity is a grammatical distinction between *inclusive* and *exclusive* first-person pronouns and verbal morphology, also called *inclusive* '*we*' and *exclusive* '*we*'. For example, inclusive 'we' means 'you and I', whereas exclusive 'we' means he, she and I, but not you.

Proto-Dravidian is believed to have separated into Proto-North Dravidian, Proto-Central Dravidian, Proto South-Central Dravidian and Proto-South Dravidian around 500 BC, while some linguists have disputed that the degree of separation between the sub-families directs to a previous divergence.

The fact that the Brahui population of Baluchistan, an ancient people who have been displaced by a later group of migrants and their descendants suggests that the Dravidian languages were formerly more widespread and were displaced by the incoming Indo-Aryan languages.

Geneticist Luigi Cavalli-Sforza discovered that the genetic tree and the linguistic tree have many impressive similarities. Talking about the expansion of the speakers of the Dravidian languages, Cavalli-Sfoza says:

> The center of origin of Dravidian languages is likely to be somewhere in the western half of India. This language family is found in northern India only in scattered pockets, and in one population (Brahui) in western Pakistan.

He continues to propose a connection between Dravidian and Elamite[4] to the West and also to the Language of the Indus civilization. But there is no archeological or linguistic evidence to prove in reality when the Dravidian language speaking people arrived India. But it is understood without doubt that they were already in Northwest India by the time the Rig Vedic Aryans entered India by 1500 BC.

Several scholars have defended that Dravidian entered India from the northwest during 2000 BC before the Aryans arrived around 1500 BC. Rasmus Rask proposes that the Dravidian languages were perhaps "Scythian",[5] generally characterizing "barbarous tribes that inhabited the northern parts of Asia and Europe".

---

4. Elamite was the primary language in modern day Iran from 2800 BC to 550 BC. The last written records in Elamite appear about the time of the conquest of the Persian Empire by Alexander the Great.
5. The Scythians were Iranian horse-riding tribes who were inhabiting large areas in the central Eurasian grasslands starting with the 700 BC up to 400 AD.

All implications proposed by scholars that the Proto-Dravidians entered Indian subcontinent from outside are based on the conception that Brahui was the result of splitting of Proto-Dravidians and the people existing at the time of Indus Civilization were Dravidians. They have concluded that for the time being, it is best to think Dravidians were the natives of the Indian subcontinent who had dispersed throughout the country by the time the Aryans entered India around 1500 BC.

Based on some indirect evidences, it is understood that modern human languages attained their present condition of development between 50,000 and 150,000 years ago. ...starting from 60,000 or 70,000 years ago modern humans began to migrate from Africa, finally reaching remote habitable places in the world.

The amount of genetic variations observed by various calculations suggest that the population would have been about 50,000 in the Paleolithic period, just before roaming out of Africa.

Nayan Chanda writes in his article that he has found his origin by tracing back through DNA testing. He found out that his ancestors started walking out of Africa some 40,000 years ago journeying through Jordan valley and then through Iran they ended up in India. By this explanation, we can assume that Proto-Dravidians were the natives of the Indian subcontinent and they split near Brahui and spread throughout India before Aryans entered the subcontinent.

Numerous theories are proposed about the origin of Sanskrit word for Dravida.

Kamil Zvelebil quotes,

> The forms such as _dramila_ (in Daṇḍin's Sanskrit work _Avanisundarīkathā_) _damiḷa_ (found in Ceylonese chronicle Mahavamsa) and then goes on to say, "The forms _damiḷa/damila_ almost certainly provide a connection of _dr(a/ā) viḍa_" and "_...tamiḷ_ < _tamiẓ_...whereby the further development might have been *_tamiẓ_ > *_damiḷ_ > _damiḷa- /_ _damila-_ and...."

Zvelebil in his earlier dissertation states:

> It is obvious that the "Sanskrit *dr(a/ā)viḍa*, Pali *damila*, *damiḷo* and Prakrit *d(a/ā)viḍa* are all etymologically connected with *tamiẓ*" and further remarks "The *r* in *tamiẓ* → *dr(a/ā)viḍa* is a hypercorrect (A pronunciation produced by mistaken analogy with standard usage out of a desire to be correct) insertion...."

Another Dravidian linguist Bhadriraju Krishnamurti in his book *Dravidian Languages* states:

> Joseph (1989: *IJDL* 18.2:134-42) gives extensive references to the use of the term *draviḍa*, *dramila* first as the name of a people, then of a country. Sinhala's prehistoric inscriptions cite *dameḍa-*, *damela-* denoting Tamil merchants. Early Buddhist and Jain sources used *damiḍa-* to refer to a people of south India (presumably Tamil); *damilaraṭṭha-* was a southern non-Aryan country; *dramiḍa-*, *dramiḍa*, and *draviḍa-* were used as variants to designate a country in the south (*Bṛhatsamhita-*, *Kādambarī*, *Daśakumāracarita-*, 400-700 AD). It appears that *damiḍa-* was older than *draviḍa-* which could be its Sanskritization.

A.L. Basham believed that the Dravidian languages were initiated in the Neolithic period by Palaeo-Mediterranean migrants who brought the skills of agriculture to Indus in 400 BC. Some examples show the possibility of such belief like the Greek word for rice is *oryza* which in Dravidian languages *arisi, ariki, akki*, etc. There are numerous evidences of sea-trade between south Indian ports on the west coast and Rome and Greece in the pre-Christian period.

Kuiper notes that Vedic Sanskrit has retroflex consonants (*ṇ*) with about 88 words in the *Rig-Veda* having unrestricted retroflexes. Several example words are *Iṭanta*, *Kaṇva*, *puṇya* and *maṇḍūka*. The Dravidian language family is a vital candidate because it is plentiful in retroflex phonemes, which can be restored back to the Proto-Dravidian stage.

In addition, a number of grammatical features of Vedic Sanskrit not found in its sister Avestan language appear to have been borrowed from Dravidian languages. These include the gerund, which has the same function as in Dravidian.

Some Dravidian languages are listed below:

Suthern Group	Central Group	Northern Group	South Central Group
Badaga	Kolami	Brahui	Gondi
Irula	(Kondekor) Gadaba	Kurux	Konda
Kannada	Naikri	Malto	Kui
Kodagu	Naikri		Kuvi
Koraga	Ollari		Manda
Kota	Parji		Pengo
Kurumba			**Telugu**
Malayalam			
Tamil			
Toda			
Tulu			

Only four of the Dravidian languages, Kannada, Malayalam, Tamil, and Telugu have recorded history and literature.

How do we know that we all are connected to each other? Is it just a speculation or real? Here is an interesting article, which was published in the newspaper *Times of India* on Jan 27, 2014. Mr. Nayan Chanda writes from where and how we came to the present location from our origins and how the genetic science has proven beyond a shadow of doubt that all humans are originated from Africa. It also helps to understand how the languages could have disseminated all around the globe.

> A simple way of finding out who you really are under the skin or under your blond or auburn hair is to send a swab from your cheek to a lab for testing. I did it. I sent a sample of my DNA to the National Genographic Project, a collaboration between National Geographic Society and IBM to map the journey of human genome. The vial I sent did not have my name or any information other than the serial number that came with the vial in the mail.
>
> A few weeks later I checked the results of the test on the web by typing in the serial number and was surprised by

what it said. They said, I was Indian because my DNA marker of M52—was an unmistakably Indian marker. What is more amazing though is that by digging deep into my DNA they found that my ancestors came from East Africa some 40,000 years ago. The earliest DNA marker I carry is the Y-chromosome marker M168, which is the marker for the earliest common ancestor of every non-African male person living today.

My ancestors, progenies of an African father, at one stage started walking out of the area they lived in, possibly in search of food and better living. That journey was carried out by successive generations ultimately leading them out of Africa and into other continents. The route my ancestors took in their thousands of years journey to reach India is etched, incredible as it may sound, in my DNA.

My DNA shows the marker M89 associated with the population living in the Middle East, Jordan Valley. The other marker that follows M89 is the marker associated with today's Iran—M201. The ancestral journey which began in Africa ended in India. This DNA trail is similar to our passport with the visas of various places we have travelled to.

The inevitable question is, how come so many of the present-day non-Africans look so different? Like detectives, scientists have figured the reasons behind the amazing diversity among what can be called an African diaspora. Exposed as they were to a great variety of environments—from extremely hot to extremely cold, dry to humid over the millennia, their body shapes, skin colors and everything that now identifies someone as African or Caucasian or Mongoloid was transformed.

Extra doses of melanin make the skin black and also protect it from the sun's ultraviolet radiation. As the skin also needs sunlight to make vitamin D people in Northern Europe lost melanin to open the skin pores to sunlight (hence their fairer complexion). The African diaspora that ended up settling in India travelled through different routes undergoing various transformations under the impact of different environments. But that does not alter the fact that 99% of all our DNA is exactly the same as that of our common African parents.

KANNADA ALPHABETS

Vowels and Vowel Diacritics with ka

ಅ	ಆ	ಇ	ಈ	ಉ	ಊ	ಋ	ೠ
ಕ	ಕಾ	ಕಿ	ಕೀ	ಕು	ಕೂ	ಕೃ	ಕೄ
a	ā	i	ī	u	ū	ṛ	ṝ
[a]	[a:]	[i]	[i:]	[u]	[u:]	[rɨ/ru]	[rɨ:/ru:]

ಎ	ಏ	ಐ	ಒ	ಓ	ಔ	ಅಂ	ಅಃ
ಕೆ	ಕೇ	ಕೈ	ಕೊ	ಕೋ	ಕೌ	ಕಂ	ಕಃ
e	ē	ai	o	ō	au	aṃ	aḥ
[e]	[e:]	[ai]	[o]	[o:]	[au]	[aŋ]	[ah]

Consonants

ಕ	ಖ	ಗ	ಘ	ಙ	ಚ	ಛ	ಜ	ಝ	ಞ
ka	kha	ga	gha	ṅa	ca	cha	ja	jha	ña
[ka]	[k^{h}a]	[ga]	[g^{ɦ}a]	[ŋa]	[ʧa]	[ʧ^{h}a]	[ʤa]	[ʤ^{ɦ}a]	[ɲa]

ಟ	ಠ	ಡ	ಢ	ಣ	ತ	ಥ	ದ	ಧ	ನ
ṭa	ṭha	ḍa	ḍha	ṇa	ta	tha	da	dha	na
[ʈa]	[ʈ^{h}a]	[ɖa]	[ɖ^{ɦ}a]	[ɳa]	[ta]	[t^{h}a]	[da]	[d^{ɦ}a]	[na]

ಪ	ಫ	ಬ	ಭ	ಮ	ಯ	ರ	ಲ	ವ
pa	pha	ba	bha	ma	ya	ra	la	va
[pa]	[p^{h}a]	[ba]	[b^{ɦ}a]	[ma]	[ja]	[ra]	[la]	[ʋa]

ಶ	ಷ	ಸ	ಹ	ಳ	ಕ್ಷ	ಜ್ಞ
śa	ṣa	sa	ha	ḷa	kśa	jna
[ɕa]	[ʂa]	[sa]	[ha]	[ɭa]	[kʂa]	[ʤna]

An Example of Conjunct Consonants

ಕ್ಕ	ಖ್ಖ	ಗ್ಗ	ಚ್ಚ	ಟ್ಟ	ತ್ತ	ತ್ರ	ಥ್ಯ	ದ್ದ	ನ್ನ
kka	khkha	gga	cca	ṭṭa	tta	tra	thya	dda	nna
ಬ್ಬ	ಮ್ಮ	ರ್ರ	ರ್ತ	ಲ್ಲ	ಳ್ಳ	ಸ್ಥ	ಸ್ಪ	ಸ್ವ	ಹ್ಹ
bba	mma	rra	rta	lla	ḷḷa	stha	spa	sva	hha

Numerals

೧	೨	೩	೪	೫	೬	೭	೮	೯	೧೦
ಒಂದು	ಎರಡು	ಮೂರು	ನಾಲ್ಕು	ಐದು	ಆರು	ಏಳು	ಎಂಟು	ಒಂಬತ್ತು	ಹತ್ತು
oṃdu	eraḍu	mūru	nālku	aidu	āru	ēḷu	eṃṭu	oṃbattu	hattu
1	2	3	4	5	6	7	8	9	10

The above Kannada numerals are taken from the conjunct consonants of *gga*, *tta*, *nna*, *lla*, *shya*, *mma*, *yya*, *kru*, and *rra*.

10

Kannada

About Kannada Language

Kannada **language** is one of the four major Dravidian languages of South India. According to the Dravidian scholars Bhadriraju Krishnamurti and Kamil Zvelebil around 800-600 BC. Kannada and Tamil split into two separate independent languages from the Proto-Tamil-Kannada subgroup.

The Ashoka rock edict dated to 230 BC found at Brahmagiri suggests that it contained words recognizable in Kannada language.

The research about the antiquity of Kannada language has recorded that the earliest copper plates inscribed in Old Kannada script dated to early 800 AD and the oldest palm leaf manuscript in Old Kannada Dhavala dated to 900 AD has been discovered. The oldest Kannada inscription dated 450 AD was discovered at Halmidi.

The writing practice of Kannada is found in various places. It is reported that Old Kannada *Nishadi* inscription dated 350-400 AD is discovered on the Chandragiri hill, Shravanabelagola. Approximately 450 AD a full-length Kannada language stone inscription (*shila shaasana*) comprising Brahmi characters with characteristics credited to Old Kannada script is found in the Halmidi inscription; Tamatekallu inscription of Chitradurga, the Chikkamagaluru inscription of 500 AD are found.

Writing

The Kannada script evolved from southern varieties of the Ashokan Brahmi script. The original script went through several ramifications.

In Kannada the word order is subject-object-verb like in any other Dravidian languages. The language uses typical Dravidian retroflex consonants (sounds pronounced with the tip of the tongue curled back against the roof of the mouth), such as *d*, *n*, and *t*.

There are three types of genders in Kannada: Masculine, Feminine, and Neutral.

Kannada language uses forty-nine phonemic letters, divided into three groups: sixteen vowels (*swara*); thirty six consonants (*vyanjana*) (includes two letters: *anusvara* ಂ and *visarga* ಃ). The character set is virtually identical to other Indian languages. The script is derived from Brahmi script and various combinations of "half-letters" (glyphs) or symbols attached to several letters appear.

Sanskrit and Prakrit have influenced Kannada language significantly on its phonetics, morphology, vocabulary, grammar and syntax.

Kadamba script was developed during the reign of the Kadambas between 400 and 600 AD.

The influence on Kannada grammar appears to be three-fold; *Panini's* grammar, *Kaatantra* and Shakarayana's *Saskatayana* grammar, and Prakrit grammar. Some examples of naturalized derived words of Prakrit origin in Kannada are *baṇṇa* derived from *vaṇṇa*, *arasu* and from Sanskrit, *varṇa*, *hunnime*, *puṇṇivā*, *paurṇimā*, *rāya* from *rāja*. Kannada has numerous borrowed identical words such as *dina*, *kopa*, *surya*, *mukha*, *nimiṣa*, *etc.*

The earlier grammatical works include portions of *Kavirajamarga* of 900 AD and Kavyavalokana and Karnataka *Bhashabhushana*, both written by Nagavarma II in 1200 AD. The most significant work of Kannada grammar is Keshiraja's *Shabdamanidarpana* written in 1260 AD.

William Reeve from London Missionary Socity compiled an early dictionary of the Kannada language, and translated Bible into Kannada with the co-author John. The dictionary was compiled from 1827 to 1834, when he was in Bangalore.

Though William Reeve compiled and published Kannada-English dictionary, another German priest Ferdinand Kittel compiled the first improved Kannada-English dictionary containing about 70,000 words in 1894. Kittel also wrote a book on Kannada grammar entitled *A Grammar of the Kannada Language* in English.

Kannada Professor G. Venkatasubbaiah has compiled and edited more than 10 dictionaries including the first modern *Kannada-Kannada Nighantu* (Kannada-Kannada Dictionary) in 1995. He also wrote a Kannada-English dictionary and a *kliṣtapadakōśa* (a dictionary of complex Kannada words) a dictionary of difficult words. It is a unique kind in Kannada language which covers different language specifications like word derivation, punctuation, phoneme and morphological patterns of Kannada language developed over the centuries.

Dialects

There is a considerable difference between the spoken forms of languages in Karnataka region and varies from region to region. Some examples are Kundagannada, Nadavar-Kannada, Havigannada, Are Bhashe, Malenadu Kannada, Soliga, Gulbarga Kannada, Dharawad Kannada, etc. All of these dialects are influenced by their regional and cultural background. Tribal langauges Badaga, Betta kurumba, Irula, Vagari, Toda, Koraga, Kota, Belari also exist.

Influence of Other Languages

Kannada has been influenced in a large degree by Sanskrit. Influences of other languages such as Prakrit and Pali also are found in Kannada language. Some foreign words are

Persian: rasta=raste>road; shumar=sumaru>approximately; shipharas=shipharasu>influence; dasavej=dastaveju>document; sibbandi=sibbandi>staff; sipayi=sipayi>soldier; jamin=jaminu>land; gumasta=gumasta>clerk, etc.

Arabic: anamat=anamattu>all together; japti>search; najuk=najuku>delicate; mamul=mamuli>as usual or bribe; daptar=daptaru>file; savkar=sahukara>rich man; chaku=chaku>knife.

Many of these words usually occur in Tamil, Telugu and Kannada. Persian and Arabic words are found in many ancient literary works of Kannada such as *Shabdamanidarpana* by Keshiraja, *Basavapurana* by Bheemakavi, *Chennabasavapurana* by Virupaksha Pandita, and *Jaimini Bharatha* by Lakshmeesha.

Development of Language by Literary Works

Three stages in the development of Kannada language are recognized: Old Kannada (Halagannada) from 450-1200 AD; Middle Kannada (Nadugannada) from 1200-1700 AD; and Modern Kannada (Navya) from 1700 AD-present.

Kannada literature began with the *Kavirajamarga* by Nripatunga in 900 AD followed by Pampa's *Bharata* in 941 AD. The earliest grammar is by Nagavarma II of early 1200 AD. *Kavirajamarga* is the earliest literary work in Kannada. It is a guide book for poets and scholars to standardize the writing styles.

Old Kannada 450-1200 AD: (Halagannada) was the language of Banavasi in Uttara Karanatka during the Satavahana and Kadamba periods.

Kappe Arabhatta was a Chalukya warrior of the 800 AD who carved stanzas on a cliff in Badami, Karnataka. The inscription consists of five stanzas written out in ten lines in Kannada script. It demonstrates nine Sanskrit words out of twelve words in Kannada. It is the oldest record of Kannada poetry in tripadi meter.

Vaddaradhane by Shivakoti Acharya dated 900 AD the earliest existing prose work in Kannada provides a detailed description of the life of Bhadrabahu of Shravanabelagola. Even though the work is estimated to be 9th century, some scholars argue that the work is pre-sixth century.

Next generation of Kannada literature with new forms of composition are Ragale and rhythms like Sangatya and Shatpadi appeared in 1200-1300 AD. The works of this period are centered on Jain and Hindu ideologies. Two noted writers of this period are Harihara and Raghavanka. A famous Jain writer of the same period is Janna who also expressed Jain religious philosophies.

In 1200 AD, the Vachana Sahitya contributed a great deal of Kannada literature to spread social reforms among all sections of society. Basavanna, Allama Prabhu and Akka Mahadevi are the important writers in this tradition. They started an awareness by creating an atmosphere for social revolution which caused to rethink the ideas of caste, creed and religious convictions.

Middle Kannada (Nadugannada): 1200-1700 AD between the 1500 and 1800 AD, literature in Middle Kannada language flourished. Kumara Vyasa, the most influential Kannada writer wrote the *Karnataka Bharata Kathamanjari* in Bhamini Shatpadi (hexa-meter).

Religious mystics such as Kanakadasa, Purandaradasa, Vyasatirtha, Sripadaraya, Vadiraja, Vijaya Dasa, and Jagannatha Dasa produced devotional poems in this period in Kannada. Kanakadasa's *Ramadhanya Charite* is a book concerning the issues of class struggle. In this period Haridasa literature made rich contribution to Carnatic music also.

Modern Kannada (Hosagannada) 1800 AD-present: 1900 AD onwards a gradual transition occurred and paved way to Hosagannada or Modern Kannada. Most notable poet Nanda-like Muddana started writing in modern Kannada, a different form of Nadugannada. Some linguists argue that Indira Bai or Gulvadi Venkata Raya are the first writers in Modern Kannada.

The first printing in Kannada appeared in 1817 when *Canarese Grammar* of William Carey printed at Serampore and the *Bible in Canarese* by John Hands in 1820.

Navodaya, Navya, Navyottara, Dalita and Bandaya literature are the versions of modern Kannada in the 2000 AD influenced by many movements. Kannada has produced a number of poets and writers such as Kuvempu, Bendre, and V.K. Gokak.

As an example Kannada script has taken to show how the scripts develop over a period of time.

KADAMBA SCRIPT—500 AD

ADI GANGA SCRIPT—400-600 AD

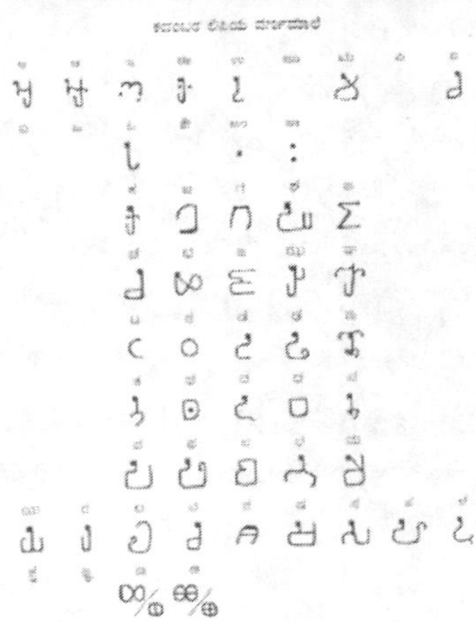

BADAMI CHALUKYA SCRIPT—600-700 AD

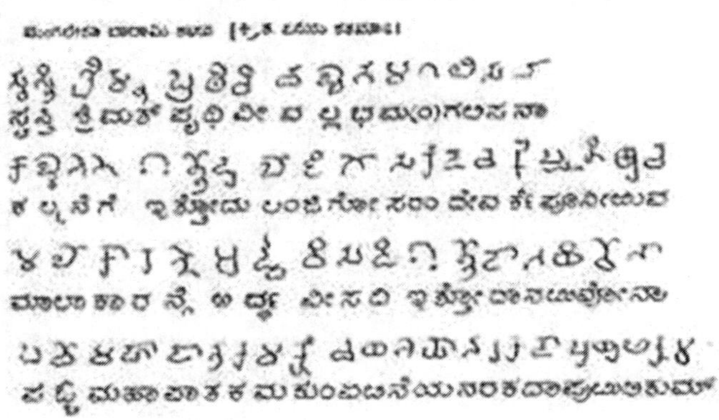

RASTRAKUTA SCRIPT—800-1000 AD

ರಾಷ್ಟ್ರಕೂಟರ ಲಿಪಿಯ ವರ್ಣಮಾಲೆ

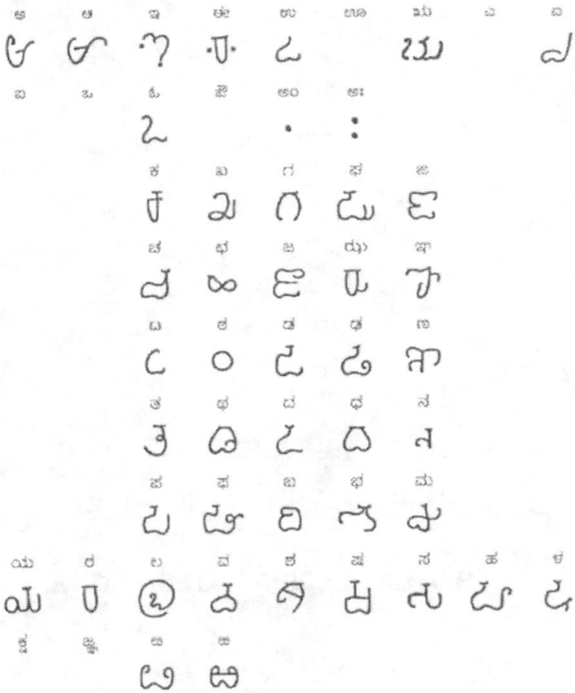

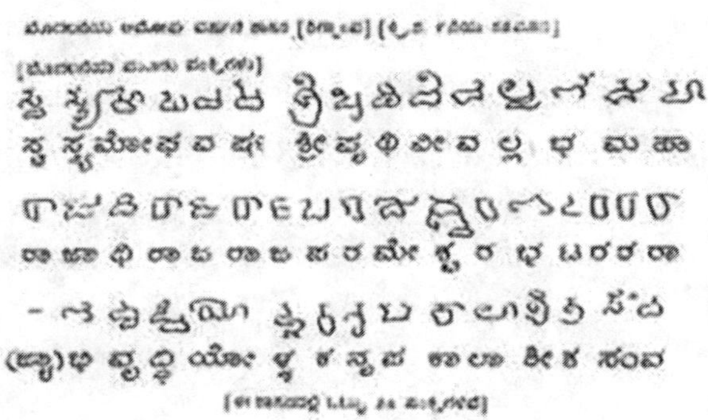

KALYANA CHALUKYA SCRIPT—1000-1200 AD

ಕಲ್ಯಾಣ ಚಾಲುಕ್ಯರ ಲಿಪಿಯ ವರ್ಣಮಾಲೆ

HOYSALA SCRIPT—1300 AD

ಹೊಯ್ಸಳರ ಲಿಪಿಯ ವರ್ಣಮಾಲೆ

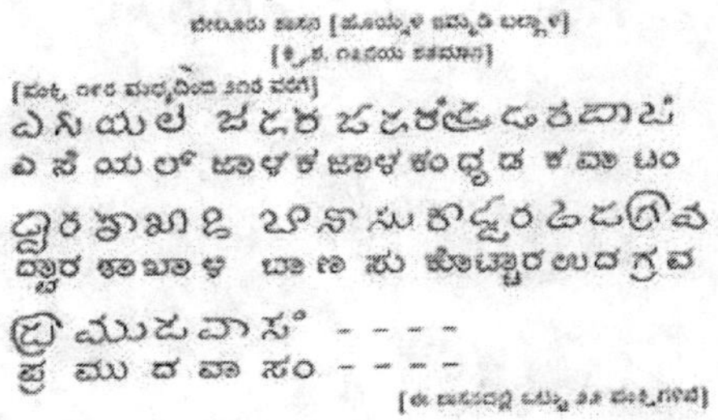

VIJAYANAGARA SCRIPT—1600 AD

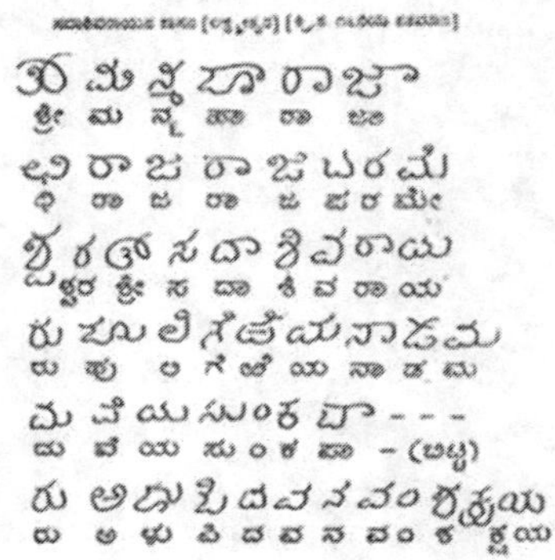

MODI SCRIPT—1900 AD

ಮೈಸೂರು ಒಡೆಯರ ಕಾಲದ ಲಿಪಿಯ ವರ್ಣಮಾಲೆ

ಚಿತ್ರ - 63 : ಕೋಲಾರದ [illegible] ಕ್ರಿ.ಶ. 1933

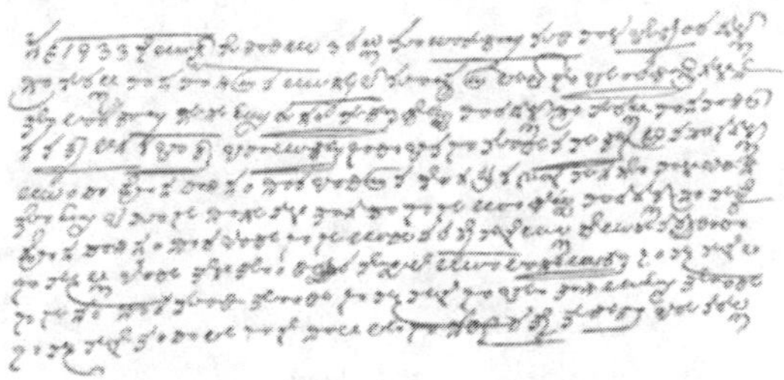

11

Tamil Alphabets

Vowels and Vowel Diacritics

அ	ஆ	இ	ஈ	உ	ஊ
a	ā	i	ī	u	ū
[ʌ]	[a:]	[i]	[i:]	[u,ɯ]	[u:]
எ	ஏ	ஐ	ஒ	ஓ	ஔ
e	ē	ai	o	ō	au
[e]	[e:]	[ʌy]	[o]	[o:]	[ʌʊ]

ப	பா	பி	பீ	பு	பூ	
pa	pā	pi	pī	pu	pū	
பெ	பே	பை	பொ	போ	பௌ	ப்
pe	pē	pai	po	pō	pau	p

Consonants

க	k [k, g, x, ɣ, h]	த	t [t̪, d̪, ð]	ல	l [l]	ஜ	j [ʤ]
ங	ṅ [ŋ]	ந	n [n̪]	வ	v [ʋ]	ஷ	ṣ [ʂ]
ச	c [ʧ, ʤ, ʃ, s]	ப	p [p, b, β]	ழ	ẓ, ḷ, ṛ [ɻ]	ஸ	s [s]
ஞ	ñ [ɲ]	ம	m [m]	ள	ḷ [ɭ]	ஹ	h [h]
ட	ṭ [ʈ, ɖ, ɽ]	ய	y [j]	ற	ṟ, R [r, t, d]	க்ஷ	kṣ [kʂ]
ண	ṇ [ɳ]	ர	r [ɾ]	ன	ṉ, N [n]		

ஃ = āytam - turns p into f and j into z, e.g. ஃபீ fi [fi:] ஃஜி zi [zi]

Numerals

௦	௧	௨	௩	௪	௫	௬
பூச்சியம்	ஒன்று	இரண்டு	மூன்று	நான்கு	ஐந்து	ஆறு
pūcciyam	o<u>n</u><u>r</u>u	iraṇṭu	mū<u>n</u><u>r</u>u	naaṉku	aintu	ā<u>r</u>u
0	1	2	3	4	5	6

௭	௮	௯	௰	௱	௲
ஏழு	எட்டு	ஒன்பது	பத்து	நூறு	எந்
ē<u>l</u>u	ettu	o<u>n</u>patu	pattu	nū<u>r</u>u	en
7	8	9	10	100	1000

Apart from the usual numeric figures, symbols for day, month, year, debit, credit, as above, rupee, and numeral are also available in Tamil language.

day	month	year	debit	credit	as above	rupee	numeral
௳	௴	௵	௶	௷	௸	௹	௺

Tamil Grantha Script

The glyphs below denote the later type of Tamil Grantha Script emerged from the Brahmi Script, which can be noticed by its similarity with the Modern Tamil Script.

Vowels

𑌅	𑌆	𑌇	𑌈	𑌉	𑌊
a	ā	i	ī	u	ū

𑌋	𑍠	𑌌	𑍡
ṛ	ṝ	ḷ	ḹ

𑌏	𑌐	𑌓	𑌔
e	ai	o	au

𑌂	𑌃
ṁ	ḥ

Consonants

TAMIL

About Tamil Language

Tamil language is a member of Dravidian language family. According to some findings, the earliest Tamil writing is found in the inscriptions from 500 BC.

Tamil descended from Proto-Dravidian language. Linguists suggest that the Proto-Dravidian was spoken around the 300 BC near lower Godavari river basin in southern India.

The earliest reference to write Tamil language is found in the Jain work Samavayanga Sutta in 300 BC and Pannavana Sutta in 168 BC.

According to Iravatham Mahadevan, Brahmī script reached the Tamil region due the southern spread of Jainism and Buddhism from North India and was adapted to match the Tamil phonetic system.

Writing

Like in other Dravidian languages, Tamil is also characterized by retroflex consonants *d*, *n*, and *t* made by curling the tip of the tongue back to the roof of the mouth. Structurally, Tamil is a subject-object-verb language. The Tamil script consists of 12 vowels, 18 consonants and one special character, the *āytam* (this old phoneme (ஃ) does not exist now). All consonants have an inherent vowel '*a*' as with other Indian scripts. In some places this inherency is eliminated in Tamil by adding a *puḷḷi* or a dot over a consonant. For example, ன is *n̲a* (with the inherent *a*) and ன் is *n̲* (without a vowel), which produces half sound.

Tamil vowels are called *uyirel̲uttu* (*uyir* = life + *el̲uttu* = letter). The vowels are classified into short *kur̲il* (neck) and long *neṭil* (head) with each five vowels and two diphthongs, *ai* and *au*.

Tamil consonants are known as *meyyel̲uttu* (*mey* = body + *el̲uttu* = letters).

The Tamil writing system evolved from the Brahmī script. The contour of the letters changed tremendously over a period of time, gradually stabilizing when printing was introduced in the 1600 AD. The main appendage to the alphabet was the integration of Grantha[1] letters to write unassimilated Sanskrit words. A script known as Vatteluttu "Round Script" was also in use.

Oldest known grammar book *Tolkāppiyam* describes the Tamil grammar extensively. Modern Tamil writing is mainly

1. Grantha is used to write a number of the Dravidian languages indigenous to southern India. The script has 35 letters, five of them vowels, and is written from left to right. Originally, it was used for writing Sanskrit, Grantha alphabet is a writing system of southern India developed in the 500 AD. The earliest inscriptions in Grantha dating from the 500-600 AD are on copper plates from the kingdom of the Pallavas (near modern Madras). The form of the alphabet used in these inscriptions classified as Early Grantha is seen primarily on copper plates and stone monuments. Middle Grantha, the form of the script used from 700-800 AD is also known from inscriptions on copper and stone. The script used from the 900-1400 AD is called Transitional Grantha. From 1300 onwards, the modern script has been in use.

based on the 1300 grammar *Nannul* which reiterated and simplified the rules of the *Tolkappiyam* with some modifications.

Dialects

Spoken Tamil has been transformed substantially over a time incorporating the changes in the phonological structure of words. This has created diglossia, the coexistence of two varieties of the same language. Often, one form is the literary or prestige dialect and other is a common dialect spoken by most of the people, a system where there is a difference between colloquial and formal/written contexts.

Tamil spoken in Kanyakumari District has more unique words and phonetic style than Tamil spoken in other parts of Tamil Nadu. Spoken Tamil tends to vary from region to region. Some examples are: Hebbar and Mandyam dialects spoken by Vaishnavites who migrated to Karnataka in the 100 AD preserve many characteristics of the Vaishnava Paribashai, a special form of Tamil developed in the 900 and 1000 AD. Tamil in Sri Lanka includes loan words from Portuguese, Dutch and English.

Influence of Other Languages

A large number of words used in classical and modern Tamil are borrowed from the languages from the countries with whom the Tamils kings had trade links such as Munda Malay Chinese, and Greek, etc. Tamil has also imported words from Urdu and Marathi, which influenced the Tamil at various points of time and from neighboring languages such as Telugu, Kannada, and Sinhala. In modern period, several words have been adapted from European languages such as Portuguese, French and English.

Development of Language by Literary Works

Scholars have distinguished three periods analyzing grammatical and lexical changes in Tamil language. They are Old Tamil from 450 BC to 700 AD, Middle Tamil from 700 to 1600 A.D, and Modern Tamil from 1600 onwards.

Inscriptions found on stone have been dated to 300 BC Famous literary works of the 400 to 600 AD include the epics *Cilappatikaram*, *Manimekalai* and the *Tirukkuraḷ*, a collection of essays on love, kinship, and ethics. In 600 to 900 AD the Alvars and Nayanars produced a huge amount of Tamil literature by composing devotional poetry and hymns to spread Vaisnava and Saiva devotional movement. From 1200-1600 AD many philosophical essays and compilation of religious mythologies were composed. From 1900 AD onwards Tamil literature was gradually influenced by Western thoughts and ideas.

Old Tamil: The earliest records in Old Tamil are short inscriptions around 200 BC found in caves and on pottery. These inscriptions are written in modified form of Brahmi script called Tamil Brahmī. The earliest text in Old Tamil is the *Tolkappiyam*, an early work on Tamil grammar and poetry. These compositions are known as Sangam literature. Scholars estimate that these poems are dated approximately between 100 and 500 AD. Other literary works in Old Tamil consist of *Thirukural*, a book of law. *Silappatikaram*, a non-religious story having moralistic connotation, and *Maṇimēkalai*, a story that provides information on the history of Tamil Nadu, Buddhism and its status during that period, contemporary arts and culture, and customs of that period. A number of other ethical and moral texts were written between 500 and 800 AD.

Middle Tamil: It is found that the evolution of Old Tamil into Middle Tamil was completed by the 800 AD and was categorized by a number of phonological and grammatical changes.

Middle Tamil was also influenced by Sanskrit. From the period of the Pallava dynasty a number of Sanskrit loanwords entered Tamil, mainly in relation to religious, political, and philosophical notions.

Tamil Brahmi and Vaṭṭeḻuttu were the main scripts used in Old Tamil inscriptions. Pallavas began using a new script, derived from the Pallava Grantha script used to write Sanskrit, which eventually replaced Vaṭṭeḻuttu.

In the 1200 AD *Tamil Ramayana* was composed by Kamban. *Naṉṉūl,* a 1200 AD grammar, became the standard grammar of literary Tamil.

Modern Tamil: The Nannul remains the standard grammar for modern literary Tamil. Interaction with European languages affected both written and spoken Tamil. Changes in written Tamil include the use of European-style punctuation. A great pressure of linguistic purism surfaced in the early 2000 AD concluding in the Pure Tamil Movement, which insisted removal of all Sanskrit and other external components from Tamil. As a result, considerable number of Sanskrit loanwords were replaced by Tamil equivalents, although some Sanskrit words still are in use.

12

Telugu Alphabets

Vowels

అ	ఆ	ఇ	ఈ	ఉ	ఊ	ఋ
a	ā	i	ī	u	ū	ṛ
[ʌ]	[a:]	[i]	[i:]	[u]	[u:]	[ri/ru]

ౠ	ఎ	ఏ	ఐ	ఒ	ఓ	ఔ
ṝ	e	ē	ai	o	ō	au
[ri:, ru:]	[e]	[e:]	[aj]	[o]	[o:]	[aw]

Vowel diacritics

క	కా	కి	కీ	కు	కూ	కృ
ka	kā	ki	kī	ku	kū	kṛ

కౄ	కె	కే	కై	కొ	కో	కౌ
kṝ	ke	kē	kai	ko	kō	kau

Consonants

క	ఖ	గ	ఘ	ఙ	చ	ఛ	జ	ఝ	ఞ
ka	kha	ga	gha	ṅa	ca	cha	ja	jha	ña
[kʌ]	[kʰʌ]	[gʌ]	[gʱʌ]	[ŋʌ]	[tʃʌ]	[tʃʰʌ]	[dʒʌ]	[dʒʱʌ]	[ɲʌ]

ట	ఠ	డ	ఢ	ణ	త	థ	ద	ధ	న
ṭa	ṭha	ḍa	ḍha	ṇa	ta	tha	da	dha	na
[ʈʌ]	[ʈʰʌ]	[ɖʌ]	[ɖʱʌ]	[ɳʌ]	[tʌ]	[tʰʌ]	[dʌ]	[dʱʌ]	[nʌ]

ప	ఫ	బ	భ	మ	య	ర	ల	వ	ళ
pa	pha	ba	bha	ma	ya	ra	la	va	ḷa
[pʌ]	[pʰʌ]	[bʌ]	[bʱʌ]	[mʌ]	[jʌ]	[rʌ]	[lʌ]	[ʋʌ]	[ɭʌ]

శ	ష	స	హ
śa	ṣa	sa	ha
[ɕʌ]	[ʂʌ]	[sʌ]	[hʌ]

Numerals

౧	౨	౩	౪	౫	౬	౭	౮	౯	౧౦
ఒకటి	రెండు	మూడు	నాలుగు	ఐదు	ఆరు	ఏడు	ఎనిమిది	తొమ్మిది	పది
okaṭi	reṅḍu	mūḍu	nālugu	aidu	āru	ēḍḍu	enimidi	tommidi	padi
1	2	3	4	5	6	7	8	9	10

TELUGU LANGUAGE

About Telugu Language

According to the Russian linguist M.S. Andronov, Telugu split from Proto-Dravidian languages between 1500-1000 BC.

Linguists have identified that some Telugu words exist in an anthology of poems *Gatha Saptashati* in Maharashtri Prakrit preserved by the 100 BC Satavahana King Hala.

It has been recorded that inscriptions comprising Telugu words dated 400 BC were discovered in Bhattiprolu in Guntur district.

Another inscription dated 575 AD was found in the Rayalaseema area and it is credited to the Renati Cholas. Cholas broke the existing custom of using Sanskrit and began writing royal declaration in the local language.

Writing

Telugu script is written from left to right. Syllables are constituted of vowels '*achchu*' or '*swaram*' and consonants '*hallu*' or '*vyanjanam*'. It is customary to write and read consonants with an inherent vowel *a*. The language consists of 14 vowels and 34 consonants. Telugu has its own digits.

Telugu words generally end in vowels similar to Pali language. In the modern language words may end with *m, n, y, w*.

The first dissertation on Telugu grammar, the *Andhra Sabda Chintamani* was written in Sanskrit by Nannayya. This grammar followed the patterns existed in *Aṣṭādhyāy* and *Vālmīki vyākaranam*. Nannayya divided his work into five parts comprising *samjnā*, *sandhi*, *ajanta*, *halanta* and *kriya*. Every Telugu grammatical rule is derived from Pāṇinian concepts. Nannayya was considered as the first Telugu poet and translator in the 1100 AD.

Dialects

Dialects of Telugu are Berad, Dasari, Dommara, Golari, Kamathi, Komtao, Konda-Reddi, Salewari, Telangana, Warangal, Mahaboobnagar (Palamuru), Gadwal (Rayalaseema mix), Narayanapeta (Kannada and Marathi influence), Vijayawada, Vadaga, Srikakulam, Visakhapatnam, Toorpu (East) Godavari, Paschima (West) Godavari, Kandula, Rayalaseema, Nellooru, Prakasam, Gunturu, Tirupati, Vadari and Yanadi (Yenadi).

Influence of Other Languages

The vocabulary of Telugu particularly in Telangana region has a repository of Persian-Arabic loanwords, which have been modified to match Telugu phonology. Words such as kaburu, javabu, etc. are found in Telugu. This is because of a prolonged Muslim rule in this region.

Development of Language by Literary Works

Telugu was influenced by Sanskrit and Prakrit. Initially, Telugu literature was found on inscriptions and poetry in the courts of the kings, and later in written works of Nannayya's *Mahabharatam* (1022 AD).

Middle Ages: During the middle period, the Telugu and Kannada scripts were separated. In the 1600 AD, during the reign of Krishnadevaraja in Vijayanagara Empire, Telugu literature experienced golden age. Annamacharya, contributed many Telugu songs during this period.

Literature is generally divided into six periods in Telugu history.

Nannaya's (1022-63 AD) translation of the Sanskrit Mahabharata into Telugu has been considered as the earliest work of Telugu literature. Nannaya died while working on the 3rd canto aranya parvam in Mahabharath. Later Tikkana of 1300 AD and Yerrapragada of 1400 AD continued and completed the translation of the Mahabharata started by Nannaya.

Later some Telugu poets translated Sanskrit poems and dramas to Telugu and others wrote original composition of poems. Srinatha (1365-1441) popularized Prabandha style by composing *Sringara Naishadham*.

The earliest translation of Ramayana in Telugu *Ranganatha Ramayana* was written by Gona Buddha Reddy. Pothana, Jakkana and Gaurana of 1400-1500 AD standardized the religious poetry. Annamayya composed many Telugu songs in this period.

Dravidian Languages

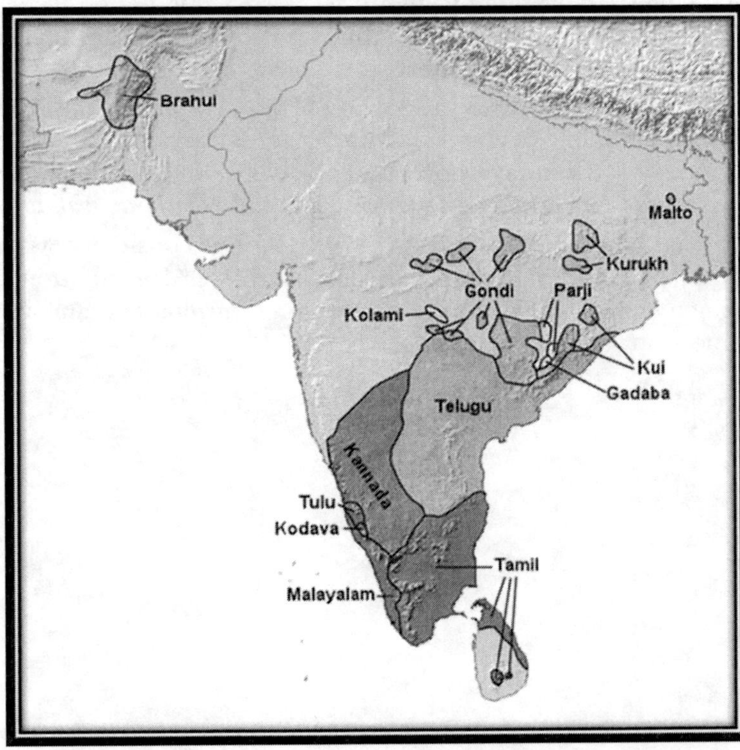

Distribution of subgroups of Dravidian languages:

North
Central
South-Central
South

Courtesy: Wikipedia Common

The 16th and 17th centuries are considered as Golden Age in Telugu literature. Krishnadevaraya's *Amukthamalayadha*, and Pedhdhana's *Manucharithra* are considered as masterpieces. Telugu literature also boomed in the southern parts such as Madurai and Tanjore. Tyagaraja's composed devotional songs in this period.

From 1850 AD a new era of transition emerged. Europeans like C.P. Brown played a significant part in the development of Telugu language and literature. During this period Telugu literature was increasingly influenced by European literary methods such as novel, short story, prose and drama.

Paravastu Chinnayya Soori (1807-61) wrote the *Bala Vyakaranam* in a new style for Andhra grammar. Other popular writings by Chinnayasoori are *Neethichandrika*, *Sootandhra Vyaakaranamu*, *Andhra Dhatumoola*, and *Neeti Sangrahamu*.

Kandukuri Veeresalingam (1848-1919) is considered as the father of Andhra Renaissance because of his contribution to Telugu literature. His novel *Rajasekhara Charitamu* became very famous in Telugu language.

13

Malayalam Alphabets

Vowels

അ	ആ	ഇ	ഈ	ഉ	ഊ	ഋ
a	ā	i	ī	u	ū	r̥
[a]	[aː]	[i]	[iː]	[u]	[uː]	[rɨ]

എ	ഏ	ഐ	ഒ	ഓ	ഔ
e	ē	ai	o	ō	au
[e]	[eː]	[ai̯]	[o]	[oː]	[au̯]

Consonants

ക	ഖ	ഗ	ഘ	ങ	ച	ഛ	ജ	ഝ	ഞ
ka	kha	ga	gha	ña	ca	cha	ja	jha	ña
[ka]	[kʰa]	[ga]	[gʱa]	[ŋa]	[ʧa]	[ʧʰa]	[ʤa]	[ʤʱa]	[ɲa]

ട	ഠ	ഡ	ഢ	ണ	ത	ഥ	ദ	ധ	ന
ṭa	ṭha	ḍa	ḍha	ṇa	ta	tha	da	dha	na
[ʈa]	[ʈʰa]	[ɖa]	[ɖʱa]	[ɳa]	[t̪a]	[t̪ʰa]	[d̪a]	[d̪ʱa]	[na, n̪a]

പ	ഫ	ബ	ഭ	മ	യ	ര	ല	വ
pa	pha	ba	bha	ma	ya	ra	la	va
[pa]	[pʰa]	[ba]	[bʱa]	[ma]	[ja]	[ɾa]	[la]	[ʋa]

ശ	ഷ	സ	ഹ	ള	ഴ	റ
śa	ṣa	sa	ha	ḷa	ḻa	ṟa
[ɕa]	[ʃa]	[sa]	[ɦa]	[ɭa]	[ɻa]	[ra]

Chillus / cillakṣaram (ചില്ലക്ഷരം)

ൺ	ൻ	ർ	ൽ	ൾ	ൿ
ṇ	n	r	l	ḷ	k
[ɳ]	[n]	[r]	[l]	[ɭ]	[k]

A *chillaksharam* represents consonants independently. These consonants are never followed by an inherent vowel.

Numerals

Vatteluttu

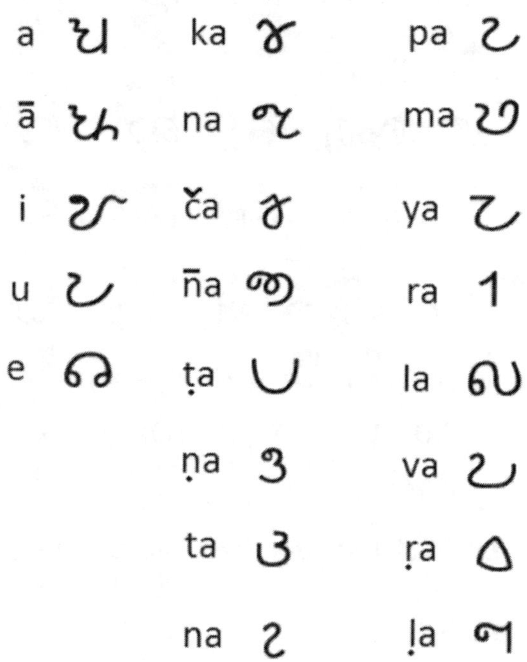

MALAYALAM LANGUAGE

About Malayalam Language

Malayalam language is a member of the family of Dravidian language mainly spoken in Kerala state of India.

There are several outlooks about the origin of Malayalam word. The first hypothesis says it originated from words *mala* meaning hill, and *alam* meaning region implying 'Hill Region' which later became the name of the language. Another hypothesis is that *mala* means Hill and '*alam* or *azham*' means deep or basin or valley or dale implying that a region below. Hill and dale. Ironically, Malayalam region is situated between Western Mountains and basin of Arabian Sea in western India. Gradually, the name of the region Malayalam transformed into Malayalam language.

An inscription dated approximately 830 AD is found in the area. It is asserted that Malayalam originated from Middle Tamil in the 600 AD.

Malayalam absorbed many components from Sanskrit for a long period of time and now it is estimated eighty percent of the vocabulary in scholarly usage of Malayalam is from Sanskrit.

Writing

Historically, several scripts were used to write Malayalam language. Among these scripts Vattezhuthu and Kolezhuthu were mainly used. Koleluttu means Rod Script derived from the Grantha script, which originated from Brahmi script. Koleluttu has letters to represent both Dravidian and Sanskrit sounds.

The earliest script used to write Malayalam was the Vatteluttu (round) script. As Malayalam progressed, it followed the rules of grammar from Sanskrit. Grantha script was accepted for writing and it was known as *Arya Ezhuttu*. Eventually, Grantha script, another Southern Brahmi variant gave rise to the modern Malayalam script.

Like other Dravidian langauges, Malayalam has retroflex consonants *d*, *n* and *t* pronounced by curling the tip of the tongue back to the roof of the mouth. It uses subject-object-verb word combination. It has a natural gender system, a method that represents the gender of humans masculine or feminine and all nonhuman nouns as neuter.

Malayalam alphabet has the largest number of letters because of its derivation of letters from both Sanskrit and Tamil languages.

Linguists have estimated that the Malayalam script consists of 578 characters. The script contains 13 vowels and 36 consonants forming 576 syllabic characters. It also contains two additional diacritic characters named anusvāra and visarga.

Dialects

Malayalam language has developed diglossia to show the difference between the formal, literary and colloquial language forms of speech.

Dialects of Malayalam are unique to regional and social levels including professional and communal distinctions. The noticeable features of many varieties of tribal speech are the speech of Muthuvans, Malayarayas, Malai Ulladas, Kanikkars, Kadars, Paliyars, Kurumas, and Vedas as well as dialects of Dalits, Brahmins, Nairs, Ezhavas, Syrian Christians (Nasrani). The Latin Christian dialect of Malayalam is influenced by Latin, Portuguese and English. The Muslim dialect is very much influenced by Arabic and Urdu.

Influence of Other Languages

Loan words and influences of other languages also come from Hebrew, Syriac and Ladino words and found in the Jewish Malayalam dialects in addition to English, Portuguese, Syriac and Greek in the Christian dialects. Arabic and Persian components also dominate in the Muslim dialects. The Muslim dialect Mappila Malayalam is used in the Malabar region of Kerala and Beary bashe is used in the extreme northern part of Kerala.

Development of Language by Literary Works

Silappatikaram[1] was written by Chera (Kerala) prince Ilango Adigal and respected as a classic in Sangam literature.

A commentary on Chanakya's *Arthasastra* in 1300 AD is the earliest literary work in Malayalam. The poetical work *Vaisikatantram* is supposed to belong to the early 1400 AD.

1. It should be noted this book appears both in Tamil and Malayalam. It is because **Tamil** language was spoken during 500 BC to 500 AD in Tamil region, which included kingdoms of Chola, Pandya and Chera (alternatively Cheral or Kerala).

Between 1200 and 1300 AD *Ramacharitam*, an epic poem was written in Malayalam. In the later centuries, Pattu, a kind of song writing literature flourished. In this period a mixture of Malayalam and Sanskrit *manipravalam* poetry was written.

In the 16th and 17th centuries, Thunchaththu Ramanujan Ezhuthachan replaced Grantha-Malayalam script in place of Tamil Vattezhuttu. Ezhuthachan started an elaborate translation of the ancient epics *Adhyatma Ramayana* and *Mahabharata* into Malayalam.

Tulu Grantha-Script was used by Nambudiris community only. A German missionary Johann Ernst Hanxleden wrote a Grammar book called *Grantha Bhashayude Vyakaranam* in 1699. Then the Nambudiri language was called Grantha Bhasha.

Between 1815 and 1820 AD, the British under Lord Monroe and Macaulay began promoting the Nambudiri Malyalam written in Tulu-Grantha Script with majority of Sanskrit words. In 1819 Benjamin Bailey a British missionary introduced the first Malayalam types to print the Tulu-Grantha Alphabet.

Dr. Hermann Gundert (1814-93 AD), a German missionary and scholar learned the language from local teachers and contributed enormously to Malayalam literature and language. His major works are *Keralolpathi* (1843), *Pazhancholmala* (1845), *Malayalabhaasha Vyakaranam* (1851), *Paathamala* (1860) (the first Malayalam school textbook), *Kerala pazhama* (1868), the *Malayalam dictionary* (1872), *Malayalarajyam* (*Geography of Kerala*) (1879), the first Malayalam newspaper *Rajya Samacharam* (1847 June), Magazine *Paschimodayam* (1879). He also translated The Bible into Malayalam.

Doctrina Christam (meaning Christian doctrine) written by Henrique Henriques in Lingua Malabar Tamil is considered to be the first printed vernacular book in India.

It was during this period that Christian missionaries made their contribution to Malayalam by compiling dictionaries in the language, translating the Bible into simple prose.

Bibliography

Andronov, M.S. (2003). *A Comparative Grammar of the Dravidian Languages*, Publisher: Lincom GmbH.

Anwesa Bagchi, M.A. (Nov. 2007). *Postpositions in Bangla, Language in India.*

Bhatt, S.C., Gopal K. Bhargava (2006). *Land and People of Indian States and Union Territories,* Gyan Publishing House, New Delhi.

Facts about the World's Languages: An Encyclopedia of the World's Major Languages, Past and Present.

Fischer, Steven Roger (2002). *A History of Writing.* Reaktion Books Ltd., London.

Heine, Bernd and Tania Kuteva Reference (2002). *World Lexicon of Gramaticalization.* Press Syndicate of the University of Cambridge, UK.

Krishnamurthy, Bhadriraju (2003). *Dravidian Languages,* Press Syndicate of the University of Cambridge Pitt Building Trumpington Street, Cambridge, UK.

Kuiper, F.B.J. (1991). *Aryans in the Rig Veda*, Rodopi.

Lieberman, D.E. (1998). "Neandertal and Early Modern Human Mobility Patterns: Comparing Archaeologial and Anatomical Evidence," in *Neandertals and Modern Humans in Western Asia.* Ed. by T. Akazawa, K. Aoki, and O. Bar-Yosef. New York, Plenum.

Mahadevan, Iravatham (1998). January 17, 1998. *The Indus Script*, Interview by Site Producer Omar Khan.

"Marathi language, alphabet and pronunciation". Omniglot.com. Retrieved on 2013-05-09.

Poole, Geoff. Article on "Thinking about Language". Noam Chomsky (1928-), Institute Professor of Linguistics, MIT, USA.

The Hindu, *Brief History—Origin and Year,* Online edition of India's National Newspaper, Friday, Oct. 14, 2005.

Toshisada, Nishida. "Local Traditions and Cultural Transmission" (18, 13).

Zvelebil, Kamil (1975), Tamil Literature, Leiden: Brill.

——. (1990). *Dravidian Linguistics: An Introduction*, Pondicherry Institute of Linguistics and Culture.

http://books.google.com/books?id=TDCKdPpbFPAC&pg=PA161&source=gbs_toc_r&cad=4#v=onepage&q&f=false

http://sangampoemsinenglish.wordpress.com/about-sangam-literature

http://www.ancientscripts.com/modi.html

http://cal1.cn.huc.edu/aramaic_language.html

Appendices

Numbers

Numbers	English	German	French	Spanish	Italian	Hindi	Japanese
0	Zero	Null	zéro	cero	nullità	shoonya	zero
1	One	eins	un	uno	uno; una	ek	ichi
2	Two	zwei	deux	dos	due	do	ni
3	Three	drei	trois	tres	tre	theen; thria	san
4	Four	vier	quatre	cuatro	quattro	chaar	yon
5	Five	fünf	cinq	cinco	cinque	paanch	go
6	Six	sechs	six	seis	sei	chhuh	roku
7	Seven	sieben	sept	siete; cribar	sette	saath	nana
8	Eight	acht	huit	ocho	otto	aat; ashta	hachi
9	Nine	neun	neuf	nueve	nove	nau	kyuu
10	Ten	zehn	dix	diez	dieci	dus; das	juu
11	Eleven	elf	onze	once	undici	gyaruh	juu ichi
12	Twelve	zwölf	douze	doce	dodici	baaruh	juu ni
13	Thirteen	dreizehn	treize	trece	tredici	trayodash; theruh	juu san
14	Fourteen	vierzehn	quatroze	catorce	quattordici	chauduh	juu yon
15	Fifteen	fünfzehn	quinze	quince	quindici	pandruh	juu go
16	Sixteen	sechzehn	seize	dieciséis; dieciseis	sedici	soluh	juu roku
17	Seventeen	siebzehn	dix-sept	diecisiete	diciassette; diciasette	sattruh	juu nana
18	Eighteen	achtzehn	dix-huit	dieciocho	diciotto	attaruh	juu hachi
19	Nineteen	neunzehn	dix-neaf	diecinueve	diciannove	unnis	juu kyuu
20	Twenty	zwanzig	vingt	veinte	venti	bees	ni juu
21	Twenty one	einundzwanzig	vingt et un	veintiuno	ventuno	ikkis	nijuu ichi
22	Twenty two	zweiundzwanzig	vingt-deux	veintidós	ventidue	baayis	nijuu ni
23	Twenty three	dreiundzwanzig	vingt-trois	veintitrés	ventitré	theyis	nijuu san
24	Twenty four	vierundzwanzig	vingt-quatre	veinticuatro	ventiquattro	chaubis	nijuu yon
25	Twenty five	fünfundzwanzig	vingt-cinq	veinticinco	venticinque	pacchis	nijuu go
26	Twenty six	sechsundzwanzig	vingt-six	veintiséis	ventisei	chubbis	niju roku
27	Twenty seven	siebenundzwanzig	vingt-sept	veintisiete	ventisette	sattaayis	niju nana
28	Twenty eight	achtundzwanzig	vingt-huit	veintiocho	ventiotto	attaayis	niju hachi
29	Twenty nine	neunundzwanzig	vingt-neaf	veintinueve	ventinove	unthees	niju kyuu
30	Thirty	dreißig	trente	treinta	trenta	thees	sanjuu
31	Thirty one	einenunddreißig	trente et un	treinta y uno	trentuno	ikthees	sanju ichi
32	Thirty two	zweiunddreißig	trente-deux	treinta y dos	trentadue	batthees	sanju ni
33	Thirty three	dreiunddreißig	trente-trois	treinta y tres	trentatré	thainthees	sanju san
34	Thirty four	vierunddreißig	trente-quatre	treinta y cuatro	trentaquattro	chaunthees	sanju yon
35	Thirty five	fünfunddreißig	trente-cinq	treinta y cinco	trentacinque	paynthees	sanju go
36	Thirty six	sechsunddreißig	trente-six	treinta y seis	trentasei	chuthees	sanju roku

37	Thirty seven	siebenunddreißig	trente-sept	treinta y siete	trentasette	saynthis	sanju nana
38	Thirty eight	achtunddreißig	trente-huit	treinta y ocho	trentaotto	adthis	sanju hachi
39	Thirty nine	neununddreißig	trente-neuf	treinta y nueve	trentanove	unchaalis	sanju kyuu
40	Fourty	vierzig	quarante	cuarenta	quaranta	chaalees	
10	Ten	zehn; zehn	dix	diez	dieci	dus; das	juu
20	Twenty	zwanzig; zwanzig	vingt	veinte	venti	bees	nijuu
30	Thirty	dreißig; dreißig	trente	treinta	trenta	these	sanjuu
40	Fourty	vierzig	quarante	cuarenta	quaranta	chaalees	yonjuu
50	Fifty	fünfzig	cinquante	cincuenta	cinquanta	pachas	gojuu
60	Sixty	sechzig	soixante	sesenta	sessanta	saath	rokujuu
70	Seventy	siebzig	soixante-dix	setenta	settanta	sattur	nanajuu
80	Eighty	achtzig	quatre-vingts	ochenta	ottanta	assee	hachijuu
90	Ninety	neunzig	quatre-vingt-dix	noventa	novanta	navve; nubbay	kujuu; kyuujuu
100	One hundred	hundert	cent	cien; ciento	cento	sau	hyaku
200	Two hundred	zweihundert	deux cents	doscientos	duecento	do sau	nihyaku
300	Three hundred	drei hundert	trois cents	trescientos	trecento	theen sau	sanbyaku
400	Four hundred	vier hundert	quatre cents	cuatrocientos	quattrocento	chaar sau	yonbyaku
500	Five hundred	fünf hundert	cinq cents	quinientos	cinquecento	panch sau	gobyaku
600	Six hundred	sechs hundert	six cents	seiscientos	seicento	chay sau	rokubyaku
700	Seven hundred	sieben hundert	sept cents	setecientos	settecento	saat sau	nanabyaku
800	Eight hundred	acht hundert	huit cents	ochocientos	ottocento	aat sau	hachibyaku
900	Nine hundred	neun hundert	neuf cents	novecientos	novecento	nau sau	kyuubyaku
1000	One thousand	tausend	mille	mil	mille	hazaar	sen; ikusen
2000	Two thousand	zwei tausend	deux mille	dos mil	duemila	do hazaar	nisen
3000	Three thousand	drei tausend	trois mille	tres mil	tremila	theen hazaar	sanzen
4000	Four thousand	vier tausend	quatre mille	cuatro mil	quattromila	chaar hazaar	yonsen
5000	Five thousand	fünf tausend	cinq mille	cinco mil	cinquemila	panch hazaar	gosen
6000	Six thousand	sechs tausend	six mille	seis mil	seimila	chchey hazaar	rokusen
7000	Seven thousand	sieben tausend	sept mille	siete mil	settemila	saat hazaar	nanasen
8000	Eight thousand	acht tausend	huit mille	ocho mil	ottomila	aat hazaar	hachisen; hassen
9000	Nine thousand	neun tausend	neuf mille	nueve mil	novemila	nau hazaar	kyuusen
100000	Hundred thousand	hundert tausend	cent mille	ciento mil	centomila	ek lakh	juu man
1000000	One million	eine million	un million	millon; millón	un milione	dus lakh	hyaku man
1000000000	One billion	eine billion	un milliard	mil millones; billón	un miliardo	ek arb	juu oku

Days and Months

English	**German**	**French**	**Spanish**	**Italian**	**Hindi**	**Japanese**
Sunday	Sonntag	dimanche	domingo	doménica	ravivar, itavar	nichiyoubi
Monday	Montag	lundi	lunes	lunedì	somavar, chandravar	getsuyoubi; getsuyou
Tuesday	Dienstag	mardi	martes	martedí	mangalavar	kayoubi
Wednesday	Mittwoch	mercredi	miércoles	mercoledí	budhwar	suiyoubi, suiyou
Thursday	Donnerstag	jeudi	jueves	giovedí	guruvar	mokuyoubi
Friday	Freitag	vendredi	viernes	venerdí	shukravar	kin'youbi
Saturday	Samstag	samedi	sábado	sabato	shanivar	doyoubi, sabato
English	German	French	Spanish	Italian	Hindi	Japanese
January	Januar	janvier	enero	gennaio	janavari	ichigatsu
February	Februar	février	febrero	febbraio	februari	nigatsu
March	März	mars	marzo	marzo	march	sangatsu
April	April	avril	abril	aprile	April	shigatsu
May	Mai	mai	mayo	maggio	May	gogatsu
June	Juni	juin	junio	giugno	June	rokugatsu
July	Juli	juillet	julio	luglio	July	shichigatsu
August	August	août	agosto	agosto	August	hachigatsu
September	September	septembre	septiembre	settembre	September	kugatsu
October	Oktober	octobre	octubre	ottobre	October	juugatsu
November	November	novembre	noviembre	novembre	November	juuichigatsu
December	Dezember	décembre	diciembre	dicembre	December	juunigatsu
English	**German**	**French**	**Spanish**	**Italian**	**Hindi**	**Hindi**
Spring	Springen	printemps	primavera	di primavera; primaverile	vasanth ritu;	haru
Summer	Summer	été	verano	estivo	greeshma ritu	natsu
Fall/Autumn	Herbst	automne	otoño	autunno	sharad ritu	aki
Winter	Winter	hiver	invierno	verno	sheeta rutu	fuyu
Solar Eclipse	Sonnenfinsternis	solaire éclipse	eclipse solar	eclissi solare	surya grahan	nisshoku
Lunar Eclipse	Mondfinsternis	lunaire éclipse	eclipse lunar	eclissi lunare	chandra grahan	gesshoku
Equinox	Tagundnachtgleiche	équinoxe	equinoccio	equinozio	vishuv	bunten

Colors

English	**German**	**French**	**Spanish**	**Italian**	**Hindi**	**Hindi**
Red	rot	rouge	tinto; rojo	vermiglio; rosso	lal	niiro; gosai; ru-
Green	grün	vert	verde	verde	hara	midoriiro; midori
Blue	blau	bleu	azul	blu	neela; aasamanee rang	aoi; ao; buru-
Navy Blue	marineblau	bleu marine	azul marino	blu marina	samudra neela rang	kon; konjou
White	weiß	blanc	blanco	bianco	saphed; shweth	howaido; shiroi

Black	böse	noir	negro; oscuro	nera; negro; nero	kala; shyama	kuroi; burakku
Brown	braun	brun	marrón; pardo;	marrone	bhura rang	kasshoku
Yellow	gelb	jaune	amarillo	giallo	peela	kiiroi; ki
Orange	orange	orange	naranja	arancia; arancione	naarangi	orenji
Pink	rosa	rose	rosado	rosa	gulaabi rang	pinku
Teal	krickente	sarcelle	verde azulado; cereta	blu verde	chaitri; kalahams	teelu
Lime	kalk	chaux	cal	calce	nimbu	raimu; sekkai
Aqua	wasser	eau	agua; berilo	verde acqua	paani; jal; vaari	suisei; suichuu
Olive	Ölzweig	olive	aceituna; oliva	oliva	jaitoon	oriibu
Silver	silber	argent	plata	argènteo; argento	chaandi	shippou; gin
Gray	grau	gray	gris	grigio	dhoosar; bhura	haiiro; gure-
Purple	purpur; purpurrot	mauve; pourpre	lila; púrpura	lilla; violet	baigani	pa-puru
Maroon	rotbraun	bordeaux; rouge foncé	granate	rosso bordeaux	maroon	kuriiro

Index